Edmund Lawrence

It May Happen Yet

A Tale of Bonaparte's Invasion of England

Edmund Lawrence

It May Happen Yet
A Tale of Bonaparte's Invasion of England

ISBN/EAN: 9783741177552

Manufactured in Europe, USA, Canada, Australia, Japa

Cover: Foto ©Andreas Hilbeck / pixelio.de

Manufactured and distributed by brebook publishing software
(www.brebook.com)

Edmund Lawrence

It May Happen Yet

IT MAY HAPPEN YET:

A TALE

OF

BONAPARTE'S INVASION OF ENGLAND.

By Edmund Lawrence.

PUBLISHED BY THE AUTHOR,

And Sold by SAMUEL E. ROBERTS,

10, Paternoster Row, London, E.C.,

And by CHARLES J. THYNNE,

Wycliffe House, 6, Great Queen Street,

Lincoln's Inn, London, W.C.

Contents.

Contents—*Continued.*

It May Happen Yet.

CHAPTER I

DRAMATIS PERSONÆ.

On an evening in February, a great many years ago—so long ago as the time about when the grandfathers and grandmothers of middle-aged people of the present time were undergoing the process of being born—two persons were sitting before a fire in the drawing-room of a house in the city of Norwich. They were a mother and her son. The lady was of the middle height, if not taller; she sat very straight on her chair, which had a straight back. She wore a dark silk gown, the waist of which was about two inches below its highest edge upon her neck; fine muslin of three or four folds protected that neck from the cold; a cap, of the kind called mob, stiff with starch, rose six or eight inches above her head. We who write this book are not a lady, and we feel ourselves incompetent to describe properly the dress of ladies; and it may be surprising to some of those who read this description that this lady, notwithstanding the hideous clothes that she wore, not only was, but looked, a lady from head to foot. Her figure was neither fat nor lean; her face was fair, and very little wrinkled; her hair, of a peculiar light brown that never turns grey; some would call it flaxen, but it was a dark flaxen, perhaps rather the colour of tow than of flax; her mouth was not large, and it had a firm look, being always kept shut, even when she smiled, and she smiled very handsomely sometimes; her nose

B

was slightly curved in outline, but not long, nor pointed; her eyes were dark blue. She was fifty-four years old, and looked fully ten years less.

This lady's name was Elizabeth Grayswell Fenthorpe; not that her middle name properly belonged to her after her marriage, although she chose to retain it. She was the daughter of a gentleman of Norfolk, a squire of moderate estate, the widow of the Reverend Henry Fenthorpe, once rector of a small parish, and one of the canons of the Cathedral of the Holy Trinity; and she was the mother of Richard Fenthorpe, doctor of medicine.

She had no other child. This Richard was in his thirty-first year. He resembled his mother in features, but his skin was brown and not fair; his hair was also dark brown—almost black; while his eyes were blue, like his mother's. He was tall, but not remarkably so, and generally well put together. His face had an intelligent look, as people ninety years ago called what is now called intellectual; it was such a face as inspired confidence in those who met him, either socially or professionally. He had been about six years in practice in Norwich, and had a good clientelle both among the well-to-do and the not so well-to-do, and both in town and country. He had studied in Edinburgh and in London; he had heard lectures from John Hunter in his first year. He adopted his profession from choice, with the approval of his father, who, however, died before Richard had graduated. The clergyman bequeathed his son four thousand pounds. Mrs. Fenthorpe had a settlement of five hundred a year, subject to poor rates. Sometimes her year's income was little more than four hundred. The associates and intimates of Mrs. Fenthorpe and her son were amongst the best people of the city and its neighbourhood. They had many friends, and a few enemies, one of whom was bitter; but they were neither vindictive nor mean, and had very little resentment against that enemy, whom they frequently enough met in society. Mrs. Fenthorpe sometimes said in allusion to him that she preferred a bitter enemy to a bitter friend.

On this February evening of the year 1805, at about a quarter before six, Mrs. Fenthorpe stirred the fire, and remarked that it was very cold. Indeed, the room in which they sat was a cold room, and the house was a cold house. It had been built about the time of the accession of the Hanoverian dynasty, at a corner where two streets cross. The walls were less thick than the walls of most eighteenth century houses; there were ever so many windows, half of which were bricked up when the window tax was imposed, with only one row of bricks. The grates were narrow, and set as far back as the perversity of architects could contrive. This room—the withdrawing-room, as it was termed—was twenty-five feet by twenty, and loftier than the average of rooms of the size, altogether difficult to warm.

"Yes," said Richard, "and the fog continues, but I think not so dense. Mother, I wish you would tell me again the particulars of Charles Fenthorpe's death."

His mother turned to him very quickly, as if surprised at the question. "What has brought that up again?" she said. "I suppose it is ten years since we spoke of it."

"I don't remember that the matter came up since we talked of it when you were settling my father's affairs, and that is more than ten years ago. Surely, mother, you don't wish to avoid the subject?"

"I do not, though it is painful. Your father was so disappointed, as well as grieved! I knew him very little—certainly did not see him more than half a dozen times, from first to last. The last time was three or four days before it happened. I liked him, and I always combated your father's suspicion, which I think had no foundation. He never was so insincere as that. It would be atrocious. But, Richard, what put it in your head now?"

"To-day old Allonby sent for me, and when I saw him I perceived that there was little the matter with him except rheumatism. He wanted to talk; and if what he thinks is true—that is, if the old miscreant is not inventing things—it puts a different colour on Charles Fenthorpe's behaviour."

"Remember, Richard, that I never doubted his good faith the last time he and your father met in the house in the close. I was disappointed, too, for all our sakes. I will begin at the beginning. You were exactly a year old——"

A double knock at the hall door interrupted Mrs. Fenthorpe, and in process of a very few seconds—the hall door of a physician's house must be well attended—the butler announced Mrs. Cardwain and the Miss Tronfords.

Mrs. Cardwain was Mrs. Fenthorpe's sister. Her husband was one of those semi-clerical lawyers who infest cathedral cities—a registrar, or a surrogate, or something of that nature. He was intensely respectable, and extremely respected. He owed much of his respectability to his stupidity, for it is a tradition of opinion among English people that there is something suspicious in brilliancy. That opinion was more a matter of faith ninety years ago than it is now; indeed, modern heresy has undermined it much, but there still remains a pretty solid substratum of the ancient belief in stupidity or mediocrity. A man "who answers to the purpose, easy things to understand," is still more likely to be an oracle in the best city society, and in those old world towns where there are fine churches and comfortable clergymen, than a smart person. In our time we have so many smart people that it is beginning to grow tiresome, and the next generation will very probably witness a reaction in favour of genuine unadulterated stupidity. But though Mr. Cardwain was of this nature, he had good qualities, which far outweighed his negative one. He was true, and a steadfast friend when he gave his friendship. He had the best Madeira and port in the diocese, except what there was in the cellars of the Palace; he would have thought it schismatic to have better wine than the bishop had. He administered his port and Madeira to his friends six times every year, eighteen friends on each occasion, one hundred and eight of both sexes in all, so that we may understand that his circle of intimate acquaintanceship was large. At that time, people's incomes were not so large as they are now, and their tastes in the matter of dinner were simple. A haunch of mutton, the produce of a sheep five years old, or sometimes one of venison, was the principal dish; entrees were unknown even by name.

They had no children, and they fixed their domestic affections chiefly on two girls, cousins of Mr. Cardwain. Helen and Frances Tronford had been left his wards. Their father had bequeathed his landed estate to the eldest, burthened with a charge for the younger sister. This estate, called Brandwood, was of several hundred acres—indeed, more than a thousand—about four miles from Norwich, in the direction of Yarmouth. There was no mansion house upon it, and these young ladies resided commonly at Yarmouth, with a duenna. Every Christmas they came to Norwich, and this winter their stay there had been prolonged for some weeks.

"I am most pleased to see you, Isabella," said Mrs. Fenthorpe to her sister, "and my dear Helen and Fanny. You have come to stay the evening, I hope?"

"Jonathan is at the Deanery," Mrs. Cardwain answered. "There is a party there; and as the girls are going home the day after to-morrow, we thought we would come to bid you good-bye. I suppose everything is ready for the festive doings to-morrow? I am glad to be out of it. I am sure Mrs. Mortland will make some mistake, and bring ill-will on some of you!"

"Are you going so soon? I thought you would stay till March, at least. Well, girls, before you go, you will see what is being done here for the education of the people, and you must make some improvement in your benighted Yarmouth. Yes, Isabella, the cakes are at this moment baking, and the apples are all bought. I undertook part of the cakes, and Mrs. Mortland undertook the tea."

"I shan't drink it, then!" exclaimed Miss Tronford the second. "I know it will be weak."

Fanny Tronford was a pretty little fat girl, nineteen years old. Helen was three years older, and much more distinguished-looking, though not above the medium height.

Both were dressed in Indian muslin, of that hue, nominally white, but, in candle-light especially, presenting a yellowish effect, at that time much admired. Their dresses were of the cut of the period, closely resembling the dressing-gown, or long bib, the regulation garment of Grosvenor Gallery angels and seraphs. Helen Tronford was of a perfect figure, as was evident even with the disadvantage of this unearthly gown, and she carried herself perfectly. She had dark brown hair and dark brown eyes; her complexion was fair; her nose straight; her lips full, but not too much so; and her expression the purest and the most loving that ever sat upon a girl's face. It was a face incapable of any but the most winning smile; it never was, and never could be, marred by a grimace or a sneer. All who saw her saw that she was made to be loved, and all who knew her loved her.

It was Fanny who made the remark about the tea.

"Three hundred children and their mothers—I suppose, half as many more!" said Mrs. Cardwain. "If nothing goes wrong it will astonish me. And oh! I heard that there is to be a gentleman from London to examine and catechise the children, and he is one of the greatest educators the world ever produced. It will be a great affair. All the ladies, the clergymen's wives and the rest, are to be invited to ask questions. What question will you ask, Elizabeth?"

"I have not thought of it," Mrs. Fenthorpe replied, smiling with her mouth shut. "Richard, ring for the candles, and I will get tea. Put on some coals. Do you know, people say coals don't make so warm a fire as they did twenty years ago. But this is not a warm room."

"It is warmer than it is outside," said Miss Tronford. "Mr. Cardwain was telling me to-day that one of the Canons, who keeps a diary of the weather, says that there never was a fog that lasted so long as this."

"I think," said Richard, "that must be the case. I do not remember such a thing. Now five days, and no wind! I was yesterday more than half-way to Yarmouth to see a patient, and I met two Yarmouth men who said that the people there are lost in wonder at it. More have sent for me this week on account of coughs and colds and rheumatism than ever did before in so short a time. But nothing deadly. Shall you not almost be amused, Miss Tronford, when I tell you that fifteen volunteers came to me to-day to consult me about their throats?"

"Oh, Dr. Fenthorpe!" replied Miss Tronford, "I do think the volunteers are growing the greatest impostors. It was all very nice at first, a year ago, when there was real enthusiasm and we were in danger, but they are keeping it up for nothing but pretence and idling. There is young Mr. Sprowls—you don't think he cares about anything but his uniform?"

"My dear Miss Tronford," replied the Doctor, "I have many friends among the volunteers; and as the medical officer of the Loyal Norwich, it is not for me to complain of them. My belief is that there was last year a very great deal less of sickness among the men of our population owing to this very volunteering. And think of another thing—how much better friends people are now than they were a few years ago. There are my relations out at Fenthorpe. We are not, as you know, extremely cordial, but it is far pleasanter not to have politics aggravating differences. Five years ago there were dozens of people in the county that would not speak to the old gentleman."

"Your Uncle Jonathan says, Richard," Mrs. Cardwain interrupted him, "that Whig is no proper description of him. Your uncle is not an illiberal man; he has no antipathy to Mr. Coke, or even to the Duke, but he cannot endure a Jacobin. I know it gave him absolute concern when young Mr. Mortland, that is, Alexander, was made a major of volunteers; I should hardly like to repeat to you what he thought."

"None of us in Norwich, I hope," said Mrs. Fenthorpe, "are illiberal. There are pretentious people enough, that set up for being more enlightened than their neighbours; but there is no place in England, I believe, where more good is being done for the common people, in educating the children, than in Norwich. That is true enlightenment, teaching them to read their Bibles. We can laugh at the amusement that we are to have to-morrow, but it is not useless to keep people in good humour. Even bringing people like the Mortlands, who are no great friends of religion or the Church, into it, is a good thing. Richard and I were saying so to-day."

The door was opened, and the tea urn was brought in. At the same moment a knock was heard at the hall door, and, on its being opened, a loud masculine voice. The five persons in the room upstairs exchanged glances, and Dr. Fenthorpe's countenance became overcast.

"Ma'am," said a gentleman who came into the room, addressing Mrs. Fenthorpe, "I am your humble servant!" He pronounced servant as if there was no vowel in the second syllable. He walked across the room awkwardly, with almost a swagger; he made a bow that was almost a nod; the same to Mrs. Cardwain, but much more profound inclinations to the two young ladies.

"You are in time for a cup of tea, Mr. Mortland," said Mrs. Fenthorpe. "Be seated near the fire; you must be cold!"

"Vastly cold, ma'am, upon m' honour; colder than char'ty. Miss Tronford, won't you be at the Yarmouth ball next week? I crave th' honour of th' first dance." Miss Tronford smiled, and said it was she that was honoured. "Agreed, then!" said the gentleman; "'t will be the last piece of hap'ness I shall enjoy before I go back to Lunnon."

He who then clipped his words, speaking while he did so loudly enough to be heard across two streets, had, two years before this, talked like any ordinary Christian, or heathen. But two years' residence in Lunnon had enabled him to transform himself into a dandy; not a buck. This was the period when bucks were going out and dandies coming in. The dandy is a product of nature—we were about to say art, but nature is more correct—superior to the buck. It is evident that this must be so, for he succeeds the buck in accordance with evolutionary law, having nearly the same relation to the latter as Cochin China fowls have to bantams, as the late Mr. Darwin and others teach. The resemblance is close. The fully developed dandy is not to be properly apprehended from the example of Mr. Robert Mortland, who was of the transition period. A far better typical case was a gentleman not much thought of in the year 1805, but known later as the first gentleman in Europe. The best portraits of him, representing his stout figure confined by the tailor's perfected art, and his neck encircled by a cravat as thick as a schooner's cable, bear a most suggestive likeness to a large Cochin China cock. The dandy was more finical than the buck. He was quite as impudent, but less aggressive; more of the *noli me tangere* about him. He dressed himself more showily, and less neatly. The buck was, perhaps, the more manly animal of the two; he would fight a duel on occasion, a thing that the other greatly disliked, not, however, from more exalted principle, but from a more affectionate regard for his skin. The external characteristic that marked the genuine difference lay in the clipping of words, and the liberal use of slang of the less vulgar forms. The buck addressed ladies with "Madam"; the dandy reduced this to a mono-syllable. This practice of shortening words rapidly spread amongst all ranks; and already, at the time we are treating of, footmen of the higher walks, and later, even hackney coachmen, employed the now universal "Marm."

Robert Mortland had gone to live in London shortly after the general election of 1802. His father, a violent Anti-Pittite, had the power of influencing seven freeholders out of thirty-two, who chose two members for a borough. Mr. Pitt would not have given him anything for his votes, for he knew that he was a Whig and something more, and had otherwise no good opinion of him. But Mr. Addington, the Prime Minister when Parliament was dissolved, had a more catholic mind, and, accordingly, bought Mr. Mortland senior's votes with a Treasury clerkship for his son. The young man had always had a desire to live in town, and suggested the transaction. It describes what kind of people the Mortlands were, that it never occurred to either of them that the business was a degrading one, and that the younger gentleman was making himself very cheap. Even had any one tried to explain this to them, they would not have understood it. Robert's ambition in life was to be thought an aboriginal Londoner, but the only person ever convinced of the correctness of that view was himself. A delicate swagger, and a turn of accent, and pretty correct slang, can be learned; a true knowledge of buttons, waistcoats, and such things, like æsthetic criticism, requires a mind of the higher order. The conversation of dandies is not interesting, and we shall not pursue an account of the remarks that Robert proceeded to entertain Helen Tronford with. She smiled in answer, now and then saying a word, and seemed amused.

At length Mrs. Fenthorpe called Robert to come and have a cup of tea; he walked to the table, and Richard Fenthorpe seized the opportunity to say four words to Helen in a low tone. She smiled, with, as Richard thought, more meaning than she had smiled on Mr. Mortland. The tea was drunk, the butler removed the urn and the rest, drew out a card table, lighted two more candles, and left the room. Richard produced cards from the drawer, and said that Miss Tronford and he were going to play chess.

"Oh, come now, Doctor," said Robert, "that's too bad, re'lly!" Richard ignored him, and opened the box of chessmen. Miss Tronford was neutral in speech, but moved towards the small table. Mr. Mortland's flank was turned.

Orthodox whist is a silent game, but three ladies, one of them very young and all of them good talkers, and Robert Mortland, did not play on the principles of Sarah Battle. The two chess players conversed in undertones; what they said was probably interesting to themselves. At half-past nine Mrs. Cardwain's footman came for his ladies, with a lanthorn. The two gentlemen also accompanied them home, the distance being less than half a mile. At Mr. Cardwain's garden gate they separated, under terms of understood armed neutrality, Doctor Fenthorpe returning to his mother's house.

"Richard," said Mrs. Fenthorpe, when her son came into the drawing-room, "I hope you are not losing time."

He looked sheepish. He was not a coward, and he was a Loyal Norwich volunteer; but there are occasions on which a brave man may look sheepish. It is no mark of want of courage to shrink from putting it to the touch.

"I don't know, mother," he replied. "Did you observe how perfectly she behaved towards——"

"Yes; and I am certain she dislikes him. Indeed, how any one could like that affected, washed-out creature, is a wonder. I thought he made very free coming here this evening; he must have known."

"I dare say. This is a small town, though forty thousand people inhabit it, and everybody knows about everybody else. I knew that Helen and Fanny are going home the day after to-morrow; they were to have gone to-morrow, but are waiting for the school feast."

"To be sure!" said Mrs. Fenthorpe, standing up. "I will go downstairs and see if everything is right. While you were out, I have been thinking about what happened thirty years ago, and I will tell you the whole thing. But, Richard, who is Allonby? I do not know the name." She sat down again.

"Allonby was lately one of the bell-ringers. He is getting old, and his son and daughter-in-law keep him; they are pretty well off. Allonby is the man who told two stories at the time; contradicted himself. When we were speaking about Charles Fenthorpe, shortly after my father died, you told me about him. I had never heard of him, and I tried to find him. He was then living near Wymondham, and I got at him with a good deal of trouble. I think he was a sexton. I could get nothing out of him. You never liked to talk about it, and I did not care to tell you I had been seeing Allonby. I have never seen him since till to-day, when he sent for me. I made him fee me, for I am perfectly sure he is capable of representing me as trying to make him give new evidence, and bribing him for it."

"Was Allonby," said Mrs. Fenthorpe, "the name of the man who said he had witnessed a will, and then denied it?"

"Yes; what did you think was his name?"

"It is so long ago; I suppose you are right. You know, the peculiarity of the whole thing is, there are not, and there never were, any letters or documents, nothing but your father's memory, and mine. It was in August, thirty years ago this year."

"Mother," said Richard, "do I mistake, or was it not this? Allonby first said he had witnessed a will, and specified the time, though not the exact day; and when he was asked who was the other witness, he said there was no other witness. He said Mr. Fenthorpe told him it was a will, and then said he had never told him it was a will, and ended his lies with saying that he had never signed anything for Mr. Fenthorpe at all!"

"It was nearly about that, but I never saw this man; I know only what your father told me. I wish we had written it down. Did I ever tell you that, some time before his death, your father wrote to Mr. Armitage to know if he had any memoranda?"

"I don't remember."

"He did; and about three months after there came a reply from a Mr. Groves, saying that Mr. Armitage was dead, and he was his executor; he had not finished going through his papers, but if he found anything about us he would let us have information. That ended it, for we never heard any more. Mr. Groves was, I believe, a very eminent lawyer; is, for he is living."

"No; you never told me of this. Did you ever hear any more of Mr. Groves, mother?"

"I think this happened when you were in Edinburgh. Every time that your father talked about Charles Fenthorpe he became restless and unhappy. He always thought him double and insincere; but at the same time, you understand, Richard, he would never totally give up the opinion that there was a will. About Mr. Groves—I think he is the same

Mr. Groves that was last year such a leader among the volunteers of Kent. I heard that Mr. Groves had given up his profession of the law, with a fortune."

"Oh, Mr. Groves, of Folkestone! I know who he is. He has a curious history. What Allonby told me to-day is, that Charles Fenthorpe got him to sign this paper as a witness, and told him he would get another witness. Now, you know a will requires two witnesses, and it is usual for them to sign together, but a will, witnessed by two who sign separately, is still valid, or was valid thirty years ago. If the law has been altered, it is since then. I am nearly sure of this. So that, unless he is still romancing, my belief is that there was a will, or perhaps still is. I hardly like to express, even to you, mother, what suspicions must arise, but not suspicions of Charles Fenthorpe."

"The difficulty is really in what Mr. Armitage thought. It was he who put it first in your father's mind that all about the will was an imposture. He said to me that your father was mistaken, which is impossible, for he repeated to me all that occurred at their last meeting the same evening. Afterwards, he dined with us, and I brought you for him to see after dinner. What kind of a night was it when you came in?"

"No change; perhaps not so cold. I did think there was a little wind. Who can that be?"

A knock at the hall door interrupted them; a call for Dr. Fenthorpe to see a country patient. He had to send for his horse; he rode two miles and two home, arriving too late for any more conversation.

CHAPTER II.

WE shall here inform our readers who the Fenthorpe family were, and what the point of doubt was concerning the will, or supposed will, of the late Charles Fenthorpe.

They were a family dating from the time of Elizabeth, a period when much property changed hands, and when the bulk of the existing race of English squires had its rise. It is believed that the changes of prices and values, produced by the Mexican and Peruvian mines of the precious metals, pouring their wealth on Europe, caused much of that revolution in property. It is said that a converse change of value is going on now, caused by scarcity of those metals; on this we offer no opinion at present; but if the present race of English country gentlemen is to be superseded by another, we have not sanguine hopes that that other will be better. Michael Fenthorpe is the first of the name that is met with. He acquired the lands of Fenthorpe, eighteen hundred acres in extent, fertile and in all ways desirable, lying near to the city of Norwich, towards the north-east, by purchase. His descendants suppose that Michael's ancestors, of whom he must have had some, had borne another surname, and that he assumed the name from his estate. His son was a man of consideration; and so was his grandson, who took the Parliament side in the war against the treacherous son of a mean-minded father; he fought at Naseby and elsewhere. The next Fenthorpe took a part in the recall of the second Charles. The next after him made that King's personal acquaintance, and the acquaintance also of the low-lived blacklegs whom he kept about him, to the dishonour of this country. After a sojourn in town of about two years, he was forced to return to Norfolk to sell his estate, or, rather, all of it except one hundred acres and the Hall. He had the pleasure, before he died, of seeing the Duke of York, who one

22

night had won from him, by the help of Dick Talbot, four hundred guineas, kicked out of England. But the fifth Fenthorpe restored the fortunes of the family.

His name was Charles, so called from the disreputable monarch. He went to Cambridge, and was called to the bar. Making a fortune by his profession, he bought back all the lands of Fenthorpe. He married, not being young, a London lady, and continued to live in town and to practise. He had two children; Charles, born in 1725, and Jane, born three or four years later. His wife died when Charles was nine years old, then he gave up the law and came to live in Norfolk. He was extremely popular, and could have got himself chosen to Parliament for Norwich, or for any open borough in the neighbourhood, had there not just before been a dissolution and general election. Not long after his removal to Fenthorpe, he married a second time, a cousin, also named Fenthorpe. A year or two later he died, leaving his estate to his son, unencumbered and unentailed, and money to his daughter, as also to his widow, with the use of Fenthorpe Hall and curtilage adjacent during her life.

The Fenthorpe who lost his property in the society of the Court had two brothers, James and Henry. The latter was a shrewd, managing man, and it was mainly by his advice and assistance that Fenthorpe Hall was not allowed to go in the elder brother's wreck. It was the daughter of James who was Charles's second wife; and Henry, and afterwards Henry's son, Henry, had always resided at the Hall, the first while he lived, and the second till Charles returned to Norfolk in 1734 or '35. This Henry was more like a brother to his cousins than a distant relative. Some time after the death of Charles, his widow married Henry, so marrying twice without changing her name. They had a son, afterwards the Reverend Henry, Canon of Norwich, and the father of Richard, with whom we are already acquainted. Charles Fenthorpe the second, though a boy, had resented his father's second marriage; and both he and his sister, then old enough to have an opinion, resented their stepmother's second marriage,

although they did not dislike Henry Fenthorpe. He was the
children's trustee and guardian, and he did his duty by them.
As they grew up it was probably irritating to them to see
one, in some measure a stranger, master of the house that
would one day be Charles's. Neither of them was amiable,
and Charles was something of a sneak. He had a propensity
towards mischievous practical jokes. Practical jokes, even
of the most harmless kind, are the very lowest form of wit;
when they are not harmless, their perpetrator goes about the
best way that could be devised to make himself hated.

The principal victim of these jokes came, as he grew up,
to be little Henry, although a child, and fifteen years
younger than Charles. They were never friends, although,
after Henry grew up, they were not enemies, and Charles had
often the manner with the young man as if he wished to atone
for former ill-treatment. When Jane was about twenty-three
or four, she got her stepmother to take her to Bath, which was
then a great journey. At Bath she met a gentleman of
North Britain, Mr. Mortland, to whom she engaged herself.
This was the cause of a serious quarrel between her and her
brother.

Mortland of Mortland came, by invitation, to Fenthorpe
Hall, and found Charles very cordial. But Charles spoke ill
of him behind his back, and this came to Jane's ears. If
the works of Dickens had been known at that time, she
would have compared her brother to Mr. Pecksniff.

Indeed, by this time, he had a character, beyond his own
family, for insincerity; but it is our opinion that a good deal
of this was owing to a kind of affectation, not, certainly, harmless, but much more innocent than anything that we read of
in the doings of the immortal Seth, the architect of Salisbury.
Our opinion is, also, that in most of what Charles Fenthorpe
said of Mortland, he was justified, and justified also in keeping on polite terms with him. Mortland was a snob; a Scotch
snob, *vide* Thackeray. How vile such a one is capable of
being we know by the example of James, sixth King of
Scotland of that name and first of England; how mean, by

another James, surnamed Boswell, laird of Auchinleck; and how vain, by another laird, Christian and surname unknown, who lived in a braw house called Cockpen.

Without being positive that Mr. Mortland united in himself all the bad qualities of these several snobs, he was a man whom, had we been a woman, we would not have married. But Miss Fenthorpe viewed him in a different light, and she accepted him with less deliberation than was exercised towards Cockpen by Mistress Jean of Clavers-ha' Lea. They were married, and went to Mortland, Ayrshire, to live. They had one son, Robert, and two or three daughters. Henry Fenthorpe and his wife died within ten or twelve years of Jane's marriage, when Charles became unlimited owner and tenant in fee of the whole estate. Young Henry went to Cambridge, and took holy orders.

After his sister's marriage, Charles Fenthorpe lived but little at home, travelling a good deal, and spending much time in London, at Bath, and at Harrogate, which was beginning, after it was introduced to the public by the adventures of Humphrey Clinker, to be a considerable resort of the semi-fashionable. He made a journey to Scotland, where he reconciled himself to some degree with his sister. When he was at home he was more friendly with his step-mother and her husband than when he had been younger, and listened, probably with some good effect, to Henry Fenthorpe's remonstrances on his almost ostentatious affection and scarcely concealed insincerity. He had, when he talked to any one, a warm, wheedling manner, as though he were that person's best friend. But his neighbours usually laughed when his back was turned.

At the time when Henry, the younger—then a beneficed clergyman and a Canon of Norwich—married Miss Greyswell, he manifested a good deal of interest in this marriage; and about the same time he visited Scotland a second time, Mortland being no longer living. He had at that time, or at some time before it, made a will, bequeathing Fenthorpe to Robert Mortland, who had just reached the age of twenty-

C

one. But on the occasion of this second visit to his sister's family, he conceived a powerful aversion to his nephew, who was the very reproduction of his father. When he returned home, he spoke of his aversion to the Reverend Henry, but said nothing about his testamentary dispositions. He maintained no great intimacy with the clergyman and his young wife.

In the summer of the year 1775, he received a letter from Scotland, which determined him on a third journey thither. Mrs. Mortland wrote that she believed her health was declining, and she should like to see her brother once more in this life. Travelling was no exertion to Charles Fenthorpe, and he made immediate preparations for departure. The principal preparation was the buying of a horse for the journey, which he estimated would require about ten days.

The day before his departure, he visited Henry and his wife at their house in the Close, and asked them to give him his dinner. While Mrs. Fenthorpe was absent from the room, perhaps on household affairs, Charles reopened the subject of his dislike of his nephew Robert, and said that he was a young man of such a disposition as to be quite unfit for an English squire. "I have thought over this for a very long time, and at length I resolved that I would not bequeath him my father's estate. It is true that he is my father's grandson, but he is neither of his name nor nation; and you, my dear, almost, brother—you will allow me to call you so— are both; and my father and I always highly valued your father. I have therefore made a will bequeathing you Fenthorpe."

Henry was much surprised, but said nothing more than ordinary words of gratitude and estimation. Charles went on with more of the same strain, and succeeded, in some measure, in reaching the other's heart by praising his wife. They were interrupted for a moment by her entrance; and when she went out of the room again, Charles said, "Armitage has my will." Then the butler came to say that dinner was on the table, and no more passed between them on the subject.

Mr. Pecksniff had Tom Pinch, who believed in him. If any one had an affection for Charles Fenthorpe, it was his groom and travelling servant, John Hamborough. They quitted home early the next morning, and arrived at an inn in the evening, a short way on the Norwich side of King's Lynn. Leaving that on the next day, they kept, after passing through Lynn, to the right, and arrived, towards afternoon, at the ferry at the mouth of the Nene below Wisbeach. There were no other passengers; the boat was large enough to have taken twenty. At some hundred yards from the Lincolnshire side, Mr. Fenthorpe's horse became uneasy. What happened exactly is known only from Hamborough's account. The boat was upset; he only escaped with his life, having taken off his coat, and being a swimmer. The accident was witnessed from the ferry station; two men put out in a small boat and picked him up, nearly exhausted.

Hamborough did not know what to do, but determined to wait till his master's body was recovered. All the bodies, three in number, were found in four or five days. At the coroner's inquest nothing was disclosed but what we relate. Hamborough procured a coffin on credit, left his master's body in it with an innkeeper, and started for Norwich, walking. He would not trust himself again on the water, and went round by Wisbeach.

Charles Fenthorpe was drowned, accordingly, fully a week before any one of his relatives knew of the accident. Hamborough had had the intelligence to request the coroner to write to Mrs. Mortland, who was the only near connection of the deceased. When Henry Fenthorpe learned what had happened, his first duty was to attend to the disposal of his cousin's remains. He quitted Norwich almost instantly for Lincolnshire, writing to Mr. Armitage, of Lincoln's Inn, fixing a day for the funeral. In his letter he informed Mr. Armitage of the last conversation that he had held with Charles.

It was September by the time that Mr. Armitage came, and the funeral was over. That gentleman was an old solicitor,

or attorney, as gentlemen of that branch of the legal profession were then called, who had been young when Charles
Fenthorpe, King's Counsel, had been practising. The great
lawyer had patronised the young attorney, and the latter
became the man of business of the family. Nothing of
moment passed in it with which he was not acquainted.

Now, it so happened that in the letter that Henry Fenthorpe had despatched to Mr. Armitage, he did not add to
his account of Charles's last communication that the deceased
had said where the will was deposited. Therefore, after the
funeral was over, and they began to business, Henry was
waiting for Mr. Armitage to produce the will, and Mr.
Armitage was waiting for Henry to produce it. Mr. Armitage
at length asked him to repeat the substance of the contents of
the letter.

He did so, when Mr. Armitage went on:

"Is it your belief that this will was executed lately?"

"You have the will, Mr. Armitage!" replied Henry.

"You must have misunderstood the deceased," replied the
attorney. "I have a will, made nearly five years ago; I have
brought it with me. I know its contents from what Charles
Fenthorpe told me, for he gave it to me in London. The will
that was made since must be at the Hall." They were in the
house in the Close.

"Charles told me that you have it," said Henry.

"I have it not, and it must be searched for," replied Mr.
Armitage. "It is not too late to go now. I suppose that
Hamborough will know where things are kept."

Henry Fenthorpe knew that Hamborough's late master had
treated him well, and, he supposed, with as much confidence
as is usually placed in retainers. The groom showed them
the drawers and desks. A short search turned over everything. There was no will. nor any document of greater value
than receipts for money paid. Hamborough had remained
while they were turning over the papers. Mr. Armitage said
to him, "We are looking for Mr. Fenthorpe's will."

"I signed his will for him—that is, your honour, I made
my mark to it—five years ago," said Hamborough.

Mr. Armitage looked up, first at him and then at Henry Fenthorpe. He made a sign to the latter to allow him to question the groom.

"You remember witnessing your late master's signature to his will, five years ago?" he said. "Where was it that that took place?"

"It was in London, at the Golden Cross. He always stayed at the Golden Cross."

"Was there any other witness—any other person besides yourself that witnessed it?"

"Yes, your honour, Mr. Fenthorpe fetched me and the boots of the inn into his room, and he said to us that he wanted us to sign his will, for he knew the boots was a scholar, though I am not; and he wrote his name, and he wrote my name, and got me to make my mark; and then the other man wrote his name. I remember the name; I knew the man well—James Stokesbury."

"And this was five years ago?"

"Yes, your honour. And he told us he had left us nothing; for, he said, it is better for you for me to give you something now than to leave you anything when I die; and he took out his purse and he gave Stokesbury two guineas, and when Stokesbury went out of the room he gave me three guineas. Three new guineas they was, and he was always good to me; and I will repent to my dying day that I advised him to buy that horse." Hamborough began to cry; and they remembered that the horse having turned rusty on the ferry-boat, was the cause of its upsetting.

"And do you not remember your master making another will lately?" said Mr. Armitage.

"Not as I know of, your honour. But how was I to know? though it would be natural like, if he did make one, for him for to get me to sign it, like the other one."

Mr. Armitage dismissed him. Henry Fenthorpe was terribly agitated. The attorney felt for him. They had never met before; but the position of a man, who for a week had supposed himself the heir of a large estate, finding that it

was a delusion, was enough to arouse commiseration or
sympathy in any one.

After a pause, "We must do nothing," he said, "till the
arrival of Mr. Mortland, or till we hear from him. I have
in my possession the will of which this man speaks; the
names to it will identify it. Indeed, Mr. Fenthorpe gave it
to me, and the envelope is endorsed. He did not employ me
to draft it; I suppose it is in his own writing. Mr.
Fenthorpe," he continued, "it is well that you have taken
no steps, nor entered on possession."

They went back to the Close. They did not converse on
the way. When they arrived at Henry Fenthorpe's house,
he sent for his wife, and told her, with what composure he
could, what they had found out or not found out.

Mr. Armitage was silent for a while, and when the husband
and wife somewhat paused in their conversation, began to ask
a few questions. Mrs. Fenthorpe replied to him.

"On the evening of the day that he dined here, which was
the day before we left for the North, we talked about it a
good deal. I think we may say that we were not much elated,
for we agreed that, having changed his mind once, he might
do it again. But, Mr. Armitage, it is a blow. What are we
to think?"

"Madam, Mrs. Fenthorpe, what, so exactly as you remember, did Mr. Fenthorpe tell you about his having deposited
the will with me?"

"Mr. Fenthorpe told me that he had said, just before they
came into dinner, that the will was in your hands."

"I have a will in my hands, that made some years ago. I
hope you trust me when I say that I have no other. It is
six months or more since I heard from the late Charles
Fenthorpe."

Both were most pressing in their assurances that they had
every confidence. "What," said Mr. Fenthorpe, "are we to
think? You have not exhausted the search of the Hall?"

"I apprehend that we have," replied Mr. Armitage. "If
you ask me what you are to think, a suspicion arises in me
that I hardly like to express, and I would not express it if Mr.

Fenthorpe had been your friend. You know his remarkable disposition; you know that every one that knew him, or nearly every one, counted him very insincere!"

"Yes," both answered.

"It is possible that he was practising a deception on you; it is possible that he had some motive in wishing to make you friendly to him. It is not pleasant to have to speak so of the dead."

"Do you mean, Mr. Armitage," Mrs. Fenthorpe said, "that he was actually playing a practical joke, such as he used to make my husband's life wretched with when he was a boy?"

"Well, madam, it occurs to me."

"I cannot believe in such monstrous insincerity! I knew him very little. He visited us after our marriage, and I saw him a few times. I could never entertain the opinion of him that most persons had. But it is not to be conceived that he should go and practise this deception, and then drown himself on purpose. No motive can be imagined that I can think of. No, Mr. Armitage, people surely do not make such communications as he made to my husband, telling the whole time falsehoods." She paused, and then continued: "I think we should not be silent about this. We have no reason to be either friends or enemies towards Mr. Mortland; that need not weigh with us. But if we let it be known that we believe there is such a will in existence, search may be made for it in places that we know nothing of, and might never think of."

She impressed Mr. Armitage very much; he was struck by so very young and very good-looking a lady talking argumentatively on the subject, not wringing her hands or sobbing or lamenting. They invited Mr. Armitage to sojourn in their house during his stay at Norwich, which must of necessity be till the arrival of Mr. Mortland, or till he was heard from. But he excused himself.

"I am going," he said, "to assist in all ways in the discovery of the last will, if such exists. But I am going to do so not, Mr. Fenthorpe, in your interest, but in the interest of justice. I would not appear to take a part; also, I have been the legal man of business of two generations of your family, and it is for your interest as much as my own that I should continue to act now, after this estate has passed to a side branch. I am as sensible of your goodness as if I accepted it. I am sure you will not misjudge me."

Henry Fenthorpe accompanied him to the principal inn in the city, and saw that he was made comfortable. He' was an old man, not much less than seventy. The journey to Norwich had been a serious undertaking to him.

In the morning, Hamborough came to the Close, and told Mr. Fenthorpe that, if any one could tell him anything, he thought it was the sexton of the church near Fenthorpe Hall, a man called Allonby. Hamborough had evidently been talking; and though he knew not the supposed contents of the missing will, he guessed them, having seen the anxiety of Henry Fenthorpe. The latter took him to the inn, where they met Mr. Armitage.

"Why do you think this man can tell anything?" said Mr. Armitage.

"The master went to him twice that I know of, lately; and John Bannox, the bailiff, said he had been with him often."

"I will go with you to him." Mr. Armitage took Henry aside, and recommended that he should permit him to go to make inquiries alone. Unwillingly enough, the clergyman consented; and we doubt if Mr. Armitage was judicious in this, for it gave Allonby the opportunity of telling more than one story. While Mr. Armitage went to put on his coat, to accompany the groom in his gig, Mr. Fenthorpe began to ask him about this Allonby.

"What kind of a man is he, John?" he inquired.

"He is a man, your honour, that I would rather know alive than know him dead!"

"What in heaven's name do you mean?"

"Sir, you won't repeat it—it might get me ill-will!" said Hamborough.

"No; I will not repeat what you tell me if you don't wish."

Hamborough whispered: "Sir, they do say that he took up a body and sold it to a doctor!"

Mr. Fenthorpe stared. Resurrection men were not so much spoken of, nor, indeed, was there so much of this outrage, at the end of the last century as there was at the beginning of this.

"And they say," Hamborough continued, "that he has done it more than once. He was away about a week not long since, and I heard it was about that. If he does anything to the master, I'll——"

Here Mr. Armitage reappeared, and they drove off, without Henry Fenthorpe having warned the attorney of the character of the man he was going to question. But he reflected that Hamborough might be as communicative with Mr. Armitage as he had been with himself.

Allonby was a man of about forty, strongly built, and very determined-looking; at the same time smooth-spoken, while he was slow of speech and of answering questions. But to those which he was asked, he replied that, about a month or six weeks ago, Mr. Fenthorpe had gone to him with a paper and had got him to put his name to it. They had gone into the vestry of the church for pen and ink. Mr. Fenthorpe had not told him, that he remembered, what the paper was. On being asked was Mr. Fenthorpe's own name on the paper signed by him, he thought it was, but was not sure. When Mr. Armitage was going away, after learning this, Allonby asked him for a fee, which Mr. Armitage refused to give him pretty positively. On this the man said he had a right to have a fee, and repeated this as the gig drove away.

Robert Mortland did not arrive in Norwich for several days, during which time Mr. Armitage continued at the inn. He repeated what Allonby had told him to the Fenthorpes. It began to be talked of at Fenthorpe Hall among the servants and out-of-door men, that a will was being searched for.

On the morning of the day that Mortland came, but before his arrival, which was not expected at any specific moment, Henry Fenthorpe, unknown to Mr. Armitage, went to pump Allonby. The story that he heard was not the same as had been told to the attorney. Perhaps Allonby had really recollected more than he had done on the first occasion. At all events, he told his questioner that Mr. Fenthorpe had made him sign " as a witness "; and being asked was it as a witness to a will, thought that it was. He was not positive that it was; then he was almost certain that it was. The interview was not satisfactory to the clergyman. Allonby did not ask for money, and Mr. Fenthorpe thought he was rather cringing in manner.

Robert Mortland arrived in Norwich, by the stage coach from Ely, on the eleventh of September. He went straight to Fenthorpe Hall, hiring a carriage from the inn. As the carriage left the inn yard, the hostler said to Mr. Armitage, who was standing near, " That must be Mr. Mortland, sir."

Mr. Armitage had not seen him, but understood, when he knew where the stranger had gone, that it was probably so. Mortland sent back the carriage. He announced himself to the servants at Fenthorpe—Hamborough, the cook, and another—as the son of the late owner's only sister, and desired a room to be prepared for him to stay all night, or longer. There was no butler, Hamborough sometimes having acted in that capacity, and sometimes a female servant, during the late master's residence. Mr. Mortland desired that the female servant should wait at table. During dinner, he asked her many questions. He ascertained that Mr. Armitage was in Norwich, which, indeed, he had known before; for he had travelled to London, and gone to that gentleman's chambers in Lincoln's Inn. Being informed of his absence, he guessed where he had gone, and left without giving his name. Then he came to Norwich by the Cambridge and Ely road, so that he might seem to have come direct from Scotland, and Mr. Armitage never knew that he had visited him in town. He was a secret man.

The servant told Mortland all the talk of the place. The latter found from her Allonby's usual whereabouts; and he wrote two letters, one to Henry Fenthorpe and the other to the attorney, requesting them to come to the Hall the next day at noon. Rising the next morning betimes, he walked over the farm with Bannox, the steward or bailiff; then, dismissing him, went alone, and for anything he himself knew, unobserved, to the church, where he found Allonby.

What passed between them is unknown. Mortland was at the Hall long before his visitors arrived. They were introduced into the principal room of the house, where they saw a tall, raw-boned young man with a pale countenance. His cheekbones were high, his nose straight and prominent, his eyes grey, his manner very pompous. He went straight to the point, telling them he was there as his mother's representative. He told of having heard of the sad accident that had befallen his uncle from the Lincolnshire coroner. He then said that he had learned from the servants that it was supposed the deceased had left a will.

"The late Charles Fenthorpe," said Mr. Armitage, "deposited with me, on the second of December, 1770, this document, which has remained with me ever since, unopened. He told me that it was his will. I do not know that it is his last will; for, on the day before he left Fenthorpe Hall on his fatal journey—you know he was going to Scotland—he told the Reverend Henry Fenthorpe that he had made another will, and told him its contents. We have taken upon ourselves to search for it, with no result. Perhaps, Mr. Fenthorpe, you will relate to Mr. Mortland what passed, and has passed since."

Henry Fenthorpe told his story, in a rather rambling and disconnected manner. Mortland did not interrupt him much. As Fenthorpe was discussing, in somewhat agitated tones, the probabilities of the case, the young Scotchman turned to Mr. Armitage and asked if it was a probable thing that his late uncle would have written a will himself without assistance.

"Quite probable," said Mr. Armitage. "I do not know, but I believe that this, which I hold in my hand, was written by himself. We shall soon know, for I see nothing to delay the opening of it. Mr. Fenthorpe was quite capable of composing his own will, for he had a good deal of legal knowledge. Only, before opening this, I recommend you, Mr. Mortland, to send for Allonby and question him."

" Do you think that necessary ? " asked Mortland. " I do not see for what purpose. He, or another, may have witnessed a will, or a dozen wills, but, if we have not the document, that is nothing to the point."

" For all that," Mr. Armitage replied, " I recommend it. It is right that everything, likely and unlikely, should be done to discover the deceased's last will, if this which I have be not his last."

Mortland objected no more, but ridiculed the idea. While they were waiting for Allonby, Henry Fenthorpe took Mr. Armitage aside and told him of the man's contradictory statement, and something about his character. Mr. Armitage was annoyed that he had been told nothing of this before; but perhaps neither of the two was prepared for what was going to happen.

Allonby came into the room, and Mr. Mortland desired the attorney to examine him. At the first question, he asked Mr. Armitage's leave to ask him, had he, Allonby, said that he had signed anything? To which Mr. Armitage answered that he certainly had.

" Your honour," said the sexton, " that is not the way of it. Mr. Fenthorpe came to me with a paper, and asked me to get him pen and ink, and he went into the vestry. Then he, Mr. Fenthorpe, wrote his own name, and said to me to write my name after it; and when I took up the pen for to write, he stopped me and said he would not get me to do it then, but some other time."

" Man," said Henry Fenthorpe amazed, " what did you tell me yesterday? You told me yesterday that he asked you to sign, and that you did sign, as a witness. Do you deny it? "

" Your reverence," replied Allonby, " when your reverence came to me yesterday, I was drunk, and I do not know what I said."

" That will do," said Mr. Armitage. He saw that the witness was not honest. " Take a pen and ink now, and write down your name on that sheet of paper."

" What for? " said the man. But Mr. Mortland told him,

quietly, to do what Mr. Armitage asked. When the writing was dry, the latter folded up the paper and put it in his pocket-book. Allonby was then allowed to depart.

"I wished," the attorney said to Mortland, "to discover whether he could write at all or not. The man is not telling the truth."

"It signifies little," said Mortland, "whether he is saying the truth or a lee." This young man was strongly moved when he unguardedly lapsed into the Ayrshire dialect.

"There is nothing now, Mr. Armitage, to prevent you from opening the will. Even if it be not my uncle's last will, no prejudice can come by reading it."

They sat down. The will, in the writing of deceased, dated 30th November, 1770, and witnessed by the mark of Hamborough and the signature of Stokesbury, bequeathed all testator's interest in the lands of Fenthorpe, and the lands themselves, and the use thereof, to his nephew, Robert Mortland of Mortland, North Britain; one thousand pounds to Henry Fenthorpe, clerk in orders; five hundred pounds to the poor of the parish; and the rest of the personal estate to Jane Mortland, widow of late Robert Mortland.

There was thus an end of the whole business, in so far as the Fenthorpes were concerned. Mr. Armitage did not believe that there was any will later than that of 1770. Mrs. Fenthorpe was less cast down than her husband. She believed that there was a will, and that it would be found at some time.

Robert Mortland and his mother came to live at Fenthorpe. In process of no long time he married, and had two sons, the acquaintance of one of whom we have already made. Richard Fenthorpe grew up and approached man's estate. The years followed one the other, and the mystery or puzzle was unexplained. In 1792 the Reverend Henry wrote to Mr. Armitage, as we have seen, to know if he had any memoranda of the circumstances. His executor, Mr. Groves, replied, saying that he knew of nothing.

CHAPTER III.

The sun rose on the morning of Tuesday, the twenty-fifth of February, through a clearer atmosphere than had been witnessed in Norfolk, or on any part of the eastern coast, for some days previous. The organisers and the guests of the treat to the school children, properly pleased with this good fortune, assembled themselves duly. Everything went off agreeably. The festivities were prolonged till nearly four o'clock, at which hour Mrs. Fenthorpe quitted the house, or barn, wherein they were held. On reaching home, she found a letter that had come by post lying on the hall table. She was somewhat surprised to see it addressed, not to herself, but to her deceased husband.

She had been one of his executors, Richard being under age at the time of his death. She opened the letter without waiting for Richard, and without scruple. The name at the foot of the letter was Augustus Groves; the date, London. There was an enclosure of some magnitude. She remembered when she had first heard of Mr. Groves, and she recognised his writing.

She was a superstitious woman; not after a vulgar manner, but a believer in coincidences and omens, like John Wesley. She doubted not but that the letter contained information about the subject that she and her son had discussed on the night before. Her heart gave a bound, and she felt as if on the verge of a discovery.

The letter told that the writer had been, as he once many years ago informed Mr. Fenthorpe, executor of Mr. Armitage, attorney, of Lincoln's Inn, who deceased in the year 1792. No papers had been found among that gentleman's effects

38

bearing in any way on any business of Mr. Fenthorpe. Mr. Groves had administered his affairs, in conjunction with Mr. Armitage's son, who succeeded to the business of his father. That son had died towards the end of 1804 and left Mr. Groves his sole executor, having no near relatives. In going through his papers a writing was found, in the hand of old Mr. Armitage, dated the 20th September, 1775. It was written on his return from Norwich, and was a history of the events that occurred there in August and September of that year. Mr. Groves now enclosed a copy of it to Mr. Fenthorpe. He desired that it should be acknowledged in course of post, not to Bloomsbury, where the letter of Mr. Groves was written, but to his house at Newgrove, Folkestone, Kent. All of which he could apprise Mr. Fenthorpe was contained in it. It might be interesting to Mr. Fenthorpe to know that Mr. Mortland had not continued, as his uncle had, to do law business, or any business, with the Armitages, who had been his (Mr. Groves's) intimate friends for a very long course of years.

Mrs. Fenthorpe read the letter and enclosure with great eagerness and rapidity. The memorandum written by Mr. Armitage was a history, with remarks, and an expression of his own conclusions, appended. There was nothing in the narrative part of it that Mrs. Fenthorpe did not find easy to recall to her recollections; but she was somewhat disturbed by Mr. Armitage's remarks.

He said that he thought it intrinsically unlikely that Charles Fenthorpe should make a second will, altering the disposition of his property, without informing him; and he had never informed him. He put aside, as worthless, the several stories that Allonby, the witness, or pretended witness, had told, and concluded generally that Henry Fenthorpe was either the victim of a delusion, which could hardly be, or had understood that Charles had actually made a will when he had no more than spoken of intending to do so. No supposition was without difficulties, but he thought this last was the most like probability.

On the night before, Richard had told his mother where

Allonby was then living; it was only three or four streets off.
Mrs. Fenthorpe had not taken off her out-of-door dress, and
she instantly went to Allonby's, after locking up the letter of
Mr. Groves.   It is not that she was an impulsive person,
who did things without consideration.   Most mothers would
have waited to consult their sons.   But Mrs. Fenthorpe
reflected that this man, having formerly told three inconsistent stories, and the day before, after the lapse of a long
time, told a fourth story, would be more credible if she
should adhere to the last story than he had been at first.

Her husband had vacillated in opinion from time to time.
Sometimes he believed that his cousin had been practising a
deception for no object that he could think of.   This notion
Mrs. Fenthorpe always combated.   At other times he believed
that there was a will, which would turn up some time; and
in talking to his wife when he was of this opinion, he dwelt
strongly on the fact of Allonby making a statement at all.
He said it showed there was something.

Every little circumstance of the events of thirty years ago
came now to Mrs. Fenthorpe's mind with great vividness.
She felt herself impelled to go forward, without a moment's
delay, in the investigation.   She believed that neglect would
be nothing but want of faith.   She felt herself equal to cross-
examine this false and crafty witness then, at once, as she
believed she would not be if she postponed the business.

A few minutes brought her to the street where he lived
with his son and daughter-in-law; and one question,
answered, brought her to the house.   It was a neat house,
comfortably furnished.   Allonby was sitting in a small
parlour by a fire.

She told him who she was, and that she had come to learn
from him again what he had imparted to Dr. Fenthorpe the
day before.

"Yes, madam," he answered, "Dr. Fenthorpe came
yesterday to see me, and we began to talk about that old
business.   You have never found any writing or will, madam,
I believe?"

"You sent for Dr. Fenthorpe, and you began to speak of this business. Dr. Fenthorpe did not come to you without being sent for, nor did he ask you questions."

"Madam, the doctor came to me at Wymondham, now a good many years ago, and he asked the questions then."

"Did you tell Dr. Fenthorpe, when you saw him some years ago, the same as you told him yesterday?" She looked the man in the face, searching his countenance as if searching his thoughts.

"Well, madam, you see, it is so long ago!" He did not meet her look.

"Look at me, Mr. Allonby." (It cost Mrs. Fenthorpe an effort to call this man Mr.; she did not do so to flatter him. She did not know but that he was used to being so addressed.) "Repeat to me, now, exactly what you told my son yesterday —if what you told him is true!"

"Certainly, madam, what I told him yesterday is true, and what I told him at Wymondham is true. I never said in my life anything that was not true."

She had presence of mind, astounding as this speech was, not to attack it, but to turn its flanks. She said:

"Then you had better not tell your first untruth to me. What I want, and what I am resolved to have, is, not the truth only, but the whole of it. I have in my possession a document, giving the entire history of the search that was made thirty years ago for Mr. Fenthorpe's will, including the various statements that you made. As they were all true, what you told yesterday cannot be inconsistent with them. But if you now, for the first time"—the man must have perceived the scorn in her voice; it shone, not ugly, but grand, in her face—"if you now vary from the truth, we have the means of putting one statement against another. This thing will not be allowed to drop. It is your interest, as it is your duty, to be open."

At the mention of a document, the man's face gave a kind of twist. He did not turn away, but he looked down.

"Madam," he said, after a short pause, "Dr. Fenthorpe

D

will have told you that I am out of health, and if it would
suit for me to tell you the whole business to-morrow, I hope I
will be better then, and I will wait on your ladyship."

"You are not so much out of health as to be unable to tell
me what you told him yesterday. Your memory is as good as
it was yesterday. Why do you not tell me now? Do you
want to see any one?"

Again the man's face gave a contortion, and Mrs. Fenthorpe wondered if she had, unknowingly, touched a sore
place. If so, it might be important.

"What does your ladyship wish exactly to know?"

"I have told you what I want to know."

He tried more fencing, but Mrs. Fenthorpe would not
answer him. Her habit of keeping her mouth shut, not as
people commonly do, but with a likeness to a shut-down and
locked lid of a box, gave her a look of great firmness, which
was not without its effect on a person who had never seen
her before. At last he began; and what he told now did not
differ from what he told the day before, although it was not
exactly the same. As he went on, he alluded, with extraordinary power of memory, to his former stories, and
contrived to give a kind of colour to his theory of their
consistency with one another. Mr. Fenthorpe, when he went
to him and brought him into the church for writing materials,
had never said positively that the document was a will. He
had a manner of talking, according to Allonby, thus: he
would say, indeed he did say, I want you to sign this for me,
after my name. Perhaps you think it is my will; well, it
may be my will. As a witness? Certainly, to sign a name
after a man's name is as a witness. Mr. Fenthorpe may have
said it was as a witness; or he may have said to Allonby
that he might call it being a witness if he liked. But what
Allonby was now clear and unhesitating about, was that Mr.
Fenthorpe told him he would get another person besides
himself to sign it also. This was not any part of any
of the various statements Allonby had formerly made, and
yet was consistent with them generally.

"What did you mean," asked Mrs. Fenthorpe, when the man had finished his story, "the first time you saw Mr. Mortland, by telling Mr. Armitage, the attorney, that you signed nothing, and that Mr. Fenthorpe only told you he would get you to sign something again?"

"The first time I saw Mr. Mortland? The attorney, Mr. Armitage, was not there the first time I saw Mr. Mortland."

Mrs. Fenthorpe must have had great presence of mind not to remark on this. She repeated the question, altering it, "When you saw them at the Hall."

"That was when they were asking me about the time I was in the church vestry with Mr. Fenthorpe. It was not there I signed it."

"Not there that you signed it! When and where did you sign it?"

"At the Hall, in the same large room."

This was new, and yet an addition rather than a contradiction. Mrs. Fenthorpe began to think this man had more shifts and moves and doubles, and perhaps more inventions, than Dr. Titus Oates.

"Why," she asked next, "did you not tell Mr. Armitage and Mr. Fenthorpe and Mr. Mortland that it was in the Hall, and not in the church, that you witnessed the document?"

"Madam, they never asked me."

"They never asked you! Mr. Armitage never asked you, nor my husband never asked you, about your signing the will, and when and where it was?"

Allonby paused; he had been frightened when he was told of a document, with which the story could be compared. Mrs. Fenthorpe went on:

"You told Mr. Armitage, the attorney, that Mr. Fenthorpe came to you and asked you had you witnessed a document. You made him believe, whatever you may have said, that you witnessed it in the church vestry. You told the same to my husband. Then you told both of them, in Mr. Mortland's presence, that you had not witnessed any document, but that Mr. Fenthorpe told you he would get you to do so. Now you say it was in the Hall that you wrote your name."

"Ma'am, don't you see, your ladyship is too hard on me. I told them that it was not in the church, and if I had said so I was wrong; and then they asked me no more about it."

"Do you know why they asked you no more about it? It is because they did not believe you. Do you know that to suppress a will is a crime?—hanging."

"Oh, ma'am, ma'am, I am an old man, and respectable! I never made away with a will. I told the gentlemen nought save the truth, and they mixed up the things I told them. And am I to get in trouble for that?"

Although alarmed, he could still argue. He was at the disadvantage of not knowing how much Mrs. Fenthorpe knew; but at every development of the conversation he was more and more impressed with her knowledge. She thought it best to be vague, and to make implications rather than to accuse him. She did not abate her commanding tone one jot.

"I did not say that you made away with a will, although many persons would think that a man who tells a story about one, at the end of thirty years, that he kept back when inquiries were made, is as likely to make away with it as to do anything else. I don't want you to be hanged, even if you deserve it. But there is another crime that I will tell you about. If you did not make away with, or hide"—here she looked at him, but he did not blench at this—"or hide, this document, but only agreed to help another person to do so, it is not hanging; but it is Bridewell."

Of all the ladies, and gentlemen too, that old Toby Allonby had ever met, or had ever heard talking, this was the only one that he felt he was not a match for. It turned out, when she made inquiry about him, that, when he was at Wymondham, and had to come before the justices as a witness in poaching and other cases, he was noted for never telling all the truth, and never perjuring himself. When he heard her words "to help another person," which she said without emphasis or as hinting at anything, he shook with excitement or fear.

"I am an old man, an old man!" he whimpered.

"So I see," said Mrs. Fenthorpe. "The next time I see you, perhaps I will say more to you." She went out of the house without more words. She thought she had gone far enough. She had succeeded in obtaining from him a repetition of what he had told Richard, and in obtaining more besides, and she had established an ascendency over him, which some would call mesmeric, but which we call moral.

But at the threshold she turned back, and came to the door of the room again. Not closing it, but looking on the old sinner as he sat by the fire, she said, loud enough to be heard by anyone else in that story of the house:

"When I come again, perhaps you will have remembered the name of the other witness."

"On my salvation!" he began; but Mrs. Fenthorpe had retreated and closed the door; and what truth, or half-truth, or equivocation, Allonby was about to aver on his salvation, we cannot tell.

Not going straight home, Mrs. Fenthorpe turned into the Cathedral yard, which was not distant, and sat down on one of the seats; it was a fine evening against that time, scarcely five o'clock. As she sat, she constructed in her mind a romance.

Mr. Mortland had seen Allonby on the day of his arrival at Fenthorpe, or on the day after, before the interview that Mr. Armitage had desired. At that interview the man had endeavoured, in a way that he now pretended was honest, to alter his previously told story. Had Allonby been tampered with? Did he know more than was yet, or ever, suspected? How did he come by his livelihood? which was something very superior for a decayed sexton or bellringer. Charles Fenthorpe had been observed going to see him twice. Was it possible that he had employed him to secrete his will? Could it be in the church, hidden behind an old register? Mrs. Fenthrope remembered that her husband had remarked that the Mortlands had got rid of Hamborough and Allonby from about Fenthorpe very soon. Now she knew that Mr.

Armitage had been got rid of. Why had Allonby sent for the doctor the day before? Was it not most probable that Allonby had given Mr. Mortland a different account from any of which she knew? Was it possible that a document missing for thirty years should be nobody knew where? She wondered how she could have forgotten Allonby's name, when Richard had told her about his visit to him the day before. Now she remembered it perfectly. She recalled to her recollection everything that took place about that time. Hamborough had told her husband that the man bore an evil reputation. He had also told her husband that he had been absent from his sextonship for a week shortly before Charles Fenthorpe's departure on his journey. She had never thought of connecting that absence with the disappearance of the will, for Hamborough had hinted that he had gone away to dispose of a corpse. It now occurred to her, could Allonby have been sent by Charles Fenthorpe to London with the will, and never gone? It was unlikely, but not impossible.

Mrs. Fenthorpe had not materials with which to complete any theory. She would find out what she could about Allonby, and see him again, and extort a written confession. She would find out, when better prepared to ask questions, what had passed when he and Mr. Mortland had first met. She would ascertain if Mr. Groves had the sheet of paper on which Mr. Armitage had made him write his name. Her resolutions were come to rapidly; not so all her conclusions. All that she was certain of was that *something was wrong.*

She walked home slowly, turning these things in her mind, and anticipating a long discussion with Richard. But near her own door she met her brother-in-law, Mr. Cardwain, who informed her of something that put Fenthorpe Hall, and Allonby, and Mr. Groves, and all except itself, out of her head.

CHAPTER IV.

ON the same night that Richard and his mother discussed the mysterious disappearance of Charles Fenthorpe's will, Augustus Groves, esquire, barrister-at-law, Justice of the Peace and Deputy Lieutenant of the County of Kent, and Colonel of the 1st Regiment of East Kent Volunteers, sat in the dining-room of his house of Newgrove, a mile and a half on the western side of Folkestone, till a late hour, alone, reading. He had that day returned from town, travelling post. He had been engaged in town for nearly a fortnight, attending to the affairs of the late Thomas Armitage, attorney, whose executor he was.

Mr. Groves was the son of a gentleman at one time high in official and political life, who had gone to Ireland in the suite of Lord Chesterfield, when that nobleman was appointed Lord Lieutenant. That gentleman outstayed Lord Chesterfield, having a permanent employment. He was brave, honourable, and popular; popular both in London and Dublin. He went much into the society of Dublin, which was then almost exclusively Protestant, but he also associated with some of the best families of the Roman Catholic religion. He fell in love with a lady of that Church, and married her, according to its forms. Till the middle of the eighteenth century, there was no law in Ireland to prohibit marriages of that kind. A priest in orders, Romish or Anglican or Hibernian, was a priest in orders, and competent to perform a valid marriage between any man and any woman.

Augustus Groves was the only child of this marriage. When he was about five years old, his parents removed to

47

England, his father having obtained an employment that was
likely to be for his life. He was much trusted by the Pelhams
and the great Whig lords. It was proposed that he should
be advanced to the Peerage, by the title of Baron Naresbrook.
He accepted the honour, and the patent of Peerage was in
preparation but a short time after his return from Ireland.

He had occasion to consult his attorney, the same Mr.
Armitage whom we met at Norwich—although this was long
before the events that we have narrated as occurring in the
Fenthorpe family, concerning the settlements of the estate
from which he was to take his title. All family matters,
births, deaths, and marriages, and their dates, were carefully
recited in the new settlement. Mr. Armitage was much
shocked to discover what he could not but think a fatal flaw.
The marriage of the future Lord Naresbrook to Lavinia
Power was celebrated on the day after the royal assent had
been given to the Act of Parliament declaring marriages of
Protestants by any but their own priesthood invalid.

Mr. —— (for his name was not Groves) was horrified. He
had no wife, and his son was illegitimate. He thought of a
re-marriage, but that would not legitimate his eldest son. He
declined the peerage, giving no reason, and kept the matter
secret between himself and Mr. Armitage. He kept it even
from his wife—we call her so, and will call her nothing else.

It is difficult to pronounce whether or not he was right.
If it were not for the persistent disposition that secrets have
to become the reverse of secret, he was, we think, right. But
his wife discovered the truth, and she died, in six months'
time, of that mixture of grief, mortification, and the dreadful
sense of helplessness, that is most truly called a broken heart.
A day or two before she died, she told her husband what she
had discovered. She had nothing, she said, to reproach him
with, but she prayed him to watch over their little son as
though he would one day succeed to a title.

We do not blame Mr. —— because he married a second
time. The boy was too young to know what he had lost. His
father placed him with a widowed sister, and changed his

name to Groves, that sister's name, sent him to Harrow and
Cambridge, gave him, after he had taken his degree, a large
annual allowance, by settlement and not at will, and kept
him as much about himself as he could a nephew, as young
Groves passed for. Mr. Armitage had always taken a deep
interest in the child, the misfortune of whose birth he had
discovered. By his advice Groves adopted the law as a profession, and became eminent as a chamber counsel. He might
have taken silk, but at the age of about fifty he withdrew
from practice, and bought a house in Kent. During the
volunteering period he took an active part in that movement,
as we have seen. He speedily became one of the most
influential and popular men in East Kent.

His father became Lord Naresbrook, and married—married
a proud, consequential lady, of a political family remarkable
for no talent but that of success in jobs. They had a son, who
succeeded his father in his estate and peerage, but in nothing
that is true honour, about the year 1798. The new lord was
the holder of a place in the royal household. His mother,
from jealousy and meanness of spirit, had filled him with a
hatred of Roman Catholics. She could not bear that the
wife whom her husband loved should have been one. When
the union between England and Ireland was effected, it is
known that Mr. Pitt and most of his colleagues contemplated
the abolition of the laws that excluded Romanists from
Parliament and from office. Lord Naresbrook knew that the
King had not been consulted about this, and that he would
disapprove it. There was an especial reason why Lord Naresbrook, of all men, should not attempt to sow disunion between
the King and the Prime Minister. But he reflected that some
one would tell his Majesty, and he determined to make favour
by being the some one. There was a quarrel. Mr. Pitt
ceased to be a Minister, and was succeeded by one of the most
incurable old women in England. Lord Naresbrook was one
of the new Ministry.

What made this behaviour of Mr. Groves's brother so base
was that he was on terms of intimate personal friendship with

Mr. Pitt. More than this, Mr. Pitt had fallen in love with Lord Naresbrook's eldest daughter, the Hon. Amelia ——. Mr. Pitt often stayed for some days at a time at Walmer, being Warden of the Cinque ports, and on his journeys backward and forward, usually visited Naresbrook, often for more than two days at a time, Naresbrook being near Maidstone. When Mr. Pitt was displaced, the match was broken off, and this in rather a contumelious manner.

Augustus Groves was often a guest at his brother's; and there he became intimate with Mr. Pitt, who formed a very high opinion of his ability and virtue. Walmer being not very far from Folkestone, Mr. Groves was frequently a guest at the Castle, and also at Downing Street when Mr. Pitt had his residence there. Mr. Groves spoke his mind very freely to Lord and Lady Naresbrook concerning their behaviour in breaking off the marriage. He was unaware of his brother's political treachery.

On this night, Monday, the 25th of February, 1805, Mr. Groves sat in his dining-room, reading, till past ten o'clock. Then he closed his book, put out one of his candles, snuffed the other, and stretched his feet towards the fire. He was a strong, hale man, and was not much fatigued with his journey of that day. He began to think.

First he thought of the memorandum that he had found, in the writing of old Mr. Armitage, about the supposed missing will of Charles Fenthorpe. Till he had received the letter from the Reverend Henry, thirteen years before this, he had never heard the name. He had mentioned the inquiry, then, to the younger Armitage, Thomas, who had recollected that there was something unusual that happened in the Fenthorpe family, which had been the occasion of the firm of Armitage & Son losing their business.

He had not mentioned to Mr. Groves the name of Mortland, and the latter did not remember it coming up on the occasion of the inquiry. But when he found Mr. Armitage's memorandum, he recognised the name of Mortland as that of a well-known gentleman of Norfolk.

He had heard no good of him. Robert Mortland had been much disappointed, when he came to live at Fenthorpe Hall, that he did not step into the popularity which, as he knew from his mother's account, his grandfather had enjoyed. He had supposed, without much reason, that his uncle had participated in the same. After the Mortlands had lived in Norfolk for many years, and after Robert's marriage and when his sons were young, Robert hit upon a device for making himself of consequence, and as he expected it would turn out, popular. He took to politics. The war was breaking out. The Whigs of the county, led by the Duke of Norfolk and Mr. Coke, opposed the war. We know now that they might as well have moved a vote of censure on a hurricane. The Duke went great lengths in his opposition. Mr. Coke went not so far, but he got up a great meeting in Norwich, at some time in 1793, to petition for peace. Robert Mortland took a part in the meeting, speaking with great energy and even violence. Mr. Coke was by no means pleased; for to advocate peace, if it could be had, was a different thing from expressing sympathy with our enemies.

For a few days, Mr. Mortland was a hero. But the more sober, even of his own party, began to look on him not as a Whig, but as a downright Jacobin. To a certain extent he was boycotted by the county. He conciliated no one; he was pompous and aggressive, and went on with his new politics—when young, like Scotch lairds of the time in general, he had been a Tory of the Lord North school—till people looked on him as actually disaffected.

When Mr. Addington came in, out of enmity to Pitt, Mortland made friends with the powers that were; and was liberal—that is, liberal for him—in the aid that he gave to the Volunteer movement when the war against Bonaparte began. People forgot their old special objection to him, and he became less unpopular than he had ever been. His wife was a great help to him; she had tried to restrain his Jacobinism, and by her candour in admitting that perhaps Mr. Mortland had gone sometimes rather farther than he meant, did him good with the county. She was anxious to unite in every public thing fit for ladies, such as schools and school feasts. In money matters, she was a mixture, of a not uncommon kind, of liberality and stinginess. One of her objects in life was to marry her son to Helen Tronford.

Mr. Groves knew the public character of Mortland, and had heard from Norfolk people that every one attributed his extreme politics to vanity. He felt an interest in being brought, by old Mr. Armitage's memorandum, into some further knowledge of this man, noticeable in his way.

After he had finished thinking about the Fenthorpes, he made up his mind that one visit more to town must wind up his executorship of the affairs of Thomas Armitage. He had, the week before, cleared all papers out of the chambers at Lincoln's Inn to the house of the deceased in Bedford Street, Bloomsbury, and parted with occupancy of the chambers to a new tenant.

Then Mr. Groves thought of the company with whom he had dined on the day before, at Mr. Pitt's. There were very few: Mr. Dundas (now Lord Melville), Lord Camden, and two or three other eminent politicians; and a Mr. Bentinck, whom Augustus Groves had not met before, and whom he took a strong liking to. Bentinck was one of Pitt's private secretaries. The conversation after dinner had been chiefly about the new turn that the war would probably take, now that the camp at Boulogne was known to be broken up, and now that the Continental powers were in a more warlike temper than they had been since Hohenlinden had ended the last struggle between France and Austria.

"So," said Mr. Groves to himself, "our volunteering is over! I am almost sorry for it. I never enjoyed anything more."

He looked at his watch, and saw that it was near eleven. He rang for the butler, and told him to put out all lamps and to lock the front door. Then, opening a shutter, he went to the window and looked out at the weather. His dining-room overlooked the Channel, at a distance of less than half a mile. The approach of the house was not in view of the dining-room windows.

It was a foggy night, otherwise fine, and no wind. Mr. Groves thought the fog was not so thick as when he had arrived from town. He was about to close the shutter, when he heard voices outside.

He listened, and heard the bar of the entrance door drawn from within; and, opening the door of the room, he heard the butler, John Holmer, in conversation with some one whose voice he did not recognise.

"Who is that at this time of night?" asked Mr. Groves.

"It is Peter Shinkwin and his son, your honour," replied Holmer.

"Come here," said the master to the servant, retreating into the dining-room. "You know this is not right."

"It is not the usual thing, sir. They want to see you."

"What does the man want with me? I have not forbidden you, you know, but I can take no part in it, nor seem to do so."

"Sir, it is not that. They want to see yourself, very special; and the old man said it was nothing wrong."

Mr. Groves went into the hall, and said to Shinkwin the elder, "This is an extraordinary thing! What do you come here for when even you ought to be in your bed?"

"Sir, Mr. Groves, your honour, my son here has got something very particular to tell you; he came from the other side to-day."

"It is not business?" asked Mr. Groves.

"No, sir, it is not. Peter, tell his honour."

Forced to this interview with known smugglers, Mr. Groves led the two men into the dining-room, and stirred the remains of the fire. "Well?" he said, looking at young Peter.

"I came from the other side to-day, sir, and was eight hours and a half coming from Bolong. I told my father what I heard there, not more than two hours ago I told him, and says he to me, this ought to be known to Mr. Groves, if to anyone."

The younger man was very unlike his father, who was a typical sea-dog in appearance. He might have been taken for a Frenchman—lean, wiry, and sharp-looking. His accent was almost French, or, perhaps, more like the tongue of the Flemings. Mr. Groves had never seen him before; his father, often. He was struck with the difference between the two, and when young Peter was proceeding, interrupted him by speaking in French:

"Dites moi qu'est ce que vous avez entendu à Boulogne. Parlez en Francais."

He answered fluently, and with a good accent. Mr. Groves then returned to English, and asked him if he were ever taken for a native on the other side.

"I have often been taken for a Dutchman or a Flushing man, sir," he said. "We have to keep up knowledge of those parties on account of business."

"I know," replied Mr. Groves. Smuggling was almost avowedly practised, although not openly in the face of day. Everybody winked at it. It was believed that many persons of position were engaged in it as capitalists. It was not a mean, demoralising pursuit like poaching, and the men who were active in it were as good subjects as King George had, in every point but the one. There was an understood code of war and etiquette with the revenue men, and those who observed it were mutually well treated, and they often talked, laughed, and drank together at the public-houses. When Mr. Groves came to Kent first, he was shocked, and would have interfered, as a magistrate, if he could have got help or information from any one person whatever. But he could not, and the coastguard officer had, with some bluntness, recommended him to let well alone. Lace, gloves, and brandy were the chief commodities, probably the largest value of brandy.

Mr. Groves, however, had not cultivated the acquaintance of the smuggling clan, and he was rather surprised at such a specimen. Shinkwin proceeded.

"I ought to tell your honour that it is as much as five weeks since I was across last. It is no matter where I was in the meantime. When I was there in January, the whole town and all round it was full of soldiers, just the same as all last year. I left Deal for Bolong on Thursday, and on Friday and Saturday I had some business to do, mostly paying of money —for they are very particular about that. Most of my friends live on the larboard side of the town, and I was not in the town till Saturday night. Now, I heard before I left Deal— I should tell your honour about this, for it caused me for to ask questions—I had heard about the camp being broken up, and the army marched to other places, though I did not hear where. Well, it happened on Sunday—that was yesterday morning—I had called to see an old chap called Cato Lappel, and he lived in a street near the basin, and we went into an *auberge* on the basin and we had something. And says I to Cato, 'The soldiers is all gone.' 'Oui,' says Cato. And I took another look at the basin, and wondered very much when I saw the boats were all gone too, which I had remarked the same before, but had no one for to speak to about it. And I asked Cato, cautious, where the boats was taken to, and he answered, cautious likewise, that there were as many boats as ever there was at Dunkirk. Now, says I to him, you know none but a very few could have gone to Dunkirk or the North Sea and us not know about it. And I tell you, Mr. Groves, there's not a man on the south coast that knows anything that does not know that the way them chaps have been watched it is only by chance that one boat could have got along the coast round Cape Grisnez except on a blind night, this many months back. And he said nothing. And I put it to him again, had they been sent Havre way, for there is no such watch kept there, although there is a watch too. And then he said, sudden, that some had gone Havre way. I asked no more about it then, and I called for Schiedam; for old Cato likes Schiedam, and he likes it at another man's charges. And he asked me again, though he knows I am not, was I never a Hollander; for those old set of chaps, that are neither Christians nor anything else, and have not even got right

Christian names, they have no regard for their country, and
they would be a Hollander, or a Dane, or even a black, to-
morrow, if so be it answered their purpose. Only they would
never be an Englishman; they know there is no use trying
that. And I assured him again, friendly, that I was no
Hollander, although I knew them; and I pointed out to him
our liquor. And he got another little glass and began to
talk. And he laughed in a silent way to himself, and he sat
a long time, the most part of two hours, before he would say
anything. And at last I hinted to him that I was curious
about the boats. And he asked me had I been in any port
on the starboard side of Bolong within a month; and I said
not. And then he assured me, positive, that all the boats had
been taken north, and the army had gone with them. And,
says I to him, do you take me for a greenhorn for to tell
cock-and-bull stories unto? But he says to me he was
telling me the truth, and I would know it soon. And he was
very positive, and very slow about saying more. And he
began to say as how the people there heard that the English
thought the whole war was going to be changed, and the
French were not going to try to come here at all. But he said
' nous verrons.' "

Here Shinkwin paused, and Mr. Groves put him a question.

"Have you any way of knowing how much of what this
person told you is true?"

"I have excellent ways of knowing, your honour; for,
after I had done with him, I went to others and heard the
same from them; they were ready enough when they found
I knew. He told me nothing that is not true, excepting for
what they expect to do; and sometimes it is hard to know
exactly what they have actually done, and what they have
only got in their heads planned, for when they get light-
headed, they are very outspoken. It was a long time before
I got it out of old Cato, that they took the boats to pieces and
carried them away on waggons with the cavalry horses. There
were three, if not four, owned it. I went to a man called
Thibaudière; he keeps an *auberge*, and when he found I

knew he kept nought back. That army that was a month ago at Bolong is now on the Scheldt, at Flushing, and in the islands, and at the Brill, and as far north as Scheveningen; and they have put their boats together again—at least, they say they have—and they expect them to try now, in this very fog. Thibaudière got quite wild talking about it, and he said, 'Tout le grand monde se souviendra de ce brouillard glorieux.'"

The man dropped his voice, and spoke with a sort of awe, as he came to the end of his communication. Mr. Groves said nothing at first; after a few minutes of silence, he asked Shinkwin if he had heard where the Consul was at that moment.

"Bonaparte, your honour?"

"Yes, Bonaparte."

"I did not ask, but I think I heard tell he is now in Holland."

"You left Boulogne this morning?"

"I left where we were anchored, though the last week we could have rode anywhere with no anchor at all. I left with the tide, and I could not have come across in the time I did without the tide. I told him"—nodding to the senior smuggler—"about this, and he recommended me for to come and tell your honour."

"I am glad that you have done so." Mr. Groves sat down, and said, after a pause, "let us hope we are not in such danger as these people think. They are always threatening."

"That is true, your honour. But, leastways, I never knowed them so cocksy about anything before."

"Where is the Channel Fleet now?" Mr. Groves asked the old man.

"Off the Needles, sir; or, mayhap, lower down, near the Start."

Mr. Groves rang the bell, and desired Holmer to take his visitors and give them something to drink—their own importation, we doubt not. The men bowed, or made legs, as that form of politeness was then called, and departed with

E

Holmer, who came back in a minute or two for the key, for there was nothing out.

"Where have you left them?" asked Mr. Groves.

"In the kitchen, sir," the butler replied.

"Holmer, I want you to tell me what you know of young Shinkwin. Is he a steady, sensible young man—I mean as much so as he could be in that business?"

"I know nought to hinder him being steady, sir. I don't know him well, not so well as I know the old one, but he bears a good character."

"Do you know anything of his way of life, by report? I mean what he does when he is not on the sea. Or do you know of any adventures beyond the common that he has had?"

"I do not, sir. I have known the father this very many years, longer far than I have served your honour. This boy was always along with him. They say he sails their craft very skilful."

"This young man has made an extraordinary communication to me, which he and his father will very likely tell to you down stairs. Let them out by the front door when they are going. Light two more candles, and bring up some coals."

When the room was again comfortably arranged, Mr. Groves began to write; and when he had finished, on half a sheet of paper, what he wanted to express, he began to copy what he had written. Before he had completed his copy, the guests of the butler came up the kitchen stairs. Mr. Groves opened the door and intercepted them.

"Will you," he said to the younger man, "wait for five minutes? Holmer, I want to speak to you."

The butler came into the room, and, in reply to his master, told how Shinkwin had repeated the same story about the army and boats. Mr. Groves got him to go through the details, and it was plain that the man was not adding to his statement. Holmer spoke as if amazed, and said there was no being up to those chaps.

"You believe that what he tells is true, and that he is not romancing?"

"I never thought of not believing him, sir. How could a man go and trump up the like of that?"

"It will not be good for him if he is telling aught but the truth," said Mr. Groves. He opened the door, and called them in.

"Shinkwin," he said, "what you told me just now is of importance, or may be so, if true. It is a very serious thing to make a statement like yours; and it is a very wicked thing to make such a statement, not being true."

He waited for an answer, which came so soon as the smuggler perceived himself expected to speak. "It is Gospel truth what I have told your honour; and, as I have a soul to be saved, I believe what the Bolong men said is the fact."

"Will you swear to it?"

"Certain, your honour. It can do me no harm to swear to the truth."

"I have written down the substance of your story. Listen to it."

Mr. Groves read the first of the papers, the completed one, slowly. "Will you swear to that?"

"Perhaps your honour would read it again?"

It was not long, and Mr. Groves read it again. Shinkwin said, "I can swear to all that, sir. I don't swear that what they told me is true, and I hope it is not. I will swear that is what I heard. I think that is the way your honour makes it."

"It is so," replied Mr. Groves. "What is your full name, age, usual place of dwelling? I describe you as a mariner."

"I live mostly here at Folkestone, at my father's. I am twenty-four. Peter, sir; no other name."

The affidavit was sworn, signed, and witnessed, Holmer being witness. Mr. Groves let it lie on the table; he meant to finish the copy before he went to bed.

"I cannot lay any commands on you three not to speak of this at present; but I recommend you, as strongly as I can, not to do so. It is my duty to give this information to those who ought to have it. You, Holmer, go now with these two Englishmen"—he raised his head as he said this, and both the Shinkwins said, "Thank your honour"—"go into the town and order a chaise to be here at six in the morning. You, young Peter, I want to come with me to town. Come up in the chaise, and don't keep it waiting."

It was now past midnight. The three men stared. For a respectable butler to walk two miles and back, at dead of night, was a new thing in Holmer's experience, and for a smuggler to travel in a post-chaise with a gentleman was a new thing in Shinkwin's. It was two o'clock before Holmer returned, and then Mr. Groves went to bed for four hours' sleep, if he could get it.

The chaise, with its two occupants, left Newgrove at about half-past six the next morning. It was not dark, nor very cold; the air was still thick, and calm. The posting on the Southern or Folkestone road was never so good as that on the great Dover road through Canterbury, but they got on for the first few stages pretty well. For their second stage they had a nice easy chaise, and Mr. Groves had a good hour's sleep. As they neared town, the fog increased.

It was very irrational, but so it was, that the thicker the fog grew, the more Mr. Groves's faith in the Boulogne men's story increased. He remarked to Shinkwin that it made one think of what might happen, when the young man shook his head and said it looked like a warning. It was as evident as anything could be that he was sincere. He asked Mr. Groves what he thought would be done if the French came. The magistrate replied merely that all men would have to do their duties.

Ten hours, the roads being in good order, or eleven hours, allowing for a halt to eat something, had been Mr. Groves's estimate of the time the journey should occupy. But, two miles short of Sevenoaks, the chaise lost a wheel by the shoeing coming lose, and they had to walk into Sevenoaks. Shinkwin carried Mr. Groves's valise. This lost an hour.

Again, still nearer town, the fog was so dense as to seriously impede their progress. The postboy stopped, and said he was afraid to go beyond a walk. A couple of half-crowns promised, and a peremptory command, got over this difficulty. It was past seven o'clock, however, before they crossed Westminster Bridge.

The chaise was turned into that narrow street on the western side of Whitehall, the principal house in which has been tenanted by some mean men, by some clever men, and by some great men. At that time it was occupied by him who was, perhaps, the greatest of them all.

Mr. Groves got out and knocked at the door. As the porter was answering his question, a gentleman came forward from within, and was passing out. But when he saw Mr. Groves he stopped and greeted him with some wonder.

"I have just arrived," said Mr. Groves; "when can I see him? I wish for no delay."

"The House," said Mr. Bentinck, for this was the secretary, "will not be late to-night. I can send to ask, if necessary. Is your business important?"

"It may be of importance. Would it do for me to wait?"

"Certainly, if you desire; but I should recommend you— you are just from a journey—to go and house yourself and get your dinner, and be here at nine. I think the house will be up by nine."

"I will do so, then. Shall you be here?"

"I shall. Tell me, Mr. Groves, where are you going to put up?"

"I generally put up in Bloomsbury, but to-night I am going to the Golden Cross. It is near, and I have a companion whom I could not bring to Bloomsbury."

"Very well; at nine o'clock."

Mr. Groves got rooms at the Golden Cross and his dinner, and ordered Shinkwin to be attended to. At the stroke of nine, they were again in Downing Street. Mr. Bentinck was there, and he and Mr. Groves went into the dining-room, where was an immense fire. Shinkwin was accommodated with a chair in the hall.

Bentinck would, of course, be present at the interview with
Mr. Pitt, and it was best to tell him the occasion of this visit.
He expressed the most complete incredulity.

"Lord Melville was saying, lately, that, during the time
the camp was at Boulogne, there was not a move they could
make that was not considered. Their whole scheme depended
on getting a naval force greater than ours into the
Channel. It even depended on getting a force into the
Channel at some moment when we should have no force in it
at all. As for their attempting to cross without any covering
fleet, the thing is too wild. And this story about breaking up
the boats and carrying them overland, and putting them
together in the small harbours on the Scheldt—really now,
sir, do you believe it?"

"Will you read this?" said Mr. Groves, taking out his
pocket-book and producing Shinkwin's affidavit.

The secretary read it twice, and handed it back. "Is this
the companion you spoke of?" he asked. "What is he?"

"He is a smuggler of respectability," Mr. Groves answered.

"Have you really come up to town for no other business
than this?" Bentinck asked in astonishment.

"I have come for nothing but this."

Bentinck opened his eyes wide, and said, after a moment's
pause, "You believe it, plainly. I should never have thought
of setting any store on information got in that way."

"Why, Mr. Bentinck," said Groves, "what is there
uncommon, or anything but very common, in getting information through spies? And this man is not even a spy!
Consider the probabilities. I have travelled to-day from
Kent with him, and he is, I say to you from observation, an
intelligent man, and one not likely to be taken in. What he
tells of his own knowledge is the truth, I am satisfied; and
it is sworn to, a thing that we lawyers set a great value on.
Where are the boats that were in the basin of Boulogne six
weeks ago? You say Lord Melville had every contingency
considered. Had he this, that has actually been done, considered?—the removal, overland, as this man has heard,

of the boats, a thing in itself not usual, but not impossible, nor even difficult to do. Has Lord Melville had it considered that a fog might last for six days without a break, in weather in which, this Shinkwin says, a catamaran might sail across the Bay of Biscay? Has he had it considered that this might happen when our fleet is in the Channel, and cannot get into the North Sea without wind? When I hear it said of anything that every contingency has been considered, I think that he who says so can have never thought that contingencies are almost infinite in variety and number. I have frequently been engaged, as counsel, in cases in which the evidence was curious; and I tell you, that I never was in a vexed case in which there was not some point that no one could have anticipated."

"I dare say," said Bentinck, "that Lord Melville means that the possibility of the French attempting to cross without a covering fleet has been considered, and set aside as a thing virtually impossible."

"Have they no covering fleet? Are there not the Texel ships?"

"No; blockaded." The secretary took up the affidavit again. "I cannot," he continued, "perceive that there is much to be alarmed at. It is a very zealous proceeding of you, Mr. Groves, to have taken this journey on this account; you will let me say how really patriotic it is, whether it be of use or of importance or not. You must be fatigued."

"Not much, Mr. Bentinck. I could not have slept in my bed another night; last night I slept not at all, though I slept for two stages this morning; without coming and imparting what I had learned. It would not do to have written; letters are not attended to like verbal communications. I, as a lawyer, know that it is so in large classes of cases. Have you curiosity to know what consideration made it imperative on me, in conscience, to tell of this, and lose no time in telling?"

"What have you to tell me? I shall be interested."

"How long have you been private secretary?"

"Less than a year; since this Ministry came in."

"To be sure; you are official private secretary. This occurred before your time, and perhaps you have not heard it. Early in spring in the year 1800, an English merchant, who had just come from the Continent, waited on Mr. Pitt, and told him that he had heard, as something more than a rumour, that the army then gathering at Dijon was not intended for service on the Rhine, but in Italy, and that it would attack the Austrians in the rear. Mr. Pitt dismissed him, and gave no attention, and, I suppose, of course, no credence, to the report. I have heard that he did not think it even worth while to apprise the Imperial Ambassador of what he had heard. That was the army that crossed the Alps and won Marengo."

Bentinck imagined that Mr. Pitt was infallible, as many others did, and as many others have imagined of other statesmen. This piece of history did not stagger him, consciously to himself, at the time, but he dropped his almost contemptuous tone and his manner of speaking of the intelligence brought from Boulogne. "What kind of a man is this mariner, or smuggler, Mr. Groves? Suppose we have him in."

"I can have no objection to that, quite the contrary; it is what I brought him for. I never saw or heard of him before last night; I know nothing of him but from himself, and from my butler, who says he bears a good character. You are aware, I presume, that there is nothing disreputable, one may call it, on the south coast, in carrying on trade under two flags?"

"I have heard some anecdotes that are not creditable to what I regard as true loyalty. No doubt, you mean that a man who runs goods is not necessarily a dishonest man in ordinary affairs."

"I do mean it, as matter of fact, and of general opinion. This man is not to be set aside as a witness because he earns his livelihood in that equivocal trade. I will admit to you that he has imparted to me a good deal of his own faith in this conjectured attempt. I am alarmed, Mr. Bentinck."

They called in Shinkwin. Mr. Groves said to him that this gentleman desired to ask him a few questions. "You have not been talking to any one, I hope?" he concluded.

"No, for certain, I have not, your honour. I will tell you all I heard, sir," he said to the secretary.

Bentinck and he had not conversed for three minutes, when the door was opened, and a tall man entered. Mr. Groves stood up, and they shook hands together. "I am told you were here before," said the gentleman.

"Leave us for the present," Groves said to the smuggler. "We may require you presently." Then he told the new-comer the object of his visit. This was a thin, rather narrow-chested man, of a good deal more than the ordinary height, with a certain eagerness in his countenance, or something that is best described as expressing an eager and sanguine disposition. He had a large, thin, prominent, but perfectly straight nose. His lips were thin, and his chin very square and firm. His eyes were remarkable for the steadiness of their gaze, not as if he searched the thoughts of his companions, but as if he were looking at something far off. His face was very pale, of an unhealthy, almost death-like hue. He looked older in the face than was in proportion to the quickness of his gestures; perhaps he was only forty, perhaps fifty-five. His voice was very sweet and full.

"This," Mr. Groves said when he had detailed Shinkwin's intelligence, "is the affidavit."

The gentleman took it and read it attentively, then said: "Lord Melville is of opinion, and so am I, that it is a practical impossibility for a landing to be attempted without the active assistance and protection of a strong fleet. Also, we know that Russia and the Emperor will shortly declare themselves in such a way that any hazardous operation by the First Consul is in the utmost degree improbable. It is due to you, Mr. Groves, who are taking so much trouble, that I should enter on this matter with you. I am not alarmed, but I will not neglect this. Is there anything more than you have told me, or than is sworn to?"

"Nothing, except that the man heard that Bonaparte is in Holland. It is known to you that the Channel Fleet is in the Channel at present, and could not get into the North Sea in this calm."

"That is the case. Suppose—to suppose the worst—that the enemy do take this opportunity, if it be an opportunity, for a landing, they can land, but they could never leave England without our permission. That should be as obvious to them as it is to us."

"I believe, sir, that it is not obvious to them. I was in France for some months during the peace, and my reading of their views is, that they would sacrifice anything for the chance, which they regard as a certainty, of making a revolution in this country."

There were a few more remarks interchanged, and Mr. Groves rose to say good evening. "Do you wish to question my informant?" he asked. "He is here."

"Oh! The man whom I saw in the hall? It is unnecessary, if he has told all he has to tell."

"I am sure there is nothing more; and if he were to tell the smallest new item now, I would disbelieve all. But, sir, you will let Lord Melville hear of this?"

"I will, of course. Mr. Bentinck, it is no more than ten o'clock; I think you had better go to Lord Melville now; he is at his house. We walked to the end of the street together." Then, turning to Mr. Groves, "You would like to see him, perhaps? Or is it too late, and are you too much fatigued?"

"I think I will go to my hotel," said Mr. Groves. He took his leave, and preceded Bentinck out of the room. He and Shinkwin stood on the steps, while the other put on his coat. "May I make so bold as ask your honour," Shinkwin said, "who was the tall gentleman who came into the room?"

"That was Mr. Pitt."

Bentinck came out, and they turned to the left at the end of Downing Street. Fifty yards farther, they saw a man on horseback. The man evidently saw them, for he pulled up and accosted them. He asked where Downing Street was. He was dressed in a red coat, like a huntsman; his horse's flanks, his coat, and his hat, were covered with patches of mud.

"I will show you," said the young secretary, and turned. The man thanked him, and said he only wanted to know. "I live in Downing Street," said Bentinck. "Have you despatches?"

"Yes, sir," said the man, "for Mr. Pitt himself."

When they got to the door, Shinkwin offered to hold the horse, and the huntsman and the secretary went in. A quarter of an hour later, while Mr. Groves was wondering would they be kept with this blown horse, which wanted grooming badly, the whole night, Bentinck opened the hall door. He looked like a man who had received a blow in the stomach, or who had seen a ghost. Mr. Groves went up the steps.

"O my God!" said Bentinck, in a terrified whisper, "it is all true. The French have landed at Harwich."

CHAPTER V.

THEY went into the house. "How many?" asked Mr. Groves.

"They don't know; they think forty thousand. The boats were still coming in when the despatch was written."

"Who sent it?"

"The commanding officer of the garrison at Harwich; no more than a battalion or a battalion and a half. It is signed by the major also, and the volunteer major."

"It is well that there is no greater garrison," said Mr. Groves. "It will be fortunate if they can get away, and be of use afterwards. But they have not come with forty thousand only. I need not keep you. We shall all have our work cut out for us."

"Oh," said Bentinck, "he would like to see you."

"Mr. Pitt?"

"Yes; he told me. Come!"

Mr. Groves would never have thought of presenting himself in the Prime Minister's presence at such a moment. But, being treated with such distinction, his brain, which worked rapidly, began, almost unconsciously to himself, to elaborate a project, assistance from Mr. Pitt in carrying out which would be necessary.

"I have desired to see you, Mr. Groves," said the Minister, "to tell you that I am giving instructions that you shall be informed of all particulars as more intelligence comes in. We shall certainly have two or three more messengers during the night. This man says that arrangements are made to have fleet horses waiting. I am sending him back, if his horse can travel, with orders, to be passed on, to the Colchester garrison and all other troops to withdraw. Mr. Bentinck is to go

68

instantly to Lord Camden's, and I am going to Lord Melville. Mr. Bentinck, order the carriage to follow me. Harry," he continued, as if speaking to himself, " must hear of this from me. Then, at six, I must go to Windsor."

Mr. Groves shuddered when he thought of the King. Would his Majesty's mind bear up? He did not know the stuff that that brave and obstinate old man was made of.

He went away to his hotel, and did not know until he was in bed how tired he was. There was in the coffee room a gentleman whom he knew pretty well, a Kent man. He told him, and no one else. He wished to judge, by even one example, what the public sentiment, or judgment, was likely to be when knowledge of the long-dreaded invasion should burst upon England.

It would be too much to say that his friend received the intelligence with composure. " Speak low," said Mr. Groves, in a tone such as one employs in the chamber of death.

" Are we prepared? " asked his friend, when the first paroxysm of astonishment was over.

" I know nothing more than that we should be, with the difference that this falls upon a part of the coast where it was never expected, and I know that in Essex there are no means of resistance. The force at Tilbury is what it has been for the last eighteen months. It will take some time to have an army in the field large enough ·to fight a pitched battle, even with volunteers. I do not know how long landing their whole force and getting it into order for marching will take. I should think four days, at least; the longer the better."

" And, Groves, may I ask what will you do yourself? "

" I will go back for my volunteers at the very first moment that I can leave town. I may say to you I must stay in town till I know what I am to do with them; and I may say that I very greatly fear that there is not going to be sufficient unity of system."

" What makes you suppose so? You know Pitt as well as any man, I suppose; and don't you think that he is equal to this emergency? "

"No man has a higher opinion of Mr. Pitt's courage and resolution than I have; and without courage and resolution military skill would be thrown away. But military skill and military knowledge—the qualities that make a great commander—can do more, when courage and resolution are joined to them, than either kind of qualities can do alone. Now, Mr. Lynton, there is no real general in England but Lord Cornwallis, and he is too old. The French will be beaten in the end, I believe, as I believe there is a God in heaven; but they will beat us first."

"God bless us! And do you think they will take London?"

"I do."

"I think I will go home," said Mr. Lynton after a pause.

"I think you had better," said Mr. Groves, shaping his voice so as not to express the half-contempt that he felt. "No business will be done in town to-morrow nor the day after, but buying and selling what people eat and drink."

Mr. Groves went upstairs and to bed, keeping his candle lighted for some time, as is the habit of many persons when they sleep in an inn. But he was asleep before the candle had burned itself down to the socket, so that he did not put it out. We have said that already a project had begun to form itself in his mind. He thought rapidly, and completed it, so far as he could then, in about an hour. But it is curious that the last subject that occupied his thoughts, was the piece of the family history of the Fenthorpes that he had found among Thomas Armitage's papers. It occurred to him that the mails would be stopped all over the east of England, and that the Reverend Henry Fenthorpe (as we have seen, he had never heard of his death) must be unable to acknowledge his letter. He felt satisfaction that he had sent a copy only of the memorandum, and kept the original.

For the present, we drop Mr. Groves, and we proceed to describe what had actually happened and was happening at Harwich at the time that intelligence of the landing reached Mr. Pitt. About daylight on the morning of the 26th of

February, the French flotilla, sounding, found themselves nearing land. They felt their way, pointing north, for they thought the currents had put them more to the south than according to reckoning. In this they were correct, and before noon they believed they were off Harwich, and very close in. The fog did not lift, but was much lighter than it had been further out at sea. The foremost boats kept towards shore, and Harwich, which was their object, was seen not more than a mile off. They instantly pressed forward, always rowing, and thirty or forty boats, each with a hundred soldiers, were in the harbour before it was known on shore that any boats were approaching. There was a row of colliers alongside the quay; as many French boats as there was room for ran up to them, grappled, and boarded them. There was no resistance.

In a very short time six or eight hundred men had landed and marched into the town. The shopkeepers stared, and most of them put up their shutters. Nobody did anything; nobody knew what to do. It was a hunting day, and the Mayor, who was a sportsman, had gone to the meet; so had the major of volunteers; so had the lieutenant-colonel commanding the garrison, which was not so large as Bentinck had told Mr. Groves—three hundred men only, being really a detachment from the garrison of Colchester, at that time always kept at full or nearly full strength. One of the few men who kept their heads, or, perhaps, who had heads to keep, was a lame sailor. As fast as he could hobble, he walked up to the barracks, and was made way for by the sentry when he told what he had come about. The second in command, a major, questioned him; at first he could not believe what he heard. He made up his mind at once, however. He turned out all his men and marched them into the town. About five hundred French were in the broad street or market-place, in a column with a front of about eight. The major halted his little army, deployed, and gave them a volley at forty yards, then closed with the bayonet.

The head of the column was cut off in no time. But the officer in command, who was in the rear, threw his column

into opener order, and advanced at double quick march from
the bottom of the street. There was then a very severe hand-
to-hand fight for half an hour. Soon the major saw that there
was no end to the enemy's numbers, for a thousand men to
three hundred was practically unlimited odds, and he thought
that the French officer perceived that he had no reinforce-
ments. He withdrew, having a perfectly free retreat, made
safe from searching shots by a turn in the street. His loss
was sixty men, perhaps twenty of them prisoners.

He began to wonder if he had done right in fighting. As
the last of the beaten detachment—not that they considered
themselves beaten—turned into the barrack-yard, the colonel,
the major of volunteers, and the Mayor were approaching from the country. When they had arrived at the meet
that morning, the master could not meet them, having been
struck down with fever thirty-six hours before; and the day
before the huntsman had broken his arm; so there was no
hunting that day; no, nor for many days. This was
providential, for had these gentlemen not returned, a disaster
would have happened. It had never occurred to the major to
withdraw to Colchester, which retreat the commanding officer,
when he understood the state of affairs, instantly ordered, so
saving the detachment from certain surrender. It is worth
mentioning that, when this circumstance came to be known
in conjunction with the plucky fight in the market-place,
which, of course, was magnified, it was much used by those
clergy, both of the Church and Dissenters, who believe that
God is the God of England as he was at one time the God of
Israel, in exhorting their people to be strong and of a good
courage, and to trust in the Lord. We have understood that
that sort of clergy was more plentiful at the beginning of this
century than it is at the present time.

The major, who was no coward, as we have seen, before
the enemy, trembled when he told his colonel of the responsi-
bility he had taken on himself, and expressed a hope that he
would get no anger. The colonel laughed.

"By God, sir, if you get anger for fighting the French,
there is no help for England with God or man."

The three sportsmen, forgetting their disappointment, turned into the barrack to hold a council. It was half-past two.

"Word must be sent at once to Colchester, and on to London," said the colonel. "Which of us has the best horse?"

"I have," said the volunteer major; "at least, for as far as Colchester. What have we got to tell? How many of them are there?"

At this instant a young gentleman, the Mayor's nephew, came into the room, asking pardon for the intrusion. He had been on the wharf when the first boats came into the harbour. He knew at once what it was. He went instantly to the top of a look-out, which had at one time been a lighthouse, and took a view. Staying there for about three-quarters of an hour—indeed, till he heard shots in the town—he tried to form an estimate of the number of the boats. He was sure there were four hundred, and he thought more; it was clear enough to see those within half a mile of shore, for since noon the fog was much less thick. He could not tell of more than he saw, but he suspected. Every one knew that each boat held one hundred men.

In a few minutes the despatch was written and sent. The major of volunteers went to a friend in Colchester who, he knew, had the fastest horse in the town, and so passed it on; then he went to the barracks, and, lastly, rode home.

It may be asked what, during all this time, was Landguard Fort doing? The weather was, as we know, foggy, and the first thirty or forty boats got into the harbour unobserved. In about half an hour the sergeant of gunners in the fort began to understand what was the matter. There were no boats within more than a mile; but, as his duty was, he opened fire. Very soon, four French frigates neared the fort, and replied. The fire on the boats was most ineffective, as they offered no target, being very little out of the water; two or three boats were struck. After the frigates had sent some shots into the fort, boats, well manned, were launched, that

F

made for the spit, to attack it in rear. The sergeant then surrendered—he had only six men—and the French took possession of the fort. It was never known who was to blame for leaving an important position so unguarded. Many ignorant persons thought the sergeant gave in too easily; but no man is justified in fighting on when utter defeat is an absolute certainty within a few minutes.

When the volunteer officer galloped off to Colchester, the colonel asked the Mayor what he was going to do. "I am going home," he answered. "They may attempt to maltreat the people, and, although I can do nothing to prevent them, a person of authority may have some moderating influence. People will be coming to ask for advice, too."

"They will take your horse, Mr. Ringland," said the colonel.

"They will not; I will have him away before that, with another despatch, and I will not have him brought back."

Mr. Ringland was not a resident in Harwich, but a squire whose estate was both in and outside of the town; he was a freeholder of the town, and had been Mayor for many years. He was very popular, and much confided in. When he arrived at his house, which was not more than half a mile from the town, twenty or thirty citizens were there, waiting to ask him what they were to do.

"I can give you no advice, except to make no resistance, which, indeed, you can't make, and to try it will do nothing but make them violent. Another thing, however, I recommend you: every one of you that has a horse, get on his back this instant, and ride away with him as far as you can, till you find a friend that will take care of him, or till you can sell him; sell him for any price at all."

The citizens walked away as fast as their legs could carry them, and those who had horses went straight to their stables; but in every instance the French had been before them. They found about a hundred and fifty horses in the town. On the next day they spread their search for horses into the neighbourhood, where they were less successful than they had expected. But we are anticipating.

When young Mr. Ringland left the barracks, after giving such information about the amount of the enemy's force as he could, he returned to the town, but hesitated about crossing it to his former look-out. Indeed, the look-out is so near the quay that he felt sure it was, by this time, in the enemy's power, and inaccessible to him. He remembered a certain builder's yard, two or three hundred yards beyond where the town ends on the road leading southwards. Going to it, he found the builder standing alone at his gate. All his men had gone into the town to satisfy themselves as to what was going on. Indeed, the prevailing feeling of the population was curiosity rather than fear, till they saw the skirmish in the market-place, and the bodies of soldiers, our own and French, lying slain. At Ringland's request, two boys were sent for the builder's men, who were found, or enough of them, easily. Ringland then, having searched the yard, got two forty-eight feet ladders carried into a field adjoining, where the ground rose somewhat, and there was a good view. He had the ladders raised, and the tops lashed together. Ropes had been fastened to the upper ends. He put five men to hold each pair of ropes, and so steady the ladders. Then he went up a ladder, and stayed at its top till it was too dark to see anything. The men held the ropes steady, and the angles of the ladders to the ground, and the angles of the ropes to them, were so arranged that there was very little swaying.

He saw as much as he had dreaded. He counted the boats, as well as he could, three times over. He did not know how many were in the harbour, nor did any one, for the French had expelled all persons from the wharf, and from the adjoining streets. Ringland guessed them, however, at eighty. There were, he was certain, more than eight hundred in the offing. He could not know how many of these contained, not the known complement of a hundred soldiers, but cavalry or field guns. He knew that there were no boats of those in sight that could carry heavy guns. He saw the four frigates close into the fort, which, he judged, must have been taken. There were five large ships besides, of what rate he could not conjecture, but all three-masters.

He came down, and, in reply to the builder, who asked how many there were, said only, "Enough to give us trouble."

The ten men lowered the ladders, and came to where they were talking. Till they heard these words, they had not understood the magnitude of the events that were happening. Some of them damned their eyes, and some blessed themselves —meaning the same by those rather dissimilar expressions of emotion. But none were loud, or boisterous, or demented.

To his uncle the Mayor's country house was about a mile and a half across fields; in the dark, it was a half-hour's walk at least. Close to the gate, a man overtook him, coming from the town; he also was going to his worship's. This was an old nautical man, who had been commander of a collier for many years, and had made money. He was a kind of oracle, and did not brag much, and was considered good authority when he said anything, with or without an oath. He told Ringland that the harbour would not give room for more than seventy boats at once; nor could all the seventy discharge at once, but the first set of seventy had discharged, and then gone up the Stour, and a second set of seventy had come in, and was about discharging then. He did not know if the landing would be proceeded with during the night.

They went into the Mayor's dining-room unannounced. The Mayor had expected visitors of another kind. The French officers had inquired for the chief magistrate of the citizens, for they wanted him to arrange billets, to save themselves trouble. But every one in Harwich knew that it was a hunting day, while no one knew that there had been no hunting. So, when the officers understood—a few of them knew English enough to gather this much—that the Mayor was absent, they took possession of every house as they went along the streets, and made these the men's quarters for the night. It was the most uncomfortable night that the inhabitants of Harwich had ever spent.

When Squire Ringland had heard his nephew's report, and what Captain Sanders had to tell, he dismissed the latter; then said, "Joe, you must take Whipcord at once, so soon as I have written. Have you any money?"

"I have three guineas, sir!" said the nephew.

The squire went to his desk and counted out thirty guineas. Joe Ringland wondered; not that the old gentleman was not liberal, but he did not know what he intended.

"You must take Whipcord, and you must not bring him back. I must stay here, for it is my duty, though I suppose they will take me prisoner. You go away, and stay away, and the Lord be with you! You and I may never see each other again."

"But, sir, and Whipcord?"

"Is it not better for you to have him than for the French to get him? I am sending word to all the country round to send away their horses."

We know not whether these two brave and cool-headed Englishmen ever met each other again; we think not.

In the morning of February, the 27th, Wednesday, all London knew that the French had landed. Word was sent to the Lord Mayor at an early hour, that, to the best of the information which his Majesty's Ministers had, a force of ninety thousand, or thereabouts, of the enemy, were in the act of disembarkation. It was known that the Privy Council was summoned for twelve o'clock, when the necessary proclamation for putting in force the Acts of Parliament relating to the emergency would be issued. A message from the King to the Houses would be delivered on their sitting.

We must now, we fear, disappoint our readers, at least such of them as may expect a description of the panic and passionate fear that a vast population may be expected to exhibit when overtaken by a tremendous calamity, because there was no panic or passionate fear exhibited by the most part of the people. There was much rather a sentiment manifesting itself, as if there had come suddenly the necessity of doing and suffering something that was very new, very unusual, and very unpleasant; but that the something to be done and suffered *must be* done and suffered, whatever it should turn out to be.

There were exceptions. A few persons wrung their hands

and shed tears when they talked to their friends, and this even before spectators, when these people ought to have stayed at home if they could not control themselves in public. Many women wept when they thought of their husbands and sons, and how they would go forth and help to fight battles, and perhaps be killed or maimed; but this was not weakness. Most of these women went to their rooms and prayed; and God, if we know anything about Him, hears such prayers when they are made properly.

A man, a Methodist preacher, who had been put out of the society that Mr. Wesley founded, for immorality, got on a waggon in Covent Garden and proclaimed that the Lord's judgment had fallen upon England, and that her last hour was come. But he was interrupted by a vigorous attack with cabbage stalks, and came down from his pulpit without an opportunity of sending round his hat, which, indeed, was his text, although he intended to bring it in at the end of his sermon, a position that the text does not usually occupy.

Covent Garden never was one of the centres of Metropolitan opinion. Let us see what was thought in the city and at the clubs. But first we must tell of a circumstance that came to be known towards three o'clock, which produced an extraordinary amount of enthusiasm, and even made men whose hearts were quaking talk as if they were brave.

Mr. Pitt went to Windsor early in the morning, as he had intended. The King was at breakfast, in the act of breaking the shell off an egg, when the arrival of the Minister was imparted to him. His Majesty was saying, "This is a bad egg, a bad egg."

When the message was given, his Majesty rose from table instantly, saying, "Mr. Pitt arrived, Mr. Pitt arrived."

Pitt was not a man of many words, when words were not required; when they were required, or when he thought they were, he could deliver more of them, and better, than any but a very few men that have ever existed. The King was not a bright man, nor quick, but he understood what was told him, and understood its portentousness.

"Mr. Pitt," he said, "this is a serious matter, a serious matter."

"Sir," replied the Minister, "it is the most serious matter that has occurred during your Majesty's reign, or during the reign of either of your Majesty's ancestors."

"Mr. Pitt," said the King, after a short pause, "I will go to London, go to London."

"Sir!" said Mr. Pitt in astonishment.

"Yes, Mr. Pitt," his Majesty continued, "and I will stay till Parliament rises, till Parliament rises."

Pitt was profoundly struck. He saw the effect that this must have on public sentiment, and there would be a considerable convenience to the public service. When the King said he would stay while Parliament sat, his Majesty probably contemplated the adjournment of the Houses to Oxford or Bristol, a contingency that had been discussed a year before. Pitt answered:

"Sir, if your Majesty shall now set such an example to your subjects of firmness and patriotism, it will resound through all Europe, and it will be spoken of with admiration by future ages. Sir, your Majesty's words give me strength."

He had rarely, if ever, been so moved. The King was not insensible to flattery, and he liked Pitt; but at that moment he thought little of Pitt's grand speech, for he was eager, and felt the tremendousness of the occasion, and was more sane than perhaps he had ever been at any moment of his life. He asked Mr. Pitt if he had a draft of the message to the Houses; he was a man who never forgot business and its forms.

It was produced, and approved, then Pitt rose to go.

"You and I must stick together, Mr. Pitt, stick together!" said his Majesty; and the Minister bowed himself out. It is not too much to say that he was elated, notwithstanding all the tons of weight of care that oppressed his mind. This would be construed as a personal compliment, and it might enable him to ride roughshod over Lord Camden, whom he despised. Pitt rather liked to ride roughshod over people, which made him enemies.

To return to the Metropolis. In the merchants' counting houses in the city no business whatever was done, nor on the Royal Exchange, except in foreign bills, which were rather freely taken. There was of talk no end. The principal point discussed was, could the enemy be kept out of London? Most seemed to think they could not; but all, except very few, were resolute that a battle must be fought to defend the Metropolis against any odds. One or two said it was impossible; the Frenchmen would be at Mile End the next evening. Four or five gentlemen were talking eagerly together, after hours, when the Exchange was thinner. One of them expressed this apprehension. At that moment, a porter came and stuck up a notice.

"The King has just arrived at Buckingham House. Half-past two p.m. 27th February."

All that were on the Exchange ran forward to read this, and to repeat it to each other; and such a cheer rose as had never shaken Sir Thomas Gresham's Palace of Commerce.

"There, you croaker, how the devil can the French be at Mile End to-morrow, when the King has come to town to-day?"

No argument less illogical could have silenced the man, who was famous for never giving up an opinion; this was effectual.

On the Stock Exchange no business was done. Consols left off at the closing quotations of the day before—about 62. Some Jew speculators were understood to offer 50, but they were scouted. If 60, or 59, or perhaps even 58, had been offered, there might have been business; as it was, there were neither buyers nor sellers. We mistake; about two o'clock the bank broker bought six hundred pounds "for money" on Chancery account; and a very considerable business indeed was done in bets. All the bets were concerning the various possible eventualities of the coming war. Would London be taken? Five to two it would. Would there be a battle first, win or not win? Forty to one there would. Would the enemy be utterly licked within three months? Even. Four months? Two to one. Many of these Stock Exchange men had time after time, during the year before, canvassed the probabilities of an invasion, and possible events; they had thus material for making bets, and all was not merely blind work. Poor fellows! Some never lived to pay, or be paid; they fell under the hurricane of shot that mowed down thousands on the banks of the river Cam. When four o'clock came, the doors were kept open till the members sang "God save the King."

People were later at the West-end than at the east, then as it is now, but the information that the frequenters of White's and Brookes's were in possession of was more matured, at two o'clock, than the city information even at four. For at the West-end, at two o'clock, it began to be said that there was another landing farther north, at Yarmouth. At four o'clock this was known to be true; but the magnitude of the enemy's force there could not be stated, nor were there even materials for surmising it. It could not be supposed to be a mere feint, nor could it be supposed to be the principal force, if there were ninety thousand at Harwich.

A military gentleman, who had said in the morning that he believed the Harwich force to be understated, reassured the minds of some of the members of White's with observations to the following effect, when he saw something like consternation at the news from Yarmouth:—"I told you this morning that I did not believe the invading army to be so small as ninety thousand men, because we know that Bonaparte always had a hundred and fifty thousand appropriated to the operation. It is impossible to tell whether he meant to keep his whole flotilla together or not. A part may have strayed north in the fog; and I am inclined to think so, because I see such an evident advantage to us in this division of force. I take for granted that the Yarmouth invasion is what we call serious—say, not under thirty thousand men; a smaller force would not be suffered to land by itself, as it might be defeated if alone, and no salvation for it. As it is, Bonaparte will not leave the coast till he has made a junction with the other army, and this gives us time. I think it gives us a week, and a week may save London."

Many members listened to him, and then sat down to whist. Let us eat and drink, for to-morrow we die.

A great many families made preparations for leaving town; those were the most hurried whose country places were the farthest off. A great many, too, who had no country places, resolved to go to Bath, Cheltenham, etc. More post-chaises left town than on the average of days, by a great deal; and so many post-horses were ordered for the next day, that the jobmasters thought of raising their prices.

All the volunteer corps of the Metropolis were ordered on parade, at their usual grounds.   There was the greatest muster, all added together, that had been yet on any occasion. Of forty-five thousand nominal, thirty-nine thousand members of the various corps paraded. Many corps passed resolutions requesting arrangements to be made for a review, so that one last opportunity, before active service, should be given for the corps to get an idea of mass movements.

This is the proper place for us to inform our readers of the sources from whence we have derived our knowledge of momentous historical events, that will be new to them, and perhaps at first incredible.

Writers of romances have means and sources of knowledge, the nature of which their allegiance to the Genius that inspires them forbids them, under fearful penalties, which they may not describe, to reveal. Writers of romances know not only the deeds and words of their actors, but their very thoughts, even those rapid thoughts that pass through men's minds unconsciously to themselves. They know their very dreams. They know not only what their actors said and thought on all occasions, but also what, in infinite variety, those actors might have thought and said, but did not.

But it is not of these general sources of our knowledge that we are about to speak. It is of those actual and tangible authorities that we have for the truth of our statements.

Why should it be intrinsically improbable that Bonaparte

was successful in compassing the invasion of England? We know (this will be admitted) that he intended to invade England if he could; and we know that pamphlets without number, English and French, have been written to prove that the invasion of England is a thing easy to accomplish. Those who reject our narrative, therefore, contend that Bonaparte, a man whose life was passed in effecting the most surprisingly difficult enterprises, was unable to effect a very easy enterprise.

But, it will be said, how is it that all memory of this event has passed away, and that it is unnoticed by historians except when they deny it?

This is specious. However, all memory of it has not passed away; at least, had not passed away twenty years ago, when some were still living who recollected it. Nor are historians actually unanimous in rejecting it. We shall come, presently, to our proof of these traditions and records. We speak here of probabilities. The non-mention of an event by historians, when there is a very general consensus in ignoring that event, is not a demonstration that the event did not happen. It is held by some eminent historical critics that a conspiracy of silence is a proof that there is something to be silent about. That eminent theologian, Bishop Warburton, founds a most powerful argument for the doctrine of a future life on the total absence of anything about it in the Pentateuch. We but use a parallel argument.

Our actual authority is thus derived—During the latter years of Louis Napoleon's reign, we spent some time in the east of France. There we made the acquaintance of two old gentlemen, who were the first to tell us what we have adopted as the real history of the year 1805. As may be supposed, we were at first incredulous. But they showed us, and eventually gave us, a book, which establishes the matter. It is badly printed on bad paper, and badly bound. It contains about 180 small pages, and is entitled "Les batailles d'Ipvich et de Cambrige; Critique Militairs par La Dousque, Colonel, Chef d'etat Major du General Barasquin, du troisième Corps de

L'Armee d'Angleterre. Librairie Napoleonienne, Paris, 1816." There is no printer's name. We studied the book carefully. We desire to be perfectly candid, and we admit that it is not without defects. It is written in an imaginative tone, not appropriate to a scientific criticism on a campaign; and there are topographical errors, which might make scoffers aver that the author had never seen the towns and rivers that he describes, nor, perhaps, maps of them. Those who are disposed to make objections may make of these admissions of ours what seemeth to them good. Our old and valued friends, who lived near Dijon, stated that they distinctly recollected the invasion; they were, at that period, not of an age to have taken a part in it. But they referred us to two gentlemen, residents of Angoulême, who had been in it, Monsieur le Capitaine Thibaudet and Monsieur Sauvagier. We hastened to Angouleme, fired with the energy of the discoverer. We regret to have to say that we met Monsieur Sauvagier coming out of his house in a coffin; the other gentleman we were unable to find—he had ceased for some time to live at that place.

We shall be accused of credulity. That pious prelate and eminent logician and most entertaining companion, Archbishop Whately, wrote a book to prove that Napoleon Bonaparte never existed. He may have erred on the side of incredulity. But that eminent man taught also that credulity and incredulity are, in reality, the same sentiment. Therefore, if we err, we err in company that does not shame us.

CHAPTER VI.

Our readers will perhaps have conjectured that the news which Mrs. Fenthorpe learned from her brother-in-law, which so absorbed her that she forgot all about the will and old Allonby, was that a French army had seized Yarmouth.

Mr. Cardwain and she turned and walked to his house, the old gentleman saying the whole time, as they went along, what a terrible thing it was, and that he did not know what they would do. Mrs. Fenthorpe replied little, excited as she was, and in suspense, knowing no more than the bare fact. On entering the house, they found on the ground-floor room, generally used as their breakfast room, Mrs. Cardwain, Helen and Fanny Tronford, and Miss Dorkington, talking eagerly. The latter lady had on her bonnet, its strings not tied; she was standing, and used gestures with both hands and feet, and also her head, with such vigour that her bonnet strings appeared like banners floating in the breeze. She seemed to have most of the conversation to herself.

"This alters our arrangements, Mrs. Cardwain. I must now leave these children under your charge. Don't interrupt me! No, I will not take them; Yarmouth is no place for them, with French officers about. We know how unprincipled they are. I must return alone. It is a bitter disappointment."

"But, Miss Dorkington," Mrs. Cardwain said in perplexity, for she thought her guest must be mad, "what do you mean? Do you really think of such a thing as going to Yarmouth?"

"To be sure I do, to defend these tender lambs' property. I have thought about the whole of it." She waved her hands,

and swung the strings of her bonnet towards Helen and
Fanny.

"It must take the French the whole of this evening and, I
dare say, a good part of the morning, to land; and I can get
to Clay House without going through the High Street, where
they will be emptying the shops, and they won't find out Clay
House at first, owing to the shrubberies. I have been round
to the stables, and have told John to have the horses ready at
seven in the morning. I shall be at home at eleven, before
any of them have got there; and when I am there, we'll see if
they will venture to attack it. Don't you think of preventing
me, Mrs. Cardwain. I know my duty to these doves. They
would come in, with nobody but servants; everybody knows it
is unguarded places that housebreakers get into. They would
break the plates and dishes, and, I dare say, the furniture.
Besides, think of the plate! There is nobody but me to
prevent it, and I am determined I will. I know it is
very annoying to you, after the girls being here so long, but I
can do far better without them."

"But, Miss Dorkington——'

"Don't imagine you can prevent me, Mrs. Cardwain. I
know my duty, and I am determined to do it." She had been
pacing up and down the room, and concluded her speech with
a stamp on the floor, and with bringing one hand down on the
palm of the other with a clap or snap, such as men use when
making bargains about the price of cattle. As Mrs. Fenthorpe and her brother-in-law listened to her, though both
knew her well, a new phase of her character opened itself to
them.

Anne Dorkington was the only daughter of a gentleman and
lady who had been married at the blacksmith's beyond Solway
Frith. Their parents on both sides took no notice of this
marriage, nor, after its accomplishment, of the parties to it.
They lived for thirty years uncomfortably but not altogether
unhappily together. Her mother managed to give Anne as
good an education as most young ladies then received; and
both mother and father bequeathed to her an independent

spirit, for, even at the worst of their fortunes, when hard put to it, in dire difficulties about lodging rent, the baker, the milk, and the rest, they had never applied to their relations. Mr. and Mrs. Dorkington died within a few days of each other of an epidemic. There was nothing left for Anne but six old silk gowns.

She was ashamed to beg, she told the clergyman who buried her parents, but she was able to dig. By this she meant that she would take service. She heard of two orphan children of a gentleman of fortune, lately deceased, who wanted a nurse. From Saffron-Waldon, where her father and mother had died, she walked all the way to Yarmouth to look for the place. When she got to Yarmouth, she was referred to a lady who lived in Norwich. She went into a baker's, bought two penny loaves, and started on her walk of twenty miles without the delay of a minute. Within five or six miles of Norwich, she broke down, and, very unwillingly, slept that night in a roadside alehouse.

During her journey of several days she had been un-molested. She did not look as if she was worth robbing, and she had a look about her as if the issue of such an attempt might be anything but certain. Nor was she of an appear-ance such as invites those attentions or insults that used most falsely to go by the name of gallantry. When she presented herself before Mrs. Cardwain as candidate for the vacant place of nurse, that lady thought she had never seen so utter and absolute a fright, and wondered if she were not a man in woman's clothes. The only feature, indeed, in which she was defective for giving the idea of such a get-up, was that she had no beard. Anne Dorkington was tall, raw-boned, with a small waist, but large hands and feet; her arms were as big in the bone, though not as powerful in muscle, as any prize-fighter's need be; and it has been conjectured that her legs were similar, although, sooner than allow verification on that subject to be reached, she would have taken life or yielded it up. Her face was cadaverous, her lips thin, and her eyes black and bright; her nose towered like the beak of an eagle, or, some said, of a vulture; and her mouth, although she had such thin lips, divided her face right across into what a Cambridge man once called two aliquot parts. But the expression of this uncommon face, at a second look, was not at all repulsive. It was honest, and even kind, and her voice was gentle and soft.

Mrs. Cardwain, after her first sensation of wonder and perhaps repugnance, took to this woman. She listened to her account of herself, and was drawn towards her by the simple way in which she told of her journey. For evidence of her statements, and for character, she referred to the rector of Saffron-Walden. Mrs. Cardwain sent for the two little children to see what they would think; this may have been a deliberately wisely put test, or may have been done without knowledge of the natures of children. However, the test determined her, for the little things made friends with the forbidding-looking scarecrow as ducklings do with a hen. Mrs. Cardwain reflected, also, that this was a servant not likely to have followers, a class which she held in abhorrence. Anne Dorkington was finally appointed nurse of Helen Tronford, aged four, and Fanny, aged eighteen months, at an emolument of five pounds a year, with a clear and understood permission, for which she stipulated, to wear silk gowns on Sundays and holidays.

At the end of a week, Mrs. Cardwain thought the new nurse was the best nurse in Norfolk; at the end of another week, that she was the best nurse in England; and at the end of a third, that she was the best nurse in the known world. By this time the carrier had brought the six silk gowns. The nurse was out with the children when he arrived, and Mrs. Cardwain sent to know what was to pay. Hearing the servant in conversation with the carrier, she went to the door to ask what was the matter.

"I sent to know what is to pay for the parcel."

"An' it please your ladyship, I won't take no money from her what's a lady, and her father and mother both died permiscuous, and her nothing at all to put on her back or in her inside—nothing but this yere parcel."

He drove away, and Mrs. Cardwain began to understand what she had suspected, that the new nurse was of a class superior to that which she assumed to belong to. Prudently, as we think, she said nothing; but she questioned Anne as to her literary attainments, and suggested that she might teach the children their letters. Gradually, the nurse became also the governess. The children became passionately fond of her, and once, when she took a fever, filled the house with their lamentations.

Clay House, at Yarmouth, had been let to a tenant, who gave it up when Helen was about ten years old. Mr. Cardwain had become tired of having the children living with himself and his wife. Accordingly, a lady housekeeper, to act as companion and duenna of the two little girls, was being looked for; a liberal payment to an eligible lady would be given.

At this very juncture Anne Dorkington received a letter by post for the first time in her life. We know her to be a brave woman, but she was very much frightened. She even cried as she handled it and read the address and the postmarks, and thought of the thirteen pence she had paid on it.

It was from an attorney, who informed her that her maternal grandfather had recently died, and, by a codicil to his will, had bequeathed her a thousand pounds. The codicil was dated a short time after his wife's death. Anne Dorkington, as she read this, recollected that her mother had frequently said it was her mother, and not her father, that was against forgiveness. She had not left off crying about the thirteen pence, and she went on crying about the thousand pounds.

But she came to a momentous resolution. Why should she not be the lady housekeeper? Why? Why should not she, Anne Dorkington, a woman of determination, so proceed as that no other than she should be the lady housekeeper?

She dried her eyes and washed her face, and put on the best and ugliest of the silk gowns, and demanded an interview with Mr. Cardwain. She told him, in a resolute yet defer-

G

ential speech, that she had been bequeathed a fortune, and could no longer act as nurse to his sweet little infant wards; but that she loved them much, and would be contented to take the situation of companion and housekeeper, which Mr. Cardwain wished to fill up, for a salary of a hundred and fifty pounds a year.

Mr. Cardwain was flabbergasted at her audacity, and would have told her to go out of the room, but that she intimidated him with her talk of her position as a lady of fortune. He was forced to take her proposal under consideration.

He went to his wife, and complained of the impertinence of the nurse. But Mrs. Cardwain advised him not to disturb himself about that, and told him Miss Dorkington's history, and said that it would be impossible to conceive a more excellent arrangement.

" But, Isabella, one hundred and fifty pounds a year ! "

" Jonathan, let me speak to her. It is a great deal, certainly; but if you talk to her—you are not used to her, you know—and I am afraid you might offend her. People with money, very often, are easily offended."

Mrs. Cardwain tried to make Miss Dorkington lower her pretensions, but with the worst success. That lady made of it a compliment even to accept a salary. She became lady housekeeper and companion at a hundred and fifty pounds a year, and went to live at Yarmouth with her little pupils in about a month. She never told how much money she had been left; but Mr. Cardwain found out, and was much disgusted. Ecclesiastical attorneys and people of that class do not use violent language when they have been taken in; but Mr. Cardwain was very near going those lengths, for if he had known it was only a thousand pounds, Miss Dorkington would never have got more than a hundred a year. Though so smart a woman of business, in other respects she had misty notions about money and the sources of wealth. She had not the least idea that her salary came from little Helen's income; she thought it came out of Mr. Cardwain's own pocket, because he was a trustee, and found out when

Helen came of age, and then with astonishment and remorse, her mistake. She wanted Helen to take back the money, every penny of which she had kept; but Helen laughed at her, and said no such thing, and if the salary were double the amount, her dearest Nannie should continue to have it, now that she was her own mistress.

Miss Dorkington was utterly unconventional; not in the common manner, for unconventional very often means rude and unfeeling. This woman never said an unkind thing, nor did one; her peculiarities were of another kind. When she was paid her thousand pounds, the first thing she did with any of it was to replenish her wardrobe. She went carefully over her six gowns, and decided that five of them could be made equal to new by cutting up the sixth, which matched none of them, into trimming. She then went to the best shop in Yarmouth and bought five shawls, one to wear with each gown. One of the gowns was of nearly a scarlet colour, and another was green; she accordingly bought a green shawl for the scarlet gown, and a scarlet shawl for the green gown; the rest in proportion. Her habit was, when she rose in the morning, to examine her stockings before putting them on. If one required mending, she would reject, not the pair, but the imperfect stocking, and select a whole one, without regard to either material or colour. She was, in consequence, known, more than once, to have gone about for a whole day in one white stocking and one black one. She was as destitute of feminine weakness as of ordinary feminine taste. She feared neither man, woman, kicking horse, savage dog, nor bull in a field. Our grandfather knew her intimately, and esteemed her most highly. He sometimes said there was not a woman in Great Britain her equal but one—Meg Dods, whose acquaintance he had made once when spending a season at St. Ronan's Well; and that the only difference between them was that one was a Scotch alewife, and the other an English lady.

Such was the lady who announced her resolution to march on the enemy at Yarmouth. As she concluded her speech,

Helen and Fanny rushed up to her, one taking each arm, and implored her to stay at Mrs. Cardwain's. Mrs. Cardwain looked inexpressibly frightened, and Mrs. Fenthorpe actually opened her mouth with amazement.

"Dear, dear Nunnie," said the girls together, "don't, don't go! What would we do if you were to be killed? What does it matter about the plate and the furniture? Don't go, there's a dear Nunnie!"

"I must go, my loves," she replied, taking the hand of one and stroking the face of the other; "you do not understand."

"Miss Dorkington," said Mr. Cardwain, who was impassive, and who rejoiced at being able to give this masterful lady the tit-for-tat for which he had been waiting for ten years, "do I gather correctly from your expressions that you intend to go to Yarmouth to-morrow?"

"I think I said so as plainly as I could, Mr. Cardwain."

"And pray, Miss Dorkington, how do you intend to travel?"

"In the coach; I have ordered John to have the horses ready at seven in the morning."

"But, Miss Dorkington, it will be impossible for you to take the horses."

"Why? Are they not my own horses—that is, Helen's horses?"

"You cannot take them, because the Mayor will this evening put out a proclamation ordering all persons who have horses to send them without delay into Cambridgeshire."

"And what right has the Mayor to order me to do this and that with my horses? He may order you, for you live in Norwich; but I live in Yarmouth, and the Mayor of Norwich shan't control me."

"My dear Miss Dorkington, it is a military measure, to prevent the French from getting them; and you will not be allowed to take horses to Yarmouth. The Yarmouth people are driving their horses this way already, as fast as ever they can, and their cattle too."

Miss Dorkington was defeated for the first time in her life. She sat down and groaned as if her heart would break. Mr. Cardwain was, so far, right, that a proclamation was about to be issued, recommending people to send away their horses; but only recommending. However, there is no doubt that, if Miss Dorkington had started on her adventurous journey, she would have been stopped and turned before she was out of the city.

The ladies and Mr. Cardwain went on talking. Mrs. Fenthorpe said little. Mrs. Cardwain and the girls uttered lamentations, and asked what they were to do. They did not yet understand that any greater calamity had fallen on them than the impossibility of moving about as freely as they had intended.

Suddenly, Miss Dorkington pulled herself together and said, "Mr. Cardwain, is it thought that they will come here?"

"I suppose they will," he replied; "this is a rich city, with no force to defend it, and all that they want is plunder. I am convinced that they will come here."

"And are you going to do nothing so that yourself and Mrs. Cardwain and these children shall have something to live on while they are here? What meat have you in the house?"

"There is the cold meat," said Mrs. Cardwain in a despondent tone.

"Then come out at once with me to the butcher's and get in as much meat, joints that will corn, as your larder will hold; and get in four or five bags of flour. You can put the flour in the attics, where the French won't think of looking for it, and when we see them coming we can hide the meat there too, but it will be better to leave it to corn in the usual place. Come, Mrs. Cardwain."

A person who proposes to do anything generally takes the command over those who let their hands hang down beside them, and neither act nor think. Sometimes mischief is worked by the passion for doing something, and sometimes it works safety. Miss Dorkington took her more timid friend "by the hair of the head," as she described it afterwards, into the street, and to the shops, and, in a short time, had the house filled with provisions for a siege. Mrs. Fenthorpe went out and walked towards home, and thought she would do the same in the morning; but there was plenty of time.

Later in the evening the Mayor called the Corporation together, having invited several of the principal inhabitants of the city to join the meeting, to give authority to the proclamation for the removal of horses. The proclamation was to be circulated not only in the city, but in the neighbourhood, and could not be mandatory. Among others, Dr. Fenthorpe was present; also, another physician, older, and with much more extensive practice, than he; and Mr. Mortland rode in to give the benefit of his advice and counsel.

Many of the gentlemen who came stated that they had already sent their horses away. Several said that they feared the farmers in the neighbourhood would be too slow of wit to take the Mayor's advice. Mr. Mortland said so, and expressed a view of the invasion that was rather new to his audience.

"Bonaparte's object in invading this country," he said, "is not, I believe, plunder or conquest, but to effect a change in our Government. Sending away horses——"

"To effect a change in our Government is conquest," said a gentleman.

"I mean," said Mr. Mortland, "that his object is one that he will try to effect, not by plunder or by anything that would, according to his expectation, set the whole country against him. I do not expect that we shall be ruthlessly treated. Sending away horses is a purely military measure, to prevent the enemy from getting them to yoke to their artillery and baggage waggons. I have sent away most of my horses. I think it as well to keep that view before us."

There was not much discussion, but these observations of Mr. Mortland, justly or unjustly, revived all the old prejudices against him. "The whole country will be against the enemy like one man," they said to one another. "This man, that says they won't behave ruthlessly, was a Jacobin once, and is no better now." From that moment forward, everything that Mr. Mortland said and did was construed by the public of Norfolk unfavourably to him. It was remembered a fortnight later, that he had said he had sent away his horses, but some of those horses reappeared, and the French did not take them; when people said, and believed most firmly, that he had never sent them away at all.

When the Corporation were leaving the council room, at about nine o'clock, and the town-clerk was going to the printer's, Richard Fenthorpe, before going away, went over to where Dr. Johnson was standing, and said a few words to him. Dr. Johnson appeared to agree with him, and both went to the Mayor, still in his chair of office.

"I think," Fenthorpe said to his worship, "that I will keep my horse. I have no doubt Norwich will be in possession of the enemy within a few days. I intend to go to the commandant and represent that I require a horse to visit my patients, and apply for a permit. Dr. Johnson thinks of doing the same. You perceive that it is no backwardness on our parts that prompts us to disregard, or appear to disregard, the proclamation."

"Certainly," said the Mayor; "if any one should be allowed to keep horses, under the circumstances that are coming on us, it should be you. But, Dr. Fenthorpe, do you believe that a French general will give any such permission?"

"I do believe it. I agree with what Mr. Mortland said, although I could perceive that it was new to many of our friends, and not palatable to them. Bonaparte's object is to make a revolution, I am confident. I know that it is as impossible for him to make a revolution, as I believe in my soul it is for him to conquer us. But he expects it, and will not begin with the harshness of a mere conqueror."

What Richard Fenthorpe said had far more effect on the Mayor than the same had had, uttered by a man who was doubtful in his principles. He said, after a few moments' pause :

"You know that Colonel —— marches to-night, or at day-break, to Ely."

"No, I did not know that!"

"And he is perfectly right. If there are, as there seems reason to think, thirty thousand of the enemy now in Yarmouth, or in the harbour ready to land, what can six hundred men do? Far better for them to be where they can be placed as part of an army. Young Mortland and Sprowles, who are two young fools, were angry, and had the impertinence to remonstrate. And they have sent to summon the six corps—no, five, for Yarmouth is out of the question—Wymondham, King's Lynn, and the rest, to come and fight a battle to defend the city! Don't repeat this. If they had any sense among them, they would go with the King's troops to Ely."

Richard went away, despondent and sick at heart. Here were four or five thousand good soldiers' lives going to be thrown away—utterly and uselessly thrown away. He must be there, a spectator of their folly, to tend the wounded. It was not his business to oppose, and he would not be listened to if he should oppose.

Nearly the whole Volunteer organisation of England had fallen, during the latter months of 1804, into a loose state. Drill was kept up, and the musters and parades were as well attended as ever. But there had been lost that feeling that the whole was an instrument that might be wanted for use at any moment; and the chief officers of the volunteers, colonels and majors of corps were no longer favoured, or harassed, with such frequent orders from the Secretary of State's Department and the Horse Guards as they had been when the invasion was first threatened. It was then a standing and every day repeated order that, if a landing of the enemy should be effected, all volunteer regiments should at once concentrate towards London, or towards such point as should be then appointed, to defend London. Of late the volunteers had been very much left to themselves. In the absence of specific orders, it is not surprising that men at a great distance from the Metropolis should come to wild resolutions. Besides, nobody had ever thought of a landing anywhere but on the south coast; the seizure of Yarmouth was a complete surprise to everybody. What made the idea of a pitched battle to defend Norwich utterly insane was that, though there was a yeomanry corps, there was no artillery but one small company, by no means too well trained, with only four six-pounders, in all Norfolk.

Richard Fenthorpe knew all this; and as he left the council house, felt that calamity was coming. But his spirit was elastic, and it was a fine night. The fog had cleared away, and the stars shone. They were steadfast, and it was his duty to be the same. Nature not unoften says these things to men.

He had to pass near his aunt's house on his way home, and he stopped to ask after the ladies. He had not been at home since four o'clock, at which time Mrs. Fenthorpe was absent on her visit to Allonby. He had then eaten his dinner hastily, and had not seen his mother since, nor had he heard of Miss Dorkington's project and disappointment.

"The ladies is in the drawing-room, sir," said the butler. But as Richard followed him up stairs, he heard Miss Dorkington's voice from the depths of the pantry scolding his aunt, and telling her she did not know how to make brine. There was no one in the drawing-room but Helen Tronford, who sat by the fire, her hands shading her face. Two candles burned on the chimney piece.

Intimate though these two persons were, this was the first time that they had ever been in a room together without a witness or witnesses. "Dr. Fenthorpe!" exclaimed Helen.

"I came to see how you are," he said. "How is Fanny?"

"She cried, and went to bed. O, Dr. Fenthorpe! What is this that is coming on us?"

"It is," he answered, "the severest trial of the courage of all of us that it could enter the mind of man we could be put to the test of. Helen, I do not think, when I think of what I shall have to do—following my volunteers and binding up their wounds—I do not think I am quite a coward; but there is one thing that would give me strength and courage if I lack them, and that is your love and sympathy."

She did not answer him, but kept her hands over her face. He spoke on: "I have loved you since you were a little child, and now I love you more than ever I did. But what do I say? All that know you, or that ever saw you, love you; but I love you as I would love my wife."

For two minutes Helen did not move; she did not, knowingly to herself, even think. But thoughts rush through the mind at those moments when mind has nearly ceased to exist, or rather when it is so merged in heart that it is all heart and not mind at all, as rapidly as the electric fluid passes from the clouds to earth. She already loved Richard, and she knew that he would say this to her. It was no shock nor surprise. But her principal feeling at the moment was rejoicing that he spoke those words then. She had been absolutely terrified at her Nunnie's wild project (they always called Miss Dorkington so); women never believe in other women as protectors, and she felt gratitude to Richard for coming and offering himself as a protector at the moment when her life, and the lives of all around her, were going to be shaken with a rudeness that she could hardly even guess at. Her loving, clinging nature was strongly appealed to, and it responded. She took away her hands from her face and looked at her lover full, but said no word.

"Helen," he said again, inspired by her glance, "may it so be? Will you love me?"

"I will," she answered. "I do." She did not even speak low. Coquetry was as far from her as all other cruelty; and as for affectation, she hardly knew what it was, or could ever perceive it in others.

He stooped and kissed her forehead, then her lips; and she blushed and half shrank, and she burst into tears, and then laughed. It was not a passionate scene. We desire to tell the truth, and we tell it as we learned it, years and years after, from Fanny, then an ancient, good old lady, with grandchildren. If we desired to present our readers with a passionate scene, we could invent one, or better, perhaps, get one out of other romances; but we hope they will pardon us, in the interests of truth.

Richard and Helen sat for an hour together, while the unconscious Miss Dorkington and Mrs. Cardwain put the rounds of beef in salt. Helen told him of the projected Yarmouth expedition, and how it was foiled. They talked no more of the coming war, but of themselves. When Richard, however, rose to go, he said to Helen that he had a presentiment that their betrothal would be the means of saving her from peril in the days that were coming.

"God knows!" she answered. "I feel safe in your hands."

As he went down stairs, Mrs. Cardwain was coming up. She stopped him to say a few words, and it struck her that his manner was queer. He replied to her hurriedly, and got out of the house.

Helen told her sister that night, who was, or pretended to be, amazed and delighted; she certainly was delighted, but was not, we believe, at all amazed. Fanny promised and vowed she would say nothing; but in the morning she told her Nunnie and her aunt. Miss Dorkington said nothing, but went to see that the beef was getting on right, and put on her bonnet; then she ordered Mrs. Cardwain to come with her to Mrs. Fenthorpe's.

The result of the conference of these three ladies, which lasted three hours, was that no one, not even Mr. Cardwain, was to be told. The secret was safe, because there were enough of ladies to talk to one another about it. Fanny even did not break counsel.

Our opinion is that this was entirely wrong. Secrets are bad things to have, and nothing should be kept secret without an overpowering reason. The mischief that arose in the future from the determination of these ladies will be seen by those who shall have the perseverance to read to the end of this book.

CHAPTER VII.

On the next day the French did not come to Norwich, as many had expected; but news came from Yarmouth, and very late at night from London. The news from London created far more apprehension for what would happen to England in general than for what would happen to Norfolk in particular, and caused the news from Yarmouth to be comparatively neglected. It was taken for granted that the portion of the invading force that had seized Yarmouth, so soon as it should have completed its landing, would march south to join the greater army at Harwich. The removal of horses to Cambridgeshire, which had commenced even on the night of Tuesday, and was proceeding during all Wednesday, almost ceased on Thursday. On Friday it was dropped altogether, and the farmers and country people for many miles on all sides of Norwich began to think that their neighbourhood was about to escape foreign occupation. Their notions were not unnaturally very vague and incorrect as to the speed with which military operations can be carried on; when they found that the French had been at Yarmouth for three days, and yet that they had seen none of them, they thought they were never going to see them at all.

It was known, so nearly as could be made out, that thirty thousand of the enemy had landed; the landing was completed, or very nearly so, during Wednesday. When the boats were first seen, a gunboat lying in Yarmouth put out to try to do some execution among them; two or three revenue cutters cruising about joined and did likewise; but there were a few large French ships that effectually protected the invading flotilla. The report was that, of the thirty thousand invaders, as many as six thousand were cavalry, which was an over-estimate, for there were fewer than three thousand. They had about sixty field guns.

The London mail coach that came by way of Ely—that by Ipswich not, of course, having arrived—brought an officer with orders from the Horse Guards that the troops at Norwich should withdraw to Ely. This movement had already been made, and the battalion and a half of the Norwich garrison, calling in one or two detachments, was far on its way southward when the despatch arrived. No instructions whatever were sent to the commanders of any of the volunteer corps of the country; this was much resented by those officers. The Mayor had heard, as we have seen, that there had not been the best agreement between the commanding officers of the King's troops and the volunteers. The officers of the latter, headed by Major Alexander Mortland, and Mr. Sprowles, the adjutant, on their desertion, as they called it, by the colonel and the garrison, sent messengers to the officers of the other regiments of the county to come and meet them and consult as to what was to be done.

Late on Wednesday, before it was known that the volunteers had been left without any orders, the officers of five regiments, or so many of them as had obeyed the summons, met at Norwich. Councils of war, it is said, never fight; but those are councils that are composed of experienced men, who know at least something about what fighting is. The young men who met at Norwich came in a temper very different. They had not the least notion of not fighting if they could find, or make, an opportunity; they would have thought themselves disgraced, now that they were left to themselves, if they had not fought one battle to defend their country. Local feeling among all the volunteers of all parts of England was very strong. These Norfolk men rejected as unnatural the idea of retreating, of their own accord, into an adjoining county. They would have obeyed orders from the Secretary of State, or from the Horse Guards, whatever they were; but here they were, without orders. Five generations before this time Cromwell and Lord Manchester had found the same local feeling throughout the east of England extremely patent and extremely difficult to deal with, and they had to overcome the difficulty by the association of the counties, an organisation that required Parliamentary authority to institute and time to perfect.

Some of the volunteer officers were for uniting the five regiments at Norwich the next day and marching straight on Yarmouth. The majority had more sense. Gradually, one of the colonels assumed the lead in the discussion; and, on its being remarked that the whole of their little army must have one commander, it was unanimously resolved to nominate him.

This man, although prepared to take one of the most fool-hardy ventures ever made in war, was by no means without some good military intuitions. He dismissed the council instantly on his appointment, to the surprise of some of the officers, who thought that war is best conducted, like mess arrangements, by a committee. He then sent, of his own men, several to scout towards Yarmouth and report to him; and he wrote circular letters to his colonels, ordering them to bring their full forces, with the very least possible loss of time, with their tents and three rations each man, to a certain point on the road east from Norwich. No doubt ever crossed his mind, or any one's mind, that the men would be as ready to fight as the officers were; and he was justified in the result, for by the Friday morning all had arrived at the rendezvous in the highest spirits. As they arrived, they pitched their tents. The colonel had provided some barrels of beer; there was not a public-house within a mile and a half, which was, perhaps, one reason why he had fixed on the position. There were three thousand three hundred infantry, two hundred and fifty horse, and four guns.

The scouts reported that the enemy were beginning to spread themselves round Yarmouth, having sent one detachment to Cromer and another towards Lowestoft; inland, they had made no advance further than two miles from the town. The fact was, General Davoust, afterwards Prince of Eckmuhl, who commanded the north division of the invasion, was waiting for orders from Bonaparte at Harwich, or he would have advanced towards the west at once. Probably he did not know till Friday morning that the landing at Harwich had been as successful as his own had been. The volunteer general was convinced—indeed, it had never occurred to him that it could be otherwise—that the Yarmouth army would attempt to join the main invasion by the coast route. But he thought at the same time that an attempt would be made, probably with a small force, on one of the principal cities of England. The notion of defending Norwich was certainly a wild one; but, with the general's views, it was not so wild, regarded nakedly, as it might be thought.

On Friday, at noon, a scout brought word that the army had begun to break up from Yarmouth, and that a part of it was coming in that direction. The general then began to draw up his little army to receive the enemy, whom he guessed that they would see the following morning. There are three roads between Yarmouth and Norwich, the most circuitous being that south of the Yare; this he had neglected altogether. Indeed, as is evident, he had means to make a stand at one point only. The next road is very nearly a straight line, and the third runs parallel to it for most of the way, meeting it at an acute angle about three or four miles from Norwich, just before the united road crosses a bridge. The bridge is over a sluggish and rather deep stream, which comes from the west, but takes a sharp turn south just above the bridge, on its way to join the Wensum. On the north side of the road, east of the bridge, there is a small acclivity, commanding both roads, the more southern of them for fully half a mile; a turn in the other road conceals all of it but a couple of hundred yards. The fields on the southern side of the road are flat.

The guns were placed on the small hill, and a regiment in

lines, four deep, flanked each side of the battery; their order was too close, for the whole front of this wing was no more than five hundred yards; the companies were far too much packed. One regiment was placed, half of it in front and the other half in rear of the bridge. The two remaining regiments were to the right, spreading as far into the fields as the general thought judicious. When his dispositions were made, he went round and spoke to the men, directing them to fire only at the word of command; the officers he desired never to open fire too soon, or at any but short distances; and, unless there were something rendering it impossible, to charge with the bayonet after firing two volleys.

The little army slept or lay awake all that night. The scouts brought word that the enemy was less than five miles off; of their number, the reports were most contradictory. Just before eleven on Saturday, noises were heard that announced their approach by the southern or direct road. In a few minutes a battalion, in marching order, with as wide a front as the road would admit of, was seen; as it came into full view from the hill, the general judged it to be of the full force of a thousand or twelve hundred men; one troop of forty horse preceded it.

The battery was ordered to fire, and a couple of rounds got pretty good range, which was not difficult, and that tremulous movement was noticed in the French column that the steadiest troops in the world are subject to when they are fired at and cannot reply at once. The cavalry troop was hurled forward against the English rather wildly; it was received as orders had been given, and rode back, a few men unhorsed. No French guns were observed, for they were far behind, and four or five battalions of foot in the line of march before them; and even when they should come up, they would be difficult to place, for the road was lined with fences of a pretty good height.

But the leading French column was pushed forward at double-quick time, and made to deploy into the fields at both sides of the road; another followed it, and another, and

another. Half the first battalion in column formation, but
with perhaps a broader front than the usual French proportion, was moved against the English regiment to the right of
the four guns. They did not fire; not even an excited man
here and there, as often happens, blazed for the mere sake of
blazing; they advanced steadily with fixed bayonets.

The English general had ordered the men of this regiment
to sit down; he now took the command of it himself. The
enemy could not see its strength from the foot of the acclivity.
When they were about sixty yards from the English, he
ordered the men up; at forty yards, the words, "Ready,
present, fire!" were for the first time heard, an as yet
unknown talisman to eight hundred Frenchman, which, in a
few weeks, they were destined to understand better. Then
the general shouted, "First line, charge with the bayonet,"
and, in half a minute more, "second line, charge with the
bayonet."

The enemy could not stand it; it was an utter surprise, and
dozens were knocked over. But a French battalion is not
put to the rout with one unexpected charge. If they fell
back so much as eighty yards, it was the utmost. The
English were not allowed to press them too closely, or to
advance too far. With hardly any loss, they were brought
back to their original position. In this the general probably
erred, for he ought to have made use of the regiment to the
left of the battery. The truth is, he had begun to understand
that he would have to fight nearly the whole French army,
and his confidence, though not his courage, was beginning to
melt away. In less time than it takes to describe it, the
French column was reformed and doubled in strength. In
their second attack on the little hill, they advanced firing,
but with not much effect, for the English were kept kneeling,
and ordered to stoop as low as possible. When the enemy
got near, two volleys were given, then a bayonet charge.
The shock of this charge was far more severe than that of
the first had been. There was a hard fight, neither giving
way, for some minutes. The French had weight, the English
position; and the English had that intrinsic superiority in

H

the use of the bayonet which no art can give to others, and which they have, as it were, by nature. The fight lasting longer than the general liked, he brought six companies of the more distant regiment into action, and ordered his cavalry to attack the French right, the mere sight of whose charge, at the moment after a reinforcement had just come into action, finished the first part of the battle.

The French retreated to re-form, and the English to carry away their wounded, who were numerous. All this time, the four English guns were being worked to some purpose; but they were useless for any real permanent advantage, as they only galled the enemy, still advancing along the road, and they could not interfere with them as they deployed into the fields. The battle on the southern side of the road had not properly begun yet, for most of the meadows had wide and deep ditches surrounding them, passages round which had to be felt for. The passages, besides, were narrow, and the forces getting through them were obliged to right about and dress their ranks as they passed each.

Each English regiment had its surgeon in attendance, and an orderly was laid off to assist each surgeon. The first man that was under Dr. Fenthorpe's care had got a bullet in his right arm; he walked steadily enough, and the wound, though sharp and disabling, was not dangerous. The next man whom Richard was called on to attend had a similar wound, but worse, and the bullet harder to find; he had to cut it out. He made the best hand of the two men that he could, tied their handkerchiefs round their necks for slings to carry their lame arms, and enjoined them to go home to Norwich as fast as they could walk, or to get on a waggon if they passed one. As these two men were about starting, a great shout arose, unlike the hoarse roar that goes on during an unsettled fight. They ran to the front, and saw the cavalry charge.

Then they raised their voices too, and walked off to Norwich, waving their hats with their sound arms.

There is a hamlet not more than a mile from this field of

battle as you go to Norwich. The villagers, seeing two
wounded volunteers, and knowing what was going on, asked
them for news, to which they answered that the French were
getting jolly well licked. Enthusiasm seized the audience,
and eighteen young fellows said they would go and see the
fun. Seventeen of them took pitchforks; the eighteenth, not
being able to find one, unchained two bulldogs. The ideas of
these peasants about how war should be waged were vague. It
was knowledge, not courage, that they were deficient in; they
really meant business. It is scarcely necessary to say that the
two faithful and courageous animals which were taken to the
battle for want of a pitchfork never after that day tackled
either man or bull. Concerning the services of the human
reinforcement, they managed among them to make a hole, a
very ugly one, in one French soldier's cheek; three or four
of them were badly wounded, and one killed outright, and the
rest were captured and taken to Yarmouth; where they
received, if not the best of care, attention which we shall
hereafter describe.

General Davoust, who was fully two miles from the bridge
at the opening of the battle, when he knew that there was
going to be one, be it ever so small, hurried forward twelve
field guns. When these arrived in view of the English army,
they were placed in position on the side of the road,
unlimbered in no time, and set to try to dismount the guns
of the four-gun battery. In a few minutes they got range,
and, within twenty minutes, two of the English guns were dismounted. During this time the French infantry, coming up
in increasing numbers, were got rapidly into the fields to their
left, or on the south side of the road. They exchanged shots
at rather long distances with the two English regiments
posted there. About an hour, or rather more, after the battle
had commenced, the first sharp fighting on this side occurred.

It was very sharp, and it was very short. The English
front was under half a mile in length; the distances from
company to company were ample. The French, now far
superior in number, tried to get between them, but could not,

for something with a clumsy, but useful, resemblance to a
square formation was used. A French company, feeling their
way round the English right, came to the brook, at the very
spot where two large trees had fallen across it. Their shouts
attracted an advancing battalion, and, though they were fired
at, in a very short time four or five hundred were across the
stream and making as hard as they could for the bridge, by
the taking of which the English would be hopelessly
surrounded.

Just as this occurred, a thousand horse came at a gallop
along the most northern of the roads from Yarmouth, and got
into view of the English left wing suddenly. Davoust by this
time was just going to open the third attack on the hill,
but, observing that something had happened in the rear of the
English right, he sent word to the officer in command of the
cavalry that he must dispose of the two regiments and the
now crippled battery, and turned his front towards the bridge.
The English right was now making for the bridge also,
almost in a rolled-up condition. Their battalion order was
utterly broken, although their companies stuck well together
still.

Only a few of them reached the bridge, or got over it. The
rest of these two thousand men, the number they had been
in the morning, were loudly called on by the French to
surrender. It was the duty of the officers to their men to do
so, but only a few of them knew that. Some companies
fought on, like the Roman dying wolf, and some hundreds
of lives were lost that should not have been. More than a
thousand prisoners were made. On the English left, the sight
of the cavalry produced an instant movement in retreat
which, however, could not be over the bridge; and the two
regiments, one of which had suffered hardly any loss, made
away as well as they could across the fields to the northwards
and north-westwards. The pursuit could be interfered with
but little, and the English cavalry were not well handled.
French dragoons, however, are not good across a country like
Norfolk, and the number of prisoners they made was less than
might have been expected. Now and then the volunteers

faced about in not very good order, and gave them a volley, when they had got into some kind of shelter; and the French cavalry commandant did not know how utter the rout at the bridge had been, and did not choose to pursue too far.

The English general and fifteen officers were slain. The general was trying to get to the bridge, with only a few followers, so soon as he saw the English right beginning to roll up; he was struck, mortally, with a musket ball, and did not live to see the end of the defeat. Alexander Mortland was severely wounded; he was the last subject that Fenthorpe had. The doctor dressed his wound, a bad one in the side, with the orderly and two of Mortland's own regiment present. Then he sent him with them to Fenthorpe Hall, less than a mile and a half from the scene of the battle, telling Mortland he would try to see him in the evening or on the next day. As the wounded major walked slowly away between his two soldiers, they passed within twenty yards of a troop of French horse, who took no notice of them.

Richard Fenthorpe and his orderly were left standing alone on the top of the hill, from whence they could see the ineffectual attempts of the English beyond the road to reach the bridge. The battle lasted, from beginning to end, an hour and three-quarters. It was as utter a rout as that of King Monmouth's army at Sedgmoor. The Loyal Norwich, and all the other regiments, had ceased to exist.

Not very long after the enemy had finished securing their prisoners, their march forward was resumed. Unknown to any of the English army, a thing that showed that their scout service was not very efficient, a French force, nearly equal to that which they had tried to interrupt, was marching on Norwich by the road south of the Yare. That division arrived, accordingly at the city, and entered it, before the division under Davoust, who, knowing the position and the distances, was not solicitous about advancing with the utmost speed. He watched, from the foot of the hill, several of his battalions defiling across the bridge, before he moved his horse as if he would accompany them. Dr. Fenthorpe was no more than a hundred and fifty yards distant. When he saw that General Davoust was going to move on, he walked quickly to him, made a military salute, and paused to see if he would be replied to. He knew French well, to read it, and enough to enable him to express himself intelligibly, although he had never spoken it, except in conversation exercises with his preceptor many years before.

We must here tell that the conjecture was perfectly correct that Bonaparte's plan for conquering England was not to strike terror, or to act so as to make the people think him their implacable enemy. It was rather, if possible, to conciliate. He had the idea, founded on no fact, but founded very deeply in his own imagination, that there was a strong French party in England, that would declare itself on its first great military success. He thought that Mr. Fox and others of what were, at one time, the new Whig party, and the bulk of the common people were of this French party, and desired a revolution and a republic. Therefore, he had given his generals orders to omit no opportunity of conciliating individuals, and to behave themselves, and make his armies behave themselves, very differently from the manner in which they had done in any of those countries which the French had of recent years overrun, except at first in Egypt. These orders were exceedingly distasteful to General Davoust, who was, of all the revolutionary generals, the most given to exercise the extreme rights of a conqueror, and the most disposed to strain the laws of war. But he would not begin his campaign by disobedience to instructions. When the doctor saluted him, he said, "Qu'est-ce que vous demandez?"

"Monsieur le General," replied Richard, "je suis le medecin d'un des regiments Anglais que vous avez defaits; je pense que mon regiment n'existe plus. Est-ce qu'il me sera permis à revenir à Norwich, ou est mon domicile?"

"Oui; ne passez pas le pont jusqu'à l'armee l'aurait traversé." He spoke brusquely, and turned his horse towards the bridge. He had looked at Fenthorpe, as though studying his face, during this short conversation.

Richard had a full hour to wait. The last part of the army that defiled along the road, except a troop of horse, was the artillery and waggons; and Richard thought that the horses that drew them were English. He distinctly recognised two or three, belonging to Yarmouth men of his acquaintance.

The French army did not halt at Norwich; they marched right across it, and advanced towards King's Lynn, leaving two thousand in the city, and no more. They spread themselves over the country as far as Wisbeach, which town they occupied, three days after the battle, with four thousand infantry. Two thousand of these were placed on the west side of the Nene, and the inhabitants were compelled, by threats and by shooting a few, to assist in throwing up intrenchments. Six thousand were left at Yarmouth and on the coast. The rest of the army, including nearly all the cavalry, was echeloned between Norwich and the Isle of Ely. The whole of Norfolk, and a considerable part of Cambridgeshire, were thus under complete military occupation. This French army, also, was unassailable. Wisbeach on the west, and the neighbourhood of the great army of invasion on the south, made it as secure as Wellington was in Portugal, after he had taken Cuidad Rodrigo and Badajoz.

Nor was this all, as describing the condition of the country and its inhabitants. Norfolk was cut off from the rest of England not alone in a military sense, but as much as if a sea rolled round it. The mail coaches, of course, were stopped, and also the local posts. There was, in one of the chief streets of Norwich, a row of six or seven large houses, the ground floors of which were occupied by shops, all but one, which was the post office. The French commandant took possession of this row of houses, turning out all the tenants; the postmaster, an old and much respected man, stood wringing his hands as he watched the profanation. A part of the garrison was encamped round the castle; the rest were dispersed through the city. The road between Wymondham and Yarmouth was constantly patrolled by cavalry, who allowed no traffic, even of pedestrians. For a whole fortnight, no news arrived in Norfolk of anything whatever that was going on in the rest of England.

CHAPTER VIII.

WHEN the House of Commons met at four o'clock on Wednesday, the 27th of February, it was remarked that, for the first time on record, as many members attended prayers as were present at the debate. But indeed there was no debate. The King's message was delivered, and Mr. Pitt said a few words, full of resolution and hope; and Mr. Fox repeated what he said before, that he had confidence in his Majesty's Government that they would entertain no proposals for an accommodation or truce so long as a foreign enemy should have a footing in England. The House adjourned till Friday.

The moment that it was known that there had been a landing of the enemy separate from that at Harwich, the orders to the garrison of Colchester to withdraw towards London were withdrawn. Orders to the contrary were sent, and all available forces were sent with all haste in that direction. The Suffolk, Essex, and Cambridgeshire volunteers were directed to concentrate between Colchester and Ipswich. Against Saturday, the second of March, there were seventy thousand troops round Colchester, and a wide temporary bridge was thrown over the river above the town. This first English army, as it was called, had a fair proportion of cavalry and of guns.

The disembarkation of the French occupied four days, and was complete only on Friday night. During the whole of the intervening days, the French had scoured the neighbourhood of Harwich for horses, with very indifferent success. A remarkable movement took place during this time all through Essex and Suffolk.

When an invasion had been daily expected, a year before the events that we are narrating, it was on the coast of Kent and Sussex that it was universally thought the enemy would land. There were positive orders that, on the first alarm, all horses should be removed from the enemy's reach. This was known all over England, and, now that the invasion had come, people remembered it. The Mayor of Harwich sent word to as many of his neighbours as he had access to, to send their horses away; and a large miller and corn-factor of Colchester, on the evening when news of the landing arrived; instantly loaded his carts with grain, and sent all he could—it was said, more than two hundred quarters—to Hertford. The movement spread like wildfire; and it was believed, though this must be a great exaggeration, that at the end of two days not more than twenty horses were left in all East Essex and Suffolk. In Norfolk, as we have seen, there was nothing of the kind.

Some curious results ultimately arose from this. Many farmers sent away their horses in charge of servants, some of whom were not perfectly honest. They would not have stolen, because they were well up in the law relating to horse stealing; but they reflected that a man cannot well steal a horse that he is given to ride. Many horses were sold for ridiculous sums, and the men who were paid for them gave but unsatisfactory accounts of what had become of their steeds. At the assizes that were held after the war was over, a more general knowledge than had ever prevailed before was diffused throughout England on the subject of the law respecting embezzlement.

The difficulty that Bonaparte was put to for want of horses was great, for he had brought but few artillery horses, and none for the waggons whatever. Besides this, it transpired afterwards that a misfortune had happened during the adventurous voyage of the flotilla, which had the effect of crippling his means still further.

One hundred and thirty thousand men of all arms had left the shores of Holland and Belgium. Of these, eighteen

thousand were cavalry. Very near the Dutch coast, the fog
had been very thick, and the sea was absolutely crowded with
craft. Two divisions of the flotilla had got confusedly mixed
up together. Nearly three hundred boats lost their way, and
put back; and it so happened that most of these were the
larger boats containing cavalry. So that the total invasion in
its two parts that actually reached England was, in all, one
hundred and ten or fifteen thousand of all arms, of whom no
more than a tenth in number at the utmost were horse. But
no accident had befallen any of the artillery boats, and there
were landed no fewer than six hundred and fifty field guns.

Some anecdotes of Bonaparte began, somehow, to ooze out.
He did not land till Thursday night, having stayed on board
a large ship, keeping a look-out, it was believed, for an
English fleet. The English had not yet thoroughly taken his
measure, and it was thought that he was prepared either to
land or to take flight to the Continent, according as he might
judge best for his personal safety. When he did land, the
first thing he did was to command the presence of the officer
who had fought the action in the market-place of Harwich.
That gentleman had strictly obeyed orders in not pressing the
English, but Bonaparte had learned that the small detachment had escaped him for want of pursuing, and he swore
at the officer for twenty minutes.

On Saturday morning all the French army but two
battalions left the coast and advanced on Colchester. On
arriving opposite to it on the eastern side, they spread themselves between that town and the river Stour. There was no
fighting that evening but a small affair of outposts. An ærial
telegraph had been established to London, and two hours
after the French began to move, it was known to the
War Office. In the middle of the night a despatch arrived
from the English commander, whom we shall call Sir D., the
tone of which Lord Camden and Mr. Pitt did not like.

Mr. Groves was still in London. On Wednesday he had
gone to Downing Street, where he heard the latest intelligence, and he pressed Mr. Bentinck to arrange for him an
interview, were it but for five minutes, with the Prime

Minister. On Thursday morning he saw Mr. Pitt for the five
minutes.

"I have a plan for making use of the Kentish volunteers
that I think is more suited to them, and that they would be
more useful in than any other way."

"What is the object of your plan, Mr. Groves?"

"It is connected with the defence of London, where, I
believe, the enemy are sure to come. It is of no use to take up
your time with it, if you are going to defend London in the
field only."

"I think you had better lay it before Lord Camden. He
will consult me if he adopts your idea. You don't know Lord
Camden? Mr. Bentinck, write, introducing Mr. Groves, and
I will sign the letter." Mr. Pitt went on writing.

Mr. Groves took the letter, and went to the Secretary of
State's office. Lord Camden was busy, but sent one of the
chiefs of the office to receive Mr. Pitt's friend. This gentleman, who was but an upper clerk, although his official title
was high-sounding, was vastly polite, and listened to Mr.
Groves without impatience, his principal business being to
act as a buffer between the Secretary and people likely to be
troublesome. Not that Lord Camden was an idler, or
incompetent, or at all deserving of the contempt that Mr.
Pitt had for him; but Secretaries of State cannot see, or spend
time with, everybody.

The first thing that the clerk said to Mr. Groves rather put
him out. "You are a resident in Folkestone, Mr. Groves, are
you not? Should you not apply at the Admiralty?"

This was so absurd that Mr. Groves feared he was talking
to an ass, but the gentleman was only totally ignorant of
everything about war, knowing no more than that the army
is a different thing from the navy. He was no ass, but a very
sensible man, as Mr. Groves had found out before half an
hour had passed; and probably his ignorance and his being
entirely free from prejudices caused him to assimilate Mr.
Groves's ideas and comprehend his projects better than if
he had been well informed in the proper business of his office.

After an hour's conversation, the clerk finished it by say-

ing, "Well, Mr. Groves, it appears, to my poor judgment,
that the idea is an excellent one, and I will lay it before Lord
Camden. It would assist me much if you would write it in
the form of a memoir or memorandum. But, as I was saying
to you, all our people think that, if we can prevent the
junction of the two invasions, London cannot be attacked,
with the force that we have now, or will have, at—where is
it?"

"Colchester," said Mr. Groves.

"Colchester. And if we can't prevent the junction, then
surely it is time enough to think of defending London or
making a resistance here?"

"Sir," said Mr. Groves, "the project that I have been laying before you could not be carried out without preparation.
There is nothing in all the world that can be done without
time to do it in. If we wait till Bonaparte has beaten the
army at Colchester, he will come thundering down upon us
before we can turn round. What we can do to-day may be of
use, and it may be impossible to do it to-morrow. Mr. ——,
may I ask you, do you think there is any systematic plan for
beating the enemy? Is there anything settled to be done in
case such a thing happens? Or anything settled in case such
another thing happens?"

"Well, you see, Mr. Groves, that is not, you understand, as
it were, my department. I could ask ——, but I should
scarcely like; it would be thought interfering."

Mr. Groves sighed. His friend went on: "I have learned,
I feel, Mr. Groves, a great deal from what you have been
saying; and though I am, as you must perceive, quite unin-
formed on these matters, I cannot but think that what you
suggest is an excellent thing. Your idea of employing the
Kentish volunteers in Kent itself, or what is the same thing,
strikes me as very good. I am a Kentish man myself, though
I have not been in Kent for twenty years. And I am very
much struck by what you say about getting things done in
proper time. All I know is—that is, now—is that Lord
Camden and Mr. Pitt are both very hopeful."

"Too hopeful!" said Mr. Groves. "Too sanguine!"

"Do you really think, now," said the clerk, "that Bonaparte will beat us in the first battle?"

"I think that we ought to make exactly what preparations ought to be made as if we were certain that he would beat us, and not on the chance of beating him in any the least degree whatever. The existence of England—the existence of England, Mr. ——, should not be left to the care of the chapter of accidents. O God! Would that people were less hopeful and more provident! I feared this. But I must go. I can let you have all in writing in three hours."

"It will do in the morning, Mr. Groves. My lord will have left this long before three hours, and I could not possibly present it to his lordship this evening; he is dining with the King. If you let me have it against ten in the morning, I shall be able to read and master it all in proper time."

"Then I will send it by the twopenny post, addressed, I suppose, to yourself?"

"My dear sir, not by the twopenny, or any post. Can you not send it by messenger?"

Mr. Groves did not know the horror that official men then had of anything coming through the post, so unlike the confidence that lawyers have in that institution; but it was not worth disputing about. "Very well," he said. "Now, I wish you good evening, and I thank you, sir, sincerely, for the manner in which you have received me."

"My good sir, don't mention it! Good evening."

Mr. Groves went out of the office a despairing man. He went to his room in the Golden Cross and began to write. There were noises, and he was restless, and he could not write so as to satisfy himself. He put out his candles—it was now past five, and a gloomy evening—and determined to go to Thomas Armitage's house in Bloomsbury and write there. As he passed out of the inn door, Shinkwin was standing in it, and touched his hat. He had forgotten all about the man, and almost started.

"Shinkwin!" he exclaimed. "I thought you had gone!"

"I did not know but your honour might have need of me," said the young smuggler, "though I don't know what, as things have turned out."

"Will you do something for me?" said Mr. Groves. "Will you go home to-night by the coach, and take a letter?"

"Certain I will, or do anything else for your honour. Shall I take a place now, for the eight o'clock coach?"

"Yes." It was curious that the sight of this man had restored Mr. Groves's spirits to par. He returned to his room and wrote to his major, telling him how he hoped that the East Kent would get something to do that would be worthy of them, but not hinting what that something was. He desired that they should be ready for marching at an hour's notice at any moment. Perhaps he would go for them, and perhaps not. Shinkwin departed with the letter, which he delivered the next morning. He entertained his fellow-travellers with an account of how he had come to London to give warning, and how he had seen Mr. Pitt in Mr. Pitt's own house; and disposed of a drink or two at every stage at some admiring passenger's expense, and was a great man entirely, as Irish people say. But he arrived at Folkestone perfectly sober.

Mr. Groves went to Bloomsbury and wrote his memoir. When he had sealed it and put it in his pocket, he turned round and opened one of the desks, of which there were many, without any particular object. A parcel caught his eye, in a hand that he remembered: "Reverend Henry Fenthorpe, Norwich. September, 1775. Memorandum."

It was old Mr. Armitage's history of his visit to Norwich, and of the search for Charles Fenthorpe's will, a copy of which had been sent to Mr. Fenthorpe. Mr. Groves read it, twice, and thought. He came to an entirely different conclusion from that which the old attorney had arrived at.

"There was a will," he said to himself. "And perhaps there was something done that should not have been done; perhaps there was a crime. The behaviour of the witness proves that there was a will. I wonder so shrewd a man as old Mr. Armitage did not see that what Henry Fenthorpe was told by his brother—was he his brother?—tallies exactly with what the witness admitted. For a man to withdraw his statement does not disprove his statement. It only proves the man to be a rogue. I have no good opinion of Mr. Mortland; it must be the same, just of age thirty years ago. It is curious, this thing coming up after so long. I wonder what was the occasion of Mr. Fenthorpe writing to me. It is curious the way it came up now among Thomas's papers. It is curious in every way. It is curious how I feel an interest in it, people that I don't know. I was thinking of it the other night. I suppose I shall never hear of it again."

He got the housekeeper to give him some tea, and walked back to his inn, thinking the whole time more of the mysterious Fenthorpe affair than of the contents of the letter in his pocket, important though they were.

At ten the next morning, Mr. Groves brought his letter to the Secretary of State's office. Mr. ——, with whom he had conversed the day before, was there, and called him into an inner room. "My lord wishes to see you," he said. "Just before he was leaving yesterday evening, I had an opportunity of telling him of your visit, and he desired you to be brought to him if you should come to-day. And my lord asked me are not you the gentleman who had the information about the landing?"

"I know what Lord Camden referred to; yes, I am."

"The gentleman that heard on Monday that they were going to take advantage of the fog, and had all the boats in Holland without our knowledge?"

"Yes," said Mr. Groves. "I learned it in a curious way."

"I had heard of it, but I did not know, Mr. Groves, that it was you, or who it was. You went to Mr. Pitt, I believe. Well, Lord Camden knows about it. I will tell his lordship you are here; you shall not have long to wait."

We must here explain the readiness that Lord Camden exhibited in receiving a visit and representations from a

gentleman whom he knew but indirectly, although favourably. We have already said that that nobleman was not the
imbecile Minister that Mr. Pitt, who was prone to depreciate
all but a few intimates, supposed. He had considerable
ability, was thoroughly disinterested, and was of sound principles. He had been a military man in his youth, but had
seen little or no active service. He had unbounded admiration
for Pitt; while the latter, when he had agreed with the King
in making him Secretary for the War Department the year
before, looked on him as a *pis aller*. Lord Camden consulted
Pitt in everything of importance, and there was no reason for
the Prime Minister to think of keeping him in his proper
place, which he never dreamed of stepping out of.

On the other hand, Mr. Pitt was not what he had been, in
some respects; and some, including Harry Lord Melville,
had remarked it, while they failed to speak of it. He had
carried on war against the Republic for nine years with but
poor success. All her allies had deserted England; two
coalitions of the Continental powers, to all appearance invincible, had been shattered, shivered, and humbled. And
England had made a peace with her enemy that was no more
than barely respectable. When, in the hour of danger, Pitt
was a second time called on by his King and country to
undertake the government and the conduct of the war, he
found, to his surprise and indignation, that many of his old
friends would not come to his assistance. He was particularly wroth with Lord Grenville, on whom he had relied;
and he vowed vengeance on him, for he was vindictive, the
only serious blot on an otherwise noble character. The direct
effect of these desertions was to undermine Pitt's confidence
in himself. He still spoke boldly, proudly, and defiantly, and
disdainfully even towards those who asked questions. This
was all external. He was sanguine by nature, but he could
not help reflecting that the war with the Republic had been a
severe strain on the strength of England, and that the First
Consul was far more powerful than the Republic had ever
been.

Besides this, Pitt's health was failing. He had led a hard life, working hard and drinking hard. Walpole drank heavily, but did not do too much work; Lord Palmerston worked hard, and lived freely enough, but took plenty of air and exercise; Mr. Gladstone worked hard, but was temperate, and always rested on Sundays. Pitt never gave himself any rest, and he drank far too much port, nearly all of it fresh bottled and fiery. Even during the three years that he was out of office, he drank his usual allowance, if allowance that can be called that had no fixed limit, and did no work but riding a good deal. In addition, his disappointment about Miss ——, the daughter of Lord Naresbrook and niece of Mr. Groves, had embittered him and impaired his moral strength. If it had not been that he slept well, his nerves could never have stood all this. But his nightly rest was extremely good. He never lay awake during his life but twice—on the night after the King had sent Mr. Fox and Lord North about their business, and made him Prime Minister, and on the night after he heard of the death of Nelson at Trafalgar.

When he had been Minister during the first war, he never consulted any one but Harry Dundas, and resented advice and even proffered information. Now he invited advice or hints, and was even too ready to take up a plan or idea from another without duly weighing it. He had inoculated Lord Camden with a good deal of the same; and neither of them had much reliance on the English general, Sir D., whom the King thought a great deal of, if that be considered any great recommendation.

When Mr. —— told Lord Camden of Mr. Groves's visit, and, in a few words, the substance of that gentleman's project, the Secretary listened with interest. He remembered Mr. Groves as the man who had warned Mr. Pitt when it was too late, and had even told him how the invasion would be effected. At Buckingham House, where he dined, there was an artillery officer, a man of the highest connections, but not much known by people in general—a studious, retiring person. Lord Camden spoke to this gentleman about the

I

subject that Mr. Groves had indirectly laid before him, and was a little surprised at his manner. " I have often thought of the same thing, my lord; but there is no use speaking of it."

" Why? " asked Lord Camden.

" It is opposed to all their ideas. I had thought of it last year, when it was expected that London would be attacked on the south, and it is far more practicable now that London will be attacked from the north. I was only yesterday, my lord, or the day before, wondering would any one else think of it."

Lord Camden was struck with this, and was struck also by this new example of what all reflecting men, military and non-military, actually took for certain when they spoke of the course of the war—that is, that London could not be preserved.

Mr. Groves was not detained for long before Lord Camden had discharged his necessary business and was ready to give him interview. " Will you, Mr. Groves," he said after the first greetings and mention of their common acquaintance, the Prime Minister, " will you tell me the particulars of your plan as shortly, at first, as you are able; then we can discuss it and the particulars."

" Should your lordship prefer to read this memoir, or that I should describe its contents by word of mouth? "

" I think I should rather hear you; you will leave the memoir, I presume? "

" Certainly, my lord. In the first place, I must remind your lordship of what is, no doubt, known to you, that there is, throughout the whole of the volunteer forces, a very strong local feeling—that is, an affection towards their own localities and counties. The feeling is nowhere stronger than it is in Kent; indeed, I believe the men of Kent will think that the French have put a personal affront on them by landing on the east coast. But the Kentish men would think that they were fighting for Kent if they were employed in London, and especially if they were employed in this way—that is, according to the plan Mr. —— spoke to you of, and on that service. Bonaparte will come into London from the north. If we cannot prevent the attack by winning a battle, we cannot prevent the attack and the capture of London. But we can, if we take measures in time, prevent, or very greatly delay, the capture of London south of the Thames."

"I understand your idea, so far. You propose to fortify and defend the bridges."

"The first thing, my lord, is to appreciate, to comprehend, the military importance of not letting the enemy, whom we cannot keep out of Middlesex, into Surrey and Kent. Once that they could get over the river there is nothing but the Kentish volunteers to keep them out of Woolwich; and I believe that they would be just as certain of getting the Medway also into their hands as of taking Woolwich. Now, the local forces of Kent are quite inadequate to defend Kent against the French that would be against them; but they would be of inestimable use in defending Kent on its frontier —that is, the Thames itself at London Bridge. Besides, it is a matter of the first necessity to the French, or it will be, to get into Kent; but if the Thames is defended properly, they cannot get there round by Richmond and Kingston, for it would expose their flank on a march of practically two and a half or three days."

"You mean that they must get into Kent as the only possible means of communicating with the Continent?"

"That is exactly what I mean, my lord. It is evident to you, and it is also evident to me, that what is necessary to them, necessary to their existence, is the very thing that we ought to erect all obstacles in our power against. I even believe that the defence of the bridges may be the vital point of the war. I think it very likely that Bonaparte will be unprepared for it. Is it not almost known to you that he has no siege or heavy guns?"

"We believe so. He has an immense number of field guns. He is short of cavalry, and he is short of waggon horses."

"If he has no heavy guns, we have them in unlimited number, and we can make London and Blackfriars Bridges impregnable. Westminster Bridge should be mined, and blown up if necessary; but I think it could be included in the same system of defence. Indeed, I am sure it could, and it should be blown up only in case of absolute necessity."

"Mr. Groves, why do you think the position of Westminster Bridge is more difficult of defence than that of the two city bridges?"

"Westminster Bridge, my lord, has no bridge-head. To defend the other two, we must occupy the Middlesex ends of them as far as Gracechurch Street and Ludgate. We should occupy also I am not quite sure how much of the mass of buildings between St. Paul's Churchyard and the river, but at least both sides of Thames Street. This would unite the defence of the two bridges in one system, and it would be impossible to attack one of them separately from an attack on the other, and both attacks would be subject to be taken in flank. Westminster Bridge is different, for want of a proper bridge-head. Palace Yard is too open for us to hold. Besides, it would spread our strength too much to try to hold Fleet Street and the Strand; the line would be too long, and would be in hourly danger of being cut. But the very first thing, an essential thing, is to remove all ships and all craft down to the wherry boats, from the Middlesex side."

"Where would you send them?"

"Down the river, anywhere they might choose to go; their captains would keep them out of fire. My lord, this ought to be begun to-day."

The effect of laying a matured plan before anybody, on that person's mind, is not always in proportion to the goodness of the plan. Very often it is in proportion much more to its apparent completeness and symmetry. Here was a good plan, complete, or nearly so, and symmetrical. Lord Camden must have been either a very wise man or a very foolish one, not to be impressed. He was not slow. During the rebellion in Ireland, he had, at one critical moment, by an act of vigour, placed Dublin beyond the reach of danger.

There was a few minutes' silence; then Lord Camden desired Mr. —— to find out where Mr. Pitt was. While Mr. —— was out of the room, there was more conversation, and Mr. Groves gave some more particulars of his project.

"And your Kentish men, Mr. Groves? How many have you?"

"I am colonel of the East Kent; but that is the name of the corps, and there are other corps in East Kent. There are in all, I am sure, four thousand—the best drilled and the readiest volunteers in all England."

Mr. —— returned. Mr. Pitt was at the Foreign Office. Lord Camden rose and put on his coat, assisted by Mr. ——; this was one of his functions.

"I am at your orders at any moment, my lord," said Mr. Groves.

"I should detain you now, sir, but that I do not know how long I should have to do so. I ought to tell you that yesterday I met at Buckingham House an artillery officer, who has very nearly the same ideas as you have about defending the Thames. I must now wish you good morning."

Lord Camden did not see Mr. Pitt that day, for he was engaged over some important despatches just arrived from Germany. They kept him till four o'clock, when he had to go to the House. A few questions were asked, to which he replied in a tone of confidence, and with some not very well suppressed asperity.

Mr. Groves, after dining that day at his inn, went to Bloomsbury, as he had done the evening before. On this occasion he could scarcely have told himself his object; it was little more than habit. He desired the housekeeper to bring him some tea, and, after drinking it, opened the same desk that he had looked through on the previous evening. Far back in the desk he found a small parcel, endorsed, like the other, in old Mr. Armitage's writing. The endorsement was, "Robert Mortland, Esquire. February, 1777."

It contained a letter, addressed to Mr. Armitage, attorney, Lincoln's Inn, and passed through the post. It contained, also, a sheet of paper, with a few words in Mr. Armitage's writing, dated as above.

"I am quite unable to think of a reason for Mr. Mortland's behaviour. I remember that he did seem to resent my insisting on his allowing me to question the supposed witness Allonby in his presence. But that will not account for this. I have made no delay, nor have I offered any objection to any of his instructions, either in the matter of the marriage settlement or otherwise."

The letter was a short one, courteous in style though not in substance, closing all business between Mr. Mortland and Mr. Armitage's firm, and directing Mr. Armitage, after furnishing his bill of costs, to hand over documents to an attorney named. The name was a Scotch one. These were the words in the letter, "I think more expedition might have been used about the settlement."

Mr. Groves read, and thought again. "What does it mean," he said to himself, "this affair turning up so often?" Then he put on his coat—unlike Lord Camden, he did so without assistance—and walked back to the Golden Cross.

CHAPTER IX.

RICHARD FENTHORPE reached home at five o'clock of the evening of the lost battle. As he passed through the streets of Norwich, blank consternation was on every face. The French were on the Castle mound, in tents, and groups of their soldiers were walking about, staring round them insolently.

His mother was at home, trembling and praying. She did not know but that he might have been among the slain, or taken prisoner. No such experience has ever been ours as waiting for a whole day, uncertain whether a son, or a father, or a brother is, or is not, in the land of the living; but those who have stood at the mouth of a coal-pit after an explosion, watching the motion of the cable that draws up the basket, know what it is.

Reassuring his mother, and after answering such questions as he could, and swallowing a glass of wine, he went to Mr. Cardwain's. Helen saw him as he passed through the garden gate, and opened the door.

"O Richard! Thank God!"

He was fain to embrace her, but restrained himself. They went into the house. They all knew that he was safe; some one who had seen him in the street had told them.

"Richard," said Mrs. Cardwain, "is it true that Major Mortland is killed?"

"No; he is severely wounded in the side. I saw him off with two men to the Hall, and I hope he was able to get there. I will see him to-morrow, if not to-night; but I fear it will be impossible to-night. We don't know yet all that have perished. Sprowles is killed, and Townsend."

"Oh, Mr. Sprowles!" exclaimed Helen, bursting out weeping; "and only the other day I said he cared for nothing but walking about in his uniform! Oh, poor Mr. Sprowles! Oh, God forgive me for what I said! Richard, how did he die?"

"He fell fighting bravely, one of our men who escaped told me. Bravely, like all the rest, but how uselessly! Let us not talk of their folly. And do you know, I just now heard that orders arrived only this morning for all the volunteers to withdraw into Cambridgeshire."

This was true. Somebody at the War Office or the Horse Guards had thought, on Thursday, of the Norfolk volunteers, and orders to retire were despatched. But the messenger, who rode post, was thrown from his horse somewhere, and the horse galloped off, and the orders came too late.

When it came to be known generally, people felt as they do when there has been delay or blundering in the launching of a lifeboat, and when lives have been lost that could have been saved; and a great and swelling feeling of resentment rose against the Government, which had neglected its duty.

As the days went on, and no news came, the anxiety and the excitement, necessarily suppressed, became unendurable; and there was greater mental suffering among all classes of people from this uncertainty and suspense, than from the feeling of enslavement under the foreign occupation. Not that the French, at first, behaved with by any means extreme, or even great, severity.

Richard stayed for some time at Mrs. Cardwain's, and was just leaving, at about seven o'clock, when a messenger came for him from the Mayor. The Mayor's house was near, and his worship was standing at his door with a French officer.

"Dr. Fenthorpe," he said to Richard, "I am sent for to the general's at the castle. I do not know what he wants, and I don't know ten words of French. I said only the word "interpreter" to this officer here, and he understood that. Will you come with me?"

"Certainly. Is it General Davoust?"

"It is not their general-in-chief, if you mean him. He is gone on with the body of their army. This is a general, or a colonel—I don't know what. This gentleman has not been uncivil. Will you ask him what is wanted with me?"

"I think it will be better for you to go without any demur," said Richard. "This is a lieutenant, and he will not have been entrusted with a message. Monsieur," he said to the officer, "je suis l'interprète."

"Allons donc," said the officer; and they started.

"I have sent all the constables," said the Mayor to Richard, "to tell the people everywhere to make no resistance, even if they go into their houses and demand food and lodging. We can't resist, and it would only bring harm on any that should attempt it. So far as I can perceive, they don't seem to feel any resentment at having been opposed; but it is hard to judge."

"I should not think that they do," said Richard; "they will feel more pride at having beaten us. Not that it is any great achievement for fourteen thousand men to have defeated three; but they can make up a fine report of it for Bonaparte."

At the name of Bonaparte, the French officer turned his head. "Il est à Harveech, messieurs," he said.

"Oui, monsieur," answered Richard, "nous en avons entendu."

By this time they were at the Castle gate, and, in a minute more, in the general's presence. He was a youngish man, with a mild expression of countenance, not at all like General Davoust, whom Richard had thought one of the most truculent-looking men he had ever seen. He rose and bowed, and desired the Mayor to be seated. Richard introduced himself as the interpreter, and sat down without being invited. The general looked at him, but said nothing. His orders were, as we know, and as Richard had a half suspicion of, to bear himself politely towards the inhabitants.

The general, addressing the Mayor through him, said he wanted billets for fourteen hundred men.

"I will billet not a man for him," said the Mayor when he heard what was wanted.

"It will not do," said Richard, "to give that flat refusal. Had you not better explain why you refuse?"

"There has not been a soldier billeted in Norwich since the time of Ket the Tanner, two hundred and fifty years ago. If I ordered billets, the people would not recognise or obey me in a thing they never heard of. And for me to order such a thing would be comforting the King's enemies, and high treason. Can you put that into your best French, Dr. Fenthorpe?"

"Sir," said Richard, "pardon me, but before I give such an answer, may I ask you have you thought of this? He may order you to be shot."

"I don't think he will. I thought it was about this that I was sent for, and I speak from premeditation. Besides, for me to mix myself up with it would be of no use whatever, and would create more confusion, besides disgracing me for the rest of my life."

An interpreter has a great deal in his power, but Richard Fenthorpe would not deceive the Mayor, whom he, and all Norwich, and half Norfolk, held in the highest estimation. He put the answer as gently as he could, making the most of the practical want of authority of the Mayor in such things, and explaining how he was a very different kind of functionary from a French Maire or a German Bergermeister.

The general knit his brows, but did not break into violent language or threats. He merely said:

"Et vous refusez, Monsieur le Maire?"

"Il est impossible, Monsieur le General, que nous pourrons nous accorder avec vos desirs." The French is not of the best quality, but it answered the purpose.

"Eh bien, c'est à votre perte, et à la perte de vos co-citoyens." Then he spoke to a clerk, and Richard heard the word "procès-verbal." The Mayor also caught it, and knew what it meant. "Tell him," he said to Richard, "that I will sign nothing. It is not according to law."

Richard repeated this, adding that, if the magistrate of an English city should do anything not according to law, his act would be invalid. He tried to puzzle the Frenchman, and succeeded, for he burst out laughing at the idea of a man being more afraid of doing an illegal act than of Bonaparte's army. He had also begun to understand that his men would be able to billet themselves just as well without assistance as with such assistance as the authorities of the city could give them. He told the Mayor and the interpreter that he had now done with them. The Mayor was making a bow, when Richard asked him to stay for a moment. "It is about my horse," he said.

Then he addressed himself to the general, telling him that he was a physician, with numerous patients; that he had a horse, which was necessary to him in making his visits; that he had learned that the French army had taken their horses from the people of Yarmouth; and that, in case they meant to do likewise at Norwich, he prayed, in the interests of humanity, that he should be permitted to keep his horse.

This French officer, general or colonel we know not, was a gentleman. Indeed, he was one of the *ancienne noblesse*, which was one reason why he was made Commandant of Norwich, as he was pretty sure to behave decently. He said at once: "C'est bien raisonnable; venez le matin pour une permission."

Richard was very much pleased, but not surprised. "Et, Monsieur le General, il y a aussi dans cette ville le Docteur Johnson, qui a une clientelle plus grande que la mienne, et je vous prie pour lui, c'est à dire pour son cheval, une permission semblable."

"Le Docteur Johnson est-il votre corrival?"

Richard forgot what this meant, and answered, "Oui, monsieur, il est mon corrival; c'est à dire il est mon ami des plus intimes et bien-aimés."

The officer smiled. A French doctor would never have thought of asking such a favour for another doctor. It would come far more natural to him to lame the other doctor's horse.

They are better now, but they were a mean, dirty lot a
hundred years ago. The permit was promised, and the
physician and the Mayor left the Castle.

Doctors Johnson and Fenthorpe were now the freest men in
Norfolk. The next day was Sunday. In the morning,
Richard rode out to the Hall to visit the wounded Mortland,
whom he found going on favourably, though the wound was
serious, and the recovery likely to be slow. On his return to
the city, after leaving his horse in the stable, he walked to
Mr. Cardwain's, guessing that his uncle and aunt, and their
guests, would have returned from church. He found the
whole family standing in the hall, with two French officers.
One of the officers had a printed paper in his hand, which he
seemed trying to induce Mr. Cardwain to take from him. Mr.
Cardwain was repelling the paper with his hand, and saying,
"No, no, no," which he perhaps knew meant the same in
French and in English. His hat was on his head, and an
umbrella in his hand. Fanny Tronford was behind him, her
back towards the officers, laughing and trying to suppress her
laughter. The other three ladies stood further back, looking
displeased; and Miss Dorkington said, "Such impudence!"

"Here, Richard," said Mr. Cardwain, "speak to them.
Helen won't, and she is right. That ladies should be exposed
to this!"

Looking at the paper, Richard read:

LE COMMANDANT ET LES OFFICIERS

DE LA GARNISON

PRIENT MONS., MME., ET LES DEMOISELLES ——

D'ASSISTER AU BAL

QUI SERA DONNÉ À L'HOTEL DE VILLE,

MARDI SOIR, LE CINQ MARS,

À HUIT HEURES PRECISES.

"Messieurs," said Richard, taking off his hat, "c'est
impossible." He turned to the hall door and opened it wide.

The officers bowed, and walked out in dudgeon. Mr. Card-wain, in towering wrath, rushed to the door to slam it, but Richard prevented him.

The evening before, they had sent to a printer's and ordered him to print five hundred copies of the circular. The man refused, till threatened with being shot. He was not paid, of course. Then in the morning, when they saw the people coming out of church, the officers divided the town into beats, and knocked at every respectable-looking house. They got a good deal of bad language that they did not understand; a few ladies who could speak French answered them politely, but with disdain. At the end of an hour, the seven or eight couples of officers who had gone on the search for victims of their hospitality met one another, all having the same blank result. They could not understand it. Some of these men had been in Italy, and remembered the glorious ball that Bonaparte's officers had given at Milan at the inhabitants' expense a few days before Marengo; others had been in Bavaria with Moreau, and had had like experience. None had ever witnessed national hatred, for the time of Prussia was not yet. Some of the more thoughtful of them wondered would conciliation be of much use with such barbarians. A brighter thought occurred to the others. As the ladies of Norwich would not come to their ball, they had recourse to those who are not ladies, some of whom can hardly be called women. Even these were shy. In the afternoon the Com-mandant heard of it, and, the only one amongst them with a feeling of shame, put a stop to the business.

Perhaps this proceeding raised more wrath and resentment than the slaughter of the volunteers, and more than what happened on the next Wednesday. On that day the French began to drive away all horses. This began at Wymondham; and against Saturday night, by sending out detachments, the French had secured, and sent away to the southwards, how far was not known, almost every horse in the county. They swept the country with incredible speed, round by Salthouse and Burnham, and its furthest corners, as well as the parts they were in occupation of. A few farmers were cunning enough and lucky enough to be able to secrete their horses; and at Cromer, which the enemy had not occupied for more than two days, a few were hidden in the bathing machines till the search was over, and escaped capture. An estimate was made that four thousand were removed, which we think very doubtful; but Bonaparte got enough of draught power for all his guns and waggons, and was at no disadvantage on that account during the rest of the time the war lasted.

The permissions to the two doctors were honourably observed. General Davoust returned from Wisbeach on Thursday, and superintended the despatch of the horses to the other army. He was for leaving none, but the Commandant of Norwich was determined not to break faith. There was no actual quarrel. The Commandant had, however, to represent that, to seize a physician's horse was like firing on an hospital. Davoust did not stay in Norwich. He had seen, coming from Yarmouth, Fenthorpe Hall, which is well within view of one point on the road, and thought it would be good, and certainly comfortable, headquarters; and he desired that his movements should not be watched by so large a population as forty thousand exasperated people. Accordingly, on Thursday evening, he and his staff and an escort went out to Fenthorpe, without any notice.

The Fenthorpe stables had not yet been emptied, and the first thing that General Davoust did was to take a survey of them, and select for his own use what he liked best. Robert Mortland had seen his approach, and, with great presence of mind, made a groom drive a wooden nail between the hoof and the shoe of one of the feet of his own favourite horse, so as to lame him for so long as the nail should be left. Thus, when the horse was led out for inspection, he was not fit, to all appearance, for even army use; and, on being rejected, the same clever groom did not long leave the nail in him. It was a risky thing, and could not be done except with a horse not very recently shod, but it turned out right in this instance. Robert disliked the visitor at Fenthorpe extremely, and so did his father. Mrs. Mortland was in a state of consternation. But the father and son determined that they would make the best of it, and they made the most deferential advances to the general. Davoust was a surly fellow, to use the very mildest term by which his manners can be described, and he received these advances without any equivalent response. There were, however, on the staff, one or two tolerable persons.

From one of these Robert learned the next day that there had been a great battle, in which the English were utterly defeated. The officer did not know where the battle had been fought, nor anything but the bare fact; nor could he tell from whom he had heard it, not knowing his informant's name. "Mais c'est vrai," he said, very positively. Robert proposed to ask the general, but this was forbidden in such peremptory terms that he durst not. Then he thought of going into Norwich to find out what he could, and to impart what he had heard. But he put this off till the next day, fearing to produce the lamed and recovered horse too soon.

In the morning he asked the officer to accompany him to Norwich, which the latter willingly agreed to on receiving leave. There was no difficulty made, for really there was very little business to do. On reaching the city one of the first men that they met was the Mayor, who stopped Mortland to inquire for his brother. After replying, Robert dismounted, and said in a low voice, "Have you heard of a battle?"

"Yes," said the Mayor, "it is rumoured that we have been beaten in a great battle, but no one knows where the rumour comes from; and nobody will ask the enemy, and they would not tell."

"Somebody will ask, and we shall hear if it is true. This gentleman had heard of it, nothing but the bare fact—that is, if it is a fact. If he goes to the Castle, he will tell me what he hears; he is talkative."

"Mr. Mortland," said the Mayor, "how do you happen to be with him?"

"We are virtually prisoners; we have to do what they tell

us. I do not think it does any harm to behave to them—well, you know, not hostilely. The general is an utter brute."

"So I have heard." They wished each other good morning, and Robert thought that his companion was going to the Castle. He was not; he stopped at the inn, and dismounted, desiring Robert to do likewise.

This officer was, in reality, what his countrymen call a "mauvais sujet," and had come into Norwich for no purpose but to get a "square meal," with something added. He dared not exceed before his general, but here was a chance. Before he and Mortland had risen from their table, they had consumed three bottles of port, that at three shillings a bottle. Mortland was candid enough in telling the landlord why he called for this wine. "The fellow," he said, "does not know the difference; and, as I pay for it, I think I may choose."

He carried his own share well enough, for he was accustomed to still greater exertions, but it did not agree with the Frenchman at all. This was no misfortune to Robert, for he helped the scamp to hide his condition, and so get a kind of pull on him, which had certain results. Captain Balutin did not, however, suffer so much from the three shilling port as to make him resolve to avoid it in future.

This happened on Saturday. On Sunday, the French being bad observers of the Lord's Day, which, indeed, is not commonly held in much respect during war-time, put up placards all over Norwich commanding all who were not customary inhabitants of the city to depart to their usual domiciles. They sent out soldiers through the city to inquire who there was then residing in it who did not belong to the town. French soldiers, and Frenchmen in general, are not quick in picking up even the least knowledge of the languages of foreigners; but the men got some kind of instruction in what they were to say, and they managed to make themselves well enough understood. Many persons, in fear, obeyed them. Among those who did not, although a sergeant and two men gave notice at the house, were Miss Dorkington and the Misses Tronford.

"How are we to go to Yarmouth," said Miss Dorkington, "when they have taken Helen's coach horses? I wonder they did not take the coach. And, besides, it is ridiculous for them to want to send ladies away. It is ridiculous the whole thing. What harm can we do them here? Let us take no notice of it."

Mr. Cardwain shook his head and said nobody could tell what they would do. "But, of course, you can't go," he added. "It is impossible for you to go. What are we to say when they come again? I don't know what we shall do."

"We'll tell them to take us," said Miss Dorkington. "Helen, you can speak French. Just you repeat to them what I say, and have it ready when they come. Tell them to take us. Tell them we are ladies, and that we always travel in a coach, and they have taken our horses and we can't go. Helen, I wish you would tell me what French to say to them, and when they hear me they won't attempt it."

"Nunnie," said Helen, "I am afraid of them. I don't know what we can do. They may attempt force. I think the best thing for us would be to start this moment and walk to Yarmouth."

At this, both Mr. Cardwain and Miss Dorkington exclaimed that that was out of the question. "You could not," Mr. Cardwain said, "and there is not a horse in all Norwich. I really don't know what is to be done."

"It would not do, Helen," said Miss Dorkington. "The road to Yarmouth is infested with them, and we should be murdered. What I say is right, let us tell them to take us, and either they will let us alone or they will give us horses to travel with. But they won't make us go. It's too nonsensical. I am not a bit afraid of them."

Fanny began to cry. Helen went and petted her, and took her out of the room. When she returned, Mrs. Cardwain, who had been at church, and Mrs. Fenthorpe, were there, hearing explanations.

"I tell you what," said Mrs. Fenthorpe; "come, all of you, Helen and Fanny and Miss Dorkington, to my house this

K

moment. Then, when they come in the morning, Isabella will say you are gone, and there will be an end of it."

They all looked at one another. "Mrs. Fenthorpe," said Helen, after a pause, "that is only postponing it. They might find it out, and it would be worse. And, Mrs. Fenthorpe"—here she drew her aside and whispered, blushing while she spoke—"don't you see it is impossible? You are very good, but don't you see it is impossible?"

"You mean, dear——" said Mrs. Fenthorpe.

"Yes; it is impossible. But you are very good to think of it." She threw her arms round the elder lady, and kissed her.

The proprieties were far more potent over the minds of men and women, and children too for that matter, ninety years ago than they are now. There was nothing impossible in their going to Mrs. Fenthorpe's house because Richard lived in it. But Helen *thought* there was, and Mrs. Fenthorpe was dumb. Perhaps she remembered that it was only an expedient that might turn out badly.

She sat down, and they had more talk, ending with no conclusion but that with which they started, that they did not know what was to be done. Even Miss Dorkington was down in the mouth.

Richard was put in possession of all this by his mother, but he was not so much alarmed as she, and thought no extremities would be proceeded with. In the morning, he left his house at his usual time, after the hour or two he gave to the poor, intending to go, amongst his first visits, to Fenthorpe Hall to see Alexander Mortland. But he was called to make a visit in the city, which took him out of his way, and, in regaining the Yarmouth road, he had to pass Mr. Cardwain's house. The gate of the garden is only about twenty yards from the hall door, which was open, and a sergeant and two soldiers were standing at it, parleying.

Richard pulled up his horse, and listened. The sergeant spoke dictatorially, and he gathered the substance of what passed. As they came out at the gate, having delivered their message, Richard stopped them.

"Monsieur," he said to the sergeant, "est-ce que vous venez de commander ces dames à se rendre à Yarmouth?"

"Oui," the man answered.

"Mais savez-vous qu'elles n'ont pas des chevaux pour voyager? Et il n'y a point de chevaux dans Norwich?"

"Qu'elles marchent donc," said the sergeant, and walked away. When Richard told of this afterwards, he said he wondered he had not struck the man with his whip, but it was as well that he had not.

He tied his horse to the gate, and went in. It was even so. If the three ladies should not have departed by the next day, they would be escorted to Yarmouth by compulsion.

He left the house. He did not grind his teeth, as some men do—in some romances; not in real life that we know of, although they often, when they get beyond the hearing of ladies, say things, calling on gods that don't exist and on devils that do or do not. He would try a thing first before he gave himself up to impotent swearing. At the worst, he could accompany the victims of military abuse to Yarmouth, and he was sure he could get Mortland, who had a horse, to do the same.

He went on to Fenthorpe Hall. After seeing the major, who was getting on slowly enough, he looked round for one of the French officers. There was none in the hall, or visible from the porch, but he heard voices in a room adjoining. Opening the door, he saw Robert Mortland and an officer drinking Madeira."

"Hollo, doctor! How is my brother doing?"

"Pretty well. Mortland, is this gentleman on the staff? Introduce me to him."

Mortland did so. Captain Balutin bowed politely. "Monsieur le Capitaine, je demande une entrevue avec le General Davoust."

"Monsieur, avec tout le plaisir du monde, s'il est possible; mais, puis je demander, quel est l'objet de cette entrevue?"

Dr. Fenthorpe told him shortly, and went into particulars in English with Mortland, who was astonished and horrified.

Captain Balutin said if orders were given, they must be carried out, and seemed very unwilling to present himself before the general. Richard said that he wanted to remonstrate against carrying out the orders, and that if the captain would not bring him to Davoust, he would go into his room unannounced.

"Balutin," said Mortland, "venez ici." He took him to a window and spoke to him in a low tone. Richard thought that Mortland spoke to the officer as if with authority, and not as beseeching him. At last the other said, "Peut-être qu'il est le mieux"; and, turning to Fenthorpe, said he would conduct him to the general's presence. The three went into the dining-room of Fenthorpe Hall, where Davoust sat over papers, alone. There was a hand-bell on the table. When Balutin introduced the visitor, the general looked at him and said nothing.

"General," said Richard, "there is an order that all persons not domiciled in Norwich shall depart to their homes. There are three ladies, of Yarmouth, now and for some weeks since sojourning with friends in Norwich. They and their friends did not, and cannot, imagine that such orders should apply to them; but this morning they received a particular direction to depart by to-morrow, or else they would be removed by force. I apply to you, in the name of humanity, and in the name of that politeness in which your nation is not deficient, to exempt them from the operation of this order."

"Who issued the order?"

"I suppose the Commandant of Norwich."

Davoust gave a kind of grin, that made his unhandsome countenance a marvel of such beauty as it would have delighted Wiertz, of Brussels, to paint. The fact is, the colonel in command at Norwich Castle was a gentleman, while Davoust was quite the contrary, and hated him. At the battle of Cambridge, not many days after this, the general managed to put him in a position of danger, where he was killed; and he expressed what was certainly not grief when he learned how his Uriah the Hittite had perished. 'You are the surgeon of English volunteers who spoke to me at the battle?" he said to Richard, when he had done grinning.

"I am, sir."

"Mr. Mortland, are you acquainted with these ladies?"

"I am, general. Captain Balutin is also acquainted with them."

Richard stared at this, but guessed that it had some meaning, although it was false. "Ah!" said Davoust, "and what sort of ladies are they, Balutin?"

"Mon general," replied the captain, "elles sont extrême-ment respectables."

Neither of the two Englishmen knew that *respectable*, in French, means far more, both socially and morally, than keeping a gig. Richard felt indignant with the captain, and thought he was very impertinent to characterise the Miss Tronfords as respectable, and took a dislike to him.

"If you and Mr. Mortland undertake that these ladies shall not communicate with Yarmouth while our army is here, I will recommend the Commandant of Norwich to make an exception in their favour. If they communicate, I will shoot them, and you two gentlemen, as spies."

"I undertake for my part," answered Richard. "What are they to do in case their servants at Yarmouth communicate with them?"

"They are to hand over to us, unopened, anything of the kind, letter or otherwise."

"Very well," said Richard. "I undertake all that; and of course, Mortland, you undertake also?"

"Certainly," said Mortland. He thought he saw a certain advantage in this, in recommending himself to Helen Tron-ford. He had no idea that matters between her and the doctor, as he always called Richard, had proceeded very far; and an idea came into his head that this was an occasion that might be improved in more ways than one.

"Allez, messieurs," said Davoust; "Balutin, restez ici."

What passed between these two worthies we do not know.

Very likely Balutin got no instructions but to go to Norwich on the business of the Yarmouth ladies, for he was a favourite of Davoust, who had before this employed him in unclean work. We are almost certain that this general's readiness in granting the exception came from the prospect that it gave him of shooting five persons in case a slip should put them in his power. He took the same pleasure in a military execution as most people take in a play.

"Are you returning immediately?" said Mortland, when they left Davoust's room.

"Yes, as fast as may be. I want to tell them. I don't think much of that captain of yours, Mortland. Did you get him to say that he knows the Miss Tronfords and Miss Dorkington?"

"I did. I thought it might be useful. Do you object to the fellow's red hair? Red hair is rather an unnatural thing for a Frenchman, is it not?"

"There are worse things than red hair," answered Richard. "Mortland, these fellows are very pushing and forward. He will want you to present him to the ladies, and I recommend you not to do it on any account."

"My dear doctor, do you think I am a fool?"

"I do not, and never did. I do not know to what degree he may be able to put a kind of compulsion on you."

"You, and the Miss Tronfords, may rely on me, be sure. Good morning."

Fenthorpe rode off, thinking of how much he would tell of his interview with the French general. When he arrived at Mr. Cardwain's, he asked for Miss Dorkington. He did not tell her all; he suppressed that he and Mortland were to be securities for their good behaviour; but he pointed out the absolute necessity of trying nothing underhand, and of informing the enemy of any communication that might possibly come from Yarmouth.

Miss Dorkington was different from what she had been the day before. Day by day she was realising to herself what their position really was. Her spirit was not quelled, but she was coming to understand that even she, like all other inhabitants of Norfolk, was helpless.

"I think it quite impossible," she said, "that the servants at Clay House could send us any message; and I don't think they would think of it, even if they could. Did you observe, Dr. Fenthorpe, that they did not order John to go back to Yarmouth? Now, how would it do to propose to the French that he should go and desire our people not to try anything, but to keep quiet? And let him stay there."

"I would let well alone, Miss Dorkington. But—I did not think of this—I am sure Mr. Mortland will come to see you, and you can consult him. I am sure he will come, because I consider our success in this is owing to him, and he will, of course, not allow his light to be eclipsed—by me, at all events." He smiled.

"I will not consult Mr. Mortland about anything," said Miss Dorkington. "Owing to him! Nonsense!"

Helen here came into the room. "Helen shall judge," said Richard. "Helen, I believe you are not to go to Yarmouth."

"Not go to Yarmouth!" She was more astonished than apparently delighted. She had bent her mind to the problem, and had thought of asking Mrs. Mortland to lend them horses, or even one horse. She had thought also of getting Mr. and Mrs. Lyniard, intimate friends of theirs living in Yarmouth, to come and stay with them at Clay House for so long a time as troubles should last. There is sometimes a feeling of disappointment that arises when one learns that something that one has planned need not be done, even though what is avoided may be very disagreeable. We have known a man to be almost angry when his surgeon told him that an operation was unnecessary. "Not go to Yarmouth!" Then a moment after, laying her hands on Richard's arm, "Richard, you have done this."

He told her what he had told Miss Dorkington. But when he came to describing how he did not think he could have succeeded without Mortland, Helen stopped him.

"Now Richard, don't tell me such a thing. Did not you

go, at once, not four hours ago? Did not you beard the lion, or the bear, in his den? Mr. Mortland! You have done it. Richard, don't you remember that evening"—here she blushed, though Miss Dorkington was rather obtuse, and would not understand the allusion—"don't you remember you told me you had a presentiment you would save me—save us, from peril? And we don't know how great a peril. No, Richard, this comes from you, and you only. Richard, I am proud of you! Nunnie, do you hear, I am proud of him!"

"Yes, love," said her Nunnie, and kissed her. "We'll talk of this again." But she looked at them as they stood together, and thought for the first time what a handsome couple they were. "Dr. Fenthorpe, this is a thing that is beyond the reach of thanks. I have been doing nothing but thinking, the last few hours, of what was before us. We don't know what we have been saved from, with all these people about."

"Could I have done less?" he answered. "But I must go now. I will come in the evening and see that it is all right."

It was all right. The Norwich Commandant cared very little for his orders being superseded. Captain Balutin brought him Davoust's message, and took Robert Mortland into Norwich with him, leaving Fenthorpe Hall as soon as they had finished the Madeira. On the way, Balutin showed his friend that he expected to be presented to the ladies; but Robert shook his head, and all that the captain saw of them was the exterior of the house where they lived.

Robert visited them, of course, that day, and almost every day after for a few weeks. But he did not take that way of recommending himself to Helen Tronford that some men less knowing would have taken. He did not try to depreciate Richard nor his services; he even represented that it was all Richard's doing, and disclaimed any merit. He did not tell how he and Richard were to answer *with their lives* for non-communication with Yarmouth. Otherwise, he was very persevering as a suitor, and Helen defended herself but badly, knowing herself impregnable, and being unsuspicious and a non-combatant by nature. Indeed, the man began to interest her, and she felt not the least alarm till he at length began to say things that are only just short of the speech in answer to which a yes or no must be said.

This did not go so far at first, however. Mortland tried a more overt attack, and one in which he did not appear first. Two days after the order and the countermand, Mrs. Mortland came in a gig to Mr. Cardwain's. Her object was to propose to the Misses Tronford and Miss Dorkington to come and stay at Fenthorpe Hall, where they would be safe from molestation, owing to the presence of General Davoust and his staff. She would send the coach, getting Robert's horse to drive with the other horse, that in the gig at the door, all the horses that they were left. She was very pressing. Mrs. Cardwain answered that there could be no safety from molestation. The girls shrank from the idea, and uttered thanks very coldly. Miss Dorkington settled the matter by saying that English ladies should not derive safety from the protection of the enemies of England. She could not help throwing a little scorn into her voice when she said this.

"That's Robert Mortland's doing," she said to Mrs. Cardwain, when their visitor had taken leave.

"No," said Mrs. Cardwain. "She is just as anxious as her son. I am very glad Richard spoke to Helen when he did; with all the trouble and uncertainty and suspense, and knowing nothing, a man like him makes one feel safe."

She did not think what an oblique compliment to her husband this was; and truly the suspense was becoming more than could be borne. For more than ten days, Norfolk had been cut off from the rest of England; no news but that doubtful and originless rumour, never confirmed and never contradicted. The inhabitants of St. Kilda are used to that kind of thing, and don't mind it; but if they were not used to it, they would not know what to make of it the first time it should come on them.

Had Mrs. Mortland been successful in inducing the Yarmouth ladies to put themselves under the joint protection of herself and General Davoust, that partnership would not have lasted long. On the evening after her visit, the general and his staff left Fenthorpe Hall without taking leave. It is true that Mrs. Mortland and Robert stood at the door as he mounted his horse, but he did not condescend to speak to them. "The devil go with him," said Robert, at the same time shaking hands with Balutin. Mr. Mortland made great moan to all who would listen to him about the French general's want of courtesy, and got laughed at. He had nothing to complain of. The enemy did no worse to him than to others whose horses they stole; they ate what was given them without complaints, though without thanks; none of them but one consumed much wine; and they broke only two dinner-plates and one breakfast-cup all the time they were there.

It was not known in Norwich that headquarters had been shifted till Saturday morning, thirty-six hours after Davoust's departure. At the same time it was rumoured that Yarmouth had been evacuated; and during the afternoon this was confirmed or half-confirmed, so that people believed it. On Sunday morning, the greater part of the garrison marched out of Norwich, and took the road to Lynn. It was understood that only four hundred were left, under the command of a major.

The Mayor met Dr. Fenthorpe coming out of church, and proposed to walk home with him. They spoke of the military movements.

"I don't believe they have entirely evacuated Yarmouth," said Richard. "Bonaparte will cling to the coast."

"This move of theirs proves the truth of the lost battle," said the Mayor. "This army is going south to join him. And the length of time that we are left mewed up this way shows that our friends have no access to us. and that is proof of disaster. Dr. Fenthorpe, do you know, I am very much alarmed at the possible consequences of their leaving so small a force here.

There are a good many of the men that were dispersed at the battle in the city, raging with anger, and the mob is infuriated. I hear things said as I walk past people; and I believe —I heard a knot of men talking about it quite loudly—that, if they are not restrained, they are mad enough, notwithstanding the lesson they have got, to attempt to storm the Castle."

"I cannot believe it," exclaimed Richard.

"I have lost all influence. If I had any, I would go among them and preach and implore them to be quiet. Hundreds would be slaughtered, and the city would be sacked. Now, it has occurred to me that you—you—have it in your power to do a great service. The permission that you have to move about, as a physician, is not limited, I believe?"

"Voyager librement—travel freely; no, no limit, as you call it. What of that?"

"Under that safe conduct, could you not go into Cambridgeshire and get information, and bring us some instructions or orders from the Government, or from some authority?"

Richard Fenthorpe was a cool man, but he thought at this moment that the Mayor was cooler. "I should have to swim the river Ouse," he said; "I don't care for that, for my horse can swim. I daresay I might get into Cambridgeshire, although how can I be sure that they will recognise my permission, if I should be questioned? They would ask me have I patients to visit so far from here? But how could I ever get back?"

This rather nonplussed the Mayor, who had not thought of it. "And if I did come back, I should not dare to show my face here, for they would treat me as a spy. I will not face hanging, though I might face shooting, if absolutely necessary."

"Not the least danger of that, for you would return as an accredited messenger from our Government. That is not the difficulty. I see what you mean—that you are running two risks of capture. I did not think of that. But I will tell you how your return could be made certain. They have not all the small places on the north shore of the country occupied; only a few at King's Lynn."

"How is it, then, that we have never heard anything through one of these small ports?"

"It must be because the people in Hull and Newcastle that they trade with are afraid to come here. They know that the enemy are in Norfolk. They don't know that they are not in every square inch of Norfolk. Besides, not only is the county cut off, as it were, but every parish is cut off from every other parish. The people are afraid to move about. There was no market last week, or hardly any. They may know something at Salthouse or some of those places that we have never heard."

"Your idea is for me to go by land and return by sea," said Richard. "I will not say no, nor will I say yes. I will tell you in the morning."

"If I could tell the people," said the Mayor, "that you, a trusty messenger, are gone to ask the Government for orders as to what we should do, they would be quiet. Everybody in Norwich knows that you have a horse."

"Then you would not attempt to keep it secret?"

"It might be kept secret for twelve hours, and when it came to be known, the French would get hold of it. I would tell the proper people, and tell them to tell everybody to keep it from the French; and the French, now there are so few, would never miss you."

"A very good plan," said Richard musingly. "Are you going? I will walk part of the way with you."

They walked along a street or two together. Richard then immediately sought one of the volunteer officers, whom he considered the most likely to engage in a desperate business. He found that the Mayor had not exaggerated, and the officer, and another who was with him, scoffed at the Mayor when he spoke of him.

"Suppose," said Richard—"you know I was against your trying to intercept the enemy the other day, but no matter about that—suppose that you were certain of hearing news, and getting orders from the Government concerning what course you should take, within, say, six or seven days from now, would the people be quiet till then?"

One of the officers said he thought they would, and the other said he was sure they would. Then they asked questions, thinking that he seemed to know something. He only answered that he was preaching patience, as he had done before, to those that would listen to him.

Undecided, but growing accustomed to the idea—who ever can tell the moment that he decides on a thing?—he rode out to see Alexander Mortland, and told him he would not visit him again for three or four days. The wounded major was doing well, and was well tended. Returning home, he went to Mr. Cardwain's; his mother was out at evening service.

"Helen," he said, after greetings, "I want to speak to you. Aunt Cardwain, may we have the library?"

"Surely, Richard. Fanny, ring for candles to be brought to the library."

He told Helen what the Mayor wanted him to do. He neither exaggerated nor minimised his own danger. He did not exaggerate the horrors dreaded by his friend of an insurrection and a sacked city. He expressed his own sanguine hope, very nearly, he said, a certainty, that he should either return or be heard from at the end of a week. "And now, Helen," he concluded, "if you say I am not to go, I will not go."

She listened to him while he spoke, without interrupting him, and she did not reply to him when he had done speaking. She went down upon her knees, and remained kneeling for many minutes. Richard, sitting on his chair, prayed also.

At last she rose up and looked at him—looked at him as the angel looked at Gideon when he was threshing wheat in the winepress—and said:

"Go—in—the—name—of God!" Then she fell upon his neck, and wept.

CHAPTER X.

MANY days before this, the battle of Ipswich had been fought and lost.

Bonaparte, as we have related, broke up from Harwich with his whole army on Saturday morning, the second of March. He brought only a hundred and fifty guns, for want of horses for more. On Sunday morning he assailed Colchester, and took it without much resistance. But his attack on the bridge above the town was unsuccessful, for the English had ten thousand men between it and the London road, and plenty of force on the other side of the river, with guns well placed. The fight had lasted all day, and was not Bonaparte's main attack, for to take Ipswich and establish a communication with Yarmouth was vital to him.

His right wing lost some time feeling for the best point at which to cross the Stour; and if Sir D—— had defended that river more scientifically, he might have made a better affair of the first great battle. Sir D—— kept too great a force north of it to threaten Bonaparte's left after the passage which the English general did not believe could be hindered altogether. Monday was occupied by Bonaparte's march on Ipswich, giving an opportunity to an active enemy to make it very troublesome. But, from time to time, he halted portions of his infantry so skilfully and so menacingly, and made such good use of his light batteries, that he gained all the profit of that day, and there was nothing but some very stiff skirmishing.

On Monday night he was close to Ipswich. There were twenty thousand men in the town, and Sir D—— thought he could hold it. But his line, from beyond Colchester to Ipswich, without a central point of support, was too long for sixty-eight thousand English to hold successfully against seventy-eight thousand French *and Bonaparte*. The French artillery were very skilfully disposed the next morning; a general battle was brought on at about eleven o'clock, and against four o'clock or five Ipswich was forced, with great slaughter. Twelve thousand of the English were killed and wounded. Few prisoners were made, for the resistance in the town itself was perfectly desperate, and a pursuit of the retreating army outside was impracticable, as we were superior in cavalry. The infantry, therefore, retreated in good order, some over the Colchester bridge towards London, but more in the direction of Sudbury, and some as far north as near Bury St. Edmunds.

The moment that cavalry could be pushed through the streets of Ipswich, eight hundred were sent with all speed north. Before reaching Yarmouth they divided, and a troop of them caught the patrols on the road from that place to Wymondham, to whom they delivered the despatches ordering the seizure of horses. But the cavalry returned to Ipswich at once, being under strict orders not to tell their fellow-soldiers of the northern invasion about the battle. These orders were remarkably well observed, although something must have leaked out. It was Bonaparte's object, we must gather from this, to completely isolate Norfolk.

The battle of Ipswich, besides opening the whole east coast to Bonaparte, sent the English army retreating excentrically, its left being practically turned. Also, by the results of this excentric retreat, it left the Colchester position untenable and the road to London open. There were materials for the English to fight a second battle before London should be given up. Only eight corps of the London volunteers had been in Sir D——'s first army; there were still fifty-two Metropolitan corps whole and untouched, besides the relics of the eight, which suffered their share in the battle, and at least thirty thousand of the regular army. London expected to be attacked, or, at least, threatened. But Bonaparte saw differently.

He pushed on, the day after the battle, a full march behind
the retreating English, in every direction except by the
London road. His progress was not so good as he had
expected, for the retreat was leisurely, and all bridges had
been broken down. In one place on the Bury road, there are
two miles where each side was then lined with beech trees,
tall, and planted not very close together. They had thus
very wide-spreading branches. These trees were all cut down
and laid across the road, delaying Bonaparte's guns for fully
half a day. He chafed and raged at this impediment. But,
by the end of the week, he had brought his whole army into
a line extending from near Bishop-Stortford to Newmarket,
headquarters being at Haverhill. He was ready for a battle
in this position, but did not invite one, although the second
English army was fast gathering at Hertford, Bedford, and
Cambridge, and he knew it would outnumber him. He was
waiting, before making an offensive movement, for the great
force of artillery left at Harwich till means of transport
should arrive.

Apparently inactive, he was by no means idle. During the
three days' fighting on the borders of Essex and Suffolk, he
had thoroughly taken the English general's measure. That
general was unenterprising, but obstinate in defence; and he
tried to do too much at one time. In other words, his instinct
was to spread his strength and try to defend every point. He
made movements according as such and such points were
menaced; he followed his enemy's moves instead of making
his enemy follow his. Already Bonaparte saw, in imagination, the very ground that the next battle would occupy, the
very manner in which the English army would be disposed,
and the very errors of its commander through which he would
defeat it. He made one or two marches of the extreme right
division of his army, so as to produce counter moves by Sir
D—— of his left, forcing, or prompting, him to bring that
wing further north and nearer to Cambridge, and thus
further away from London. At the same time, the garrison
of Wisbeach made demonstrations as if meditating an

advance, and the left wing of the English, in reply, was moved almost as far as Peterborough.

All this enables us to comprehend Bonaparte's plan. The separate invasion of Norfolk was not owing to a part of the flotilla having wandered astray in the fog; it was designed. Norfolk is covered by the Isle of Ely and the rivers; Norfolk, therefore, enabled Bonaparte to keep the left wing of his main army unassailable. It is true that to unite with the Norfolk army was inconsistent with making a rush on London. But to make a rush on London was not his project. The invasion of England on the east coast is a totally different thing from the invasion of Sussex or Kent. The English Government and military authorities had never thought of this, and they believed that London must, as a matter of course, be Bonaparte's first and, indeed, only object.

A foreign army, landing south of London, must advance on London or wait to be attacked and almost certainly destroyed. It cannot march into the centre of England, or even towards Portsmouth, without exposing its right flank to attack—overwhelming attack—from London. If, after taking London, it cannot maintain itself, it has its retreat open by the way that it came. Besides this, London north of the Thames is at the mercy of an enemy holding the Surrey side, while the Surrey side is not, as we shall see, necessarily at the mercy of an enemy in Middlesex. Moreover, the capture of London from the south involves the capture of Woolwich and the loss of Chatham, which are not necessarily results of the capture of the north side of the Thames, even from Blackwall to Hammersmith.

Therefore London should be placed in a state of defence now, in this year 1899, while we still have peace, by a series of works beginning at Kingston, going round by Redhill, and meeting the river at Woolwich, not neglecting defences towards the north and north-east, in case of accidents. We hope—we do not say we expect—to see this, or something on this principle, done before we die.

But a foreign army landing on the east coast presents its right flank to the whole of England if it advances on London,

L

and it leaves itself without retreat, and in danger of annihila-
tion, if England does not surrender on the mere capture of the
Metropolis. Bonaparte knew all this; indeed, there is hardly
anything in war that he did not know. Therefore his design
was not to conquer England through London, but to conquer
London through England. If he could fight and win a great
battle away from London, and then enter London, he thought
that he could force England to a treaty. He felt certain that
he could draw on such a battle when, and very nearly where,
he should like; and he felt certain that he would win it. The
greater the English army, the greater would be its defeat;
for, after leaving garrisons, he had ninety thousand men, the
best France had ever produced. And he had also—himself.

There was only one military or strategetic flaw in this plan.
Bonaparte's rear and right wing—the Norfolk army being
brought up—were absolutely secure; his left wing was liable
to attack at any moment—and a thing that may happen at
any moment is apt to happen at an awkward moment—from
London. But Bonaparte calculated, and he was right in the
calculation, that it would not be so attacked. However, he
made things as safe as he could by bringing a preponderance
of his artillery to that side; and he personally harangued the
extreme left division, pointing out its weak place, and making
every soldier understand the position of affairs.

It was not till the twentieth of March that he made a
general forward movement into Cambridgeshire. And in the
meantime, much had been done in London itself, nothing of
which he knew or suspected.

When Mr. Groves rose on the Saturday morning, after the
day of his interview with Lord Camden, he said to himself,
"Am I doing any good by remaining in town?" He could
not answer. He had fallen into one of those fits of despond-
ency that sanguine men are of all men the most liable to.
He had presented his plan, which he believed to be, if not
perfect, at least founded on sound principles, to the highest
authorities. He was told to wait, and they would consider of
it. The very fact of their being willing to consider it proved

that they had no plan of their own. Was England going to the verge of perdition because men would not think?

All that day he sat in his room, knowing not what more to do, except that he went out for half an hour, and asked at Downing Street, where he was always attended to, for news. It was meagre. He was not even told that Bonaparte had left Harwich, although he asked about that particularly.

On Sunday, after eating his breakfast, he inquired of the waiter the hour of morning service at St. Martin's-in-the-Fields. It was time to go, and he went to that church. As the rector, who was to preach, was reciting the words of that noble prayer that breathes the very spirit of the Psalm of the patriot prophet and king, "Save and deliver us, we humbly beseech Thee, from the hands of our enemies; abate their pride, assuage their malice, and confound their devices; that we, being armed with Thy defence, may be preserved evermore from all perils, to glorify Thee, who art the only giver of all victory; through the merits of Thy only Son, Jesus Christ our Lord," and as hundreds of the worshippers vainly endeavoured to suppress their sobs, as they poured out their hearts to their God, in their distress for their dear country, which, perhaps, too many of them loved more than they loved Him, some one walked rapidly up the aisle, and, rather to the surprise of the congregation, spoke to the officiating minister. They whispered together.

"Is Mr. Groves, of Folkestone, in this church?" said the rector in a loud voice.

Mr. Groves started up, and opened the door of the pew he sat in. He saw Mr. Bentinck at the reading desk. That gentleman saw him, and they walked out of the church together.

We pause to tell that the rector in his sermon, told how that the interruption had been caused by a message for a gentleman, to him unknown, about important business connected with the defence of the country. He was a clergyman very fond of improving an occasion, and did not allow this to slip, bringing in an exhortation to the people to stand up, with their lives if necessary, for their God, their King, and their country.

Mr. Bentinck brought the colonel of volunteers to Downing Street, where were Mr. Pitt, Lord Camden, and a military gentleman whom Mr. Groves did not know.

"Colonel Blessingburn, of the artillery—Mr. Groves," said Lord Camden.

"Mr. Groves," said Pitt, "we are going to adopt the plan of defending the south of London of which you have spoken to Lord Camden. You propose to bring up the Kentishmen to help. They are not enough. We have consulted Colonel Blessingburn as to the force that will be required. He places it at thirty thousand men, and as many guns of all sizes as may be from time to time required. There are twenty corps of volunteers of Surrey, counting the Borough. You have four thousand men, you say. We can spare ten thousand of the regular army; ten thousand, perhaps, certainly eight, by drafts from Woolwich and Chatham, and otherwise. Colonel Blessingburn wants at least six companies of sappers at once —to-day, indeed. I have, you may not have heard, got myself sworn in as one of his Majesty's Secretaries of State, under the provisions of the unrepealed Act of 1782, by arrangement with Lord Harrowby. Lord Camden and I can therefore give any order for anything not requiring the spending of money. You have recommended the instant removal of all shipping from the north side of the river. We are just now issuing orders to that purpose. Is there anything that you wish to recommend further?"

"Sir," answered Mr. Groves, "am I to be in command, subject to a superior officer, of all the Kentish regiments?"

"Do you think it advisable?" asked Mr. Pitt.

"I think it advisable that some one should be. If you and Lord Camden nominate me, I will serve."

"Do you think it advisable that you should be nominated?"

"If you have no one else that you prefer, I do."

Mr. Pitt and Lord Camden consulted. "Why," said Pitt,

when they had whispered together for a minute, "why do you think it advisable to appoint you?"

"Sir, the moment that I leave you and my Lord Camden now, I shall go to Folkestone for my men. If you give me, or promise me, a commission to command the Kentish volunteers, I shall bring up not my own men only, but two thousand more with them. If you give me no such commission, how long will be required for you to resolve whom to put them under, and to bring them up?"

"We should have to consider about that, Mr. Groves."

"And while you are considering, Bonaparte will be marching."

Mr. Groves never, from first to last, could contrive to get either Mr. Pitt, or any one else in authority, to understand the value of time. The end of this matter was, that the commission was promised. And Mr. Groves left London with the knowledge that the north shore of the river was to be cleared of shipping; which was, so far, satisfactory.

Colonel Blessingburn and he left the Prime Minister and the Secretary, the former to proceed to Woolwich with an order to send "so many pieces of ordnance as the bearer shall direct" to London. Mr. Groves thought it well worth while to go a little out of his way on his journey to Folkestone to travel so far with this gentleman. He was not a very talkative man, and he had a dispirited manner; but his heart was in his country's service, and his ideas were sound. During the three hours of their drive to Woolwich they decided on many things, which we need not specify, as they were chiefly about details—important details, certainly. It was to these two men that London south of the Thames owed its safety during the next month. This is not more extraordinary than the improvisation of the defence of Sebastopol by Todleben.

What had caused the sudden access of activity and decision on Mr. Pitt's part was the despatch of Sir D——, written on Saturday evening when he saw Bonaparte's army for the first time. It would not be right to say that the English general was frightened, but he saw that he was expected to do two things that might be incompatible with each other—to prevent Bonaparte from advancing on London, and to prevent him from joining hands with the northern invasion. He wrote undecidedly, and as if he did not expect to be successful. Neither Mr. Pitt nor Lord Camden held him in more than moderate estimation. It was three in the morning of Sunday when they read the despatch together.

"He expects to be beaten," said Pitt.

"And he will be beaten," replied Lord Camden.

"Then," said Pitt, "let us think of London, if it be possible to save it."

Let us begin to think of how to fight Hannibal when Hannibal is at our gates! Fatuity! Madness! But, Englishmen of the year 1899, you are practising the very same kind of folly at this moment.

Mr. Groves reached Folkestone at one in the morning. He did not go straight home to Newgrove, but into the town, and knocked up his major, and ordered him to get the East Kent into order for instant marching, and to send word, without a minute's loss of time, to the other corps to march also. "I am," he said, "to command all the Kentish corps. If any of them do not like me, I shall not insist. You, however, obey my orders, major."

When the major was thoroughly awake and understood what was to be done, he exhibited all the joy that a good soldier should when he beholds the enemy. "Colonel Groves," he said, "I believe all Kent and Sussex, and part of Surrey, would be delighted to serve under you."

"I shall not be able to leave this till the afternoon, and may not see you or the corps before you march. March by the Ashford road, and I will overtake you. Now, good night."

He even went to the colonel of one of the other corps, who lived a few miles distant. That officer was willing, and more than willing, to serve under him. So were all the rest; and so were three corps of West Kent, which he had not asked to be included in his commission. In all, Mr. Groves brought up to help to defend the bridges of London, six thousand men.

And two hundred more that he had not counted on. Just

as he was quitting Newgrove, at four in the afternoon of
Monday, for all that he knew never to return there, a crowd
of seafaring-looking men came up the avenue. Mr. Gróves
got out of the post-chaise, and recognised amongst them our
acquaintances, the two Shinkwins, father and son.

"Sir," said Peter senior, "your honour is going to
Lunnon?"

"I am," answered Mr. Groves.

"Sir," the man continued, "we hope as how your honour
will take huz with you." He had held his hands behind
his back; now he reached forward his right arm, holding a
cutlass, bright and keen. Young Peter did the same, and
made a sign to the crowd, who made their cutlasses visible.

"Sir, your honour," Peter senior continued. "we know the
mounseers, and we can even understand their lingo when
they talk. We think as how we could do some good down
yonder."

Mr. Groves recognised several of the crowd; some of them
he knew as of fair character, some not so good, and some very
bad. All were, he was sure, of the same profession. But that
was not the question. "What arms have you?" he asked.
He saw that they were the very men for a street fight.

"Every man on us has this," said Shinkwin, "and a pair of
pistols likewise. Good they are too, your honour." He produced his.

"And you propose to put yourselves under my command
during the war as volunteers?"

"That is just so, your honour."

"All of you?" He spoke loudly, and looked down the
crowd.

"All on us," said a hundred voices.

"How many of you are there here? And are there any
more?"

"We are here, your honour, two hundred belike."

"I take you, on certain conditions—you must take the oath,
which binds you to obey me as your commander."

"All right and tight, your honour."

"Do you all say so?" said Mr. Groves. "All men that are

willing to take the oath, walk past me round this grass plot."

All walked past.

"Now," he said, as the last man defiled past, "you are to march to London now, this minute."

"Hooray!" shouted two or three, and all joined in a cheer. "This is business," one or two said to each other.

"Two hundred is too many for a company," the commander said. "Are you all Folkestone men?" He thought they were not.

"Some on us, your honour, is Folkestone, and some is Dover, and some comes from as far as near Deal," said a big man.

"Split yourselves into two companies, according to your dwelling places, Folkestone one side here, and Dover the other side the grass plot," said the commander.

"Dover and Deal men to starboard, Folkestone men to larboard," roared the big man, who was of Folkestone.

"Now," said Mr. Groves, the movement accomplished. "you Folkestone men choose a captain, whose orders you will have to swear to obey, and he will have to obey my orders, and I will give no orders but through him; and you, Dover and Deal men, choose a captain in like manner. I can give you ten minutes to make your choice of captains." He went into the house, and came out at the end of ten minutes precisely. Two men stood in front of the rest, one of them the big man of Folkestone.

"Well," said Mr. Groves, "have you chosen captains?"

"Please your honour, I be captain of Folkestone men," said the big man.

"Folkestone company call yourselves when you are in London. What is your name?"

"Sam Gulder, and please your honour."

"And are you captain of the Dover company? What is your name?"

"Billy Blugg, sir."

"Captain Gulder and Captain Blugg, divide your companies into tens, and appoint sergeants to each ten; that is, a sergeant and nine men make ten. Appoint them yourselves;

the men are not to choose them. Give orders always to the men through their sergeants, unless the sergeant happens to be knocked over and no sergeant to give orders through; then do the best way you can. March for London at once. I cannot wait to swear you now, for I have to be in town, as you understand, about the King's business, as soon as I can. I must swear you in this county, because I am not a magistrate of Surrey. Therefore, when you come near London, stay in Kent till you have sent for me, and I will swear you. It is only about four miles on this side of town. I shall expect you in about three days."

He entered the post-chaise, and drove off. The enthusiasm of the men was great when they heard Gulder and Blugg addressed by the title of captain, and they were in the best spirits, anticipating some business exactly to their mind. On the evening of Thursday, Mr. Groves was sent for to swear in the two companies. They had halted at the last public-house in Kent. We do not know if its address be now "Old Kent Road," or some other road or street, but it is still there. Perhaps had it not been for this corps of volunteers and their visit, the public-house would not be there now, for it was in a decaying state at that time; but the smugglers and their expenditure put it on its legs. All of them had a few guineas about them; guineas, not bank notes, which they eschewed as not being properly appreciated on "the other side."

After the swearing-in, Commander Groves addressed his recruits thus:—"Captain Gulder and Captain Blugg, you and the men of your companies are now sworn volunteers in the service of King George. I believe that some of your men have, now and then, robbed the King of his dues. You are now going to risk your lives for him; and perhaps, if you do your duty properly, and his Majesty comes to hear of it, he will say nothing about the dues you have not paid. Come to me to-morrow at eight o'clock at headquarters, at the Elephant and Castle, for orders."

King George got these men as cheap as Queen Elizabeth ever got soldiers or sailors. And the article, though cheap, was not bad.

CHAPTER XI.

RICHARD FENTHORPE did not see his mother to tell her of his proposed expedition till after Helen had pronounced her blessing upon it. He knew that Mrs. Fenthorpe would make no objection. She believed that those who are doing their duty are under the peculiar protection of Almighty Providence; and her enthusiastic and impulsive, yet well-ballasted nature was such as to make her regard an adventure, unselfish and self-denying, in such a cause as this, with sympathy and almost delight.

"What luggage will you take?" she asked her son when they had finished the discussion of the business in most of its aspects. "You will take the saddle-bags?"

"That would be advertising myself as a traveller, and I think I should avoid that. I will dress in my black leather breeches, and wear an under-waistcoat; and I will take my largest greatcoat, and put a few things in the pockets; the coat will be easy to strap to me. And I will take my instruments."

"Your instruments!"

"Yes; they will prove that my permit is genuine, if I should be questioned by any of the enemy. I do not think they are likely to make a prisoner of a surgeon or physician."

"And, Richard, where will you go first? What direction?"

162

"I am thinking about that, and will not decide yet. I think Wymondham first."

"But that is a great round."

"Yes, if I were going by Wisbeach; but that is the very place I must avoid. Do you know Mr. Tomlinson's house at Wymondham? It is just before you get into the street. I think of going there, both because it is on this side of the village—there may be French there, you know—and he is a very likely person to give me hints. He is one of the shrewdest and most intelligent men I know."

"He is not one of your patients?"

"No, Dr. Johnson's. I must go to Dr. Johnson about taking care of some of my patients, Mortland among the rest, if I am away more than a week. I will tell Dr. Johnson I am going to see Tomlinson."

"And about money?"

"I will take forty-five guineas."

"Forty-five guineas! What for? And suppose you should be robbed?"

"That risk I run, mother, with forty-five guineas or forty-five shillings. I am taking more than I may want, no doubt; but I may want it all if I have to buy a horse."

"Oh, Richard! Poor John Hunter!"

"John Hunter may founder; I hope not. But I am going to spare neither myself nor him. If it were not for that, twenty would do."

"Well, Richard, whatever else you take, you take the three best things in the world, in earth or heaven. You take Faith and Hope and Love; you know Charity in the Corinthians ought to be love."

He smiled; of course, his mother alluded to Helen, or he thought so. But he did not take that opportunity to explain to her the difference between Agapæ and Eros.

In the morning, he saw the Mayor and Dr. Johnson. He requested the former to tell Lieutenant Fordman—the same who had been for fighting a fortnight before, and would be for fighting again—the very first person, of his departure.

"To-morrow morning will be time enough. I shall leave
Norwich at five this evening in broad daylight. He seemed to
think yesterday, when I was talking to him, that I had more
to say than I was saying. I think it possible that any contempt that he may have for me, as counselling peace, may be
removed when he hears of my journey."

"I will, Dr. Fenthorpe. If he holds you in any contempt
—bless my soul, how can he? Certainly not after this. And
I will take care that everybody is to know that the enemy
are not to be informed. But "—here he whispered—" I fear
—I fear, only—that they have spies."

"Spies! English spies! Among our own people?"

"I only fear; I can hardly say I suspect. One does not
know what to think."

They dined, Dr. Fenthorpe and his mother, at three. Mrs.
Fenthorpe was very impatient and restless till the cloth was
removed.

"Richard," she said, as the butler left the room, "what do
you think happened to-day?"

"A moment, mother," he interrupted her. "William, send
Sam to me."

The groom, in a minute or two, put half of his person into
view, the other half remaining concealed by the door.
"Sam," said his master, "when was John Hunter shod?"

"The day before we heard about the French, sir."

"That is three weeks. Take him immediately to have his
shoes removed, and come home with him straight and bring
him round saddled. I am going a long ride this evening, and
shall not be back to-night, and he must not cast a shoe. Be
sharp, Sam; I want to leave at five. Now, mother," so soon
as Sam had shut the door, "pardon me."

"Am I to say nothing about it to-night?"

"Better not, mother. I am all impatience to hear what
happened to-day."

"I was, about one o'clock, in Turpin Street, where that
man, Allonby, you know, lives. I was walking slowly; and,
just as I was three or four houses from his house, who do you
think came out of it?"

"Who?" The whole subject of Charles Fenthorpe's will, and Allonby's stories, had never occupied or even entered Richard's mind since his mother had told him of her interview with the witness. But it never was out of Mrs. Fenthorpe's mind.

"Robert Mortland."

"Robert Mortland!"

"He turned, as he came out of the house, towards me, and I stopped him. I asked him about his brother. He was not the least discomposed; spoke to me just as if he was coming out of any house, or a shop. Then, Richard, what do you think I did?"

"Well, mother, I suppose you went into the same house that Mortland came out of."

Mrs. Fenthorpe laughed. "How did you know?"

"Oh, I only guessed. You have never been with Allonby since that day?"

"Never since; but I have thought a deal about it, even with all we have had to think about. I went to the house, knocked, and went in. The old man was sitting just where he was the last time. I said to him, 'Mr. Allonby,' I said, 'the last time I was here I told you I expected you to tell me the name of the other witness; but I shall not trouble you, for I know a person that can tell me.'"

"Mother, did you say that?"

"And he looked perfectly like a stone. I kept looking at him to wait to hear what he would say; and he drew himself up in his chair a little, and said if I knew some one that could tell, he did not, and how could he, for he did not know himself."

"And what did you say to that?"

"I said, 'Oh yes, you do, and you have seen him quite lately.' And he looked—I cannot describe how he looked. He looked disturbed, and I thought he was thinking of what he would say next. But I thought I had not enough to go upon to mention any name, and just said good morning and came away, and shut the door after me."

"Mother," said Richard, after a pause, "it is a mere conjecture. I am very glad you did not mention Mortland's name. You think you frightened him?"

"I am sure I did. I was not long there, you know, and I did not threaten him, as I did the other time—how long?—three weeks ago. Richard, answer me this: what was Robert Mortland doing there?"

"Mother, you leap to the conclusion that the man was bribed thirty years ago to suppress something, and is still getting the wages of his falsehood. I know what you think, but it is all guess and conjecture."

"Look at what I have found out! I have found out that Mr. Mortland saw him on that morning, the last day your father ever was at the Hall, and concealed it. This old man let it out to me, and was very much put out because he let it out, though I took no notice. I have found out from Mr. Groves that Mr. Armitage was got rid of. Are there not people in London, thief-catchers, that can be employed to watch people?"

"Dearest mother, do you really think of such a thing?"

"It could not be done now, of course; but the French won't be here for ever. It is a pity, too, for if we had a good spy, perhaps we could find out a weak point at the Castle. However, we need not talk of that. But, Richard, is it not a most remarkable thing this turning up now?"

"Now? Now, in the middle of this war?"

"It is a most remarkable thing—Mr. Groves's letter coming on the very day! Richard, I remembered, after I was able to think, that the first time we heard from Mr. Groves, when your father was living, it was the very same day we heard that those awful people had murdered the French King. And then the war broke out. And now it was the very day that they invaded Yarmouth that the second letter came. It is a very remarkable thing—coincidence. And I have a firm impression, that nothing could convince me there is not something in it, that this journey of yours will be, somehow, connected with this mystery, and perhaps soon it will be a mystery no longer."

To this Richard could reply nothing, nor did he attempt it. All the reason in the world, though it be as unanswerable as the reasoning in Euclid's Elements, will not overturn or even affect an idea that a person has founded not on fact but on impression. Coincidences are, to some people—and those often wise and clever and good—evidence stronger than evidence that is real, logical proof. You cannot argue any one out of a presentiment or an impression.

"Whatever information I may pick up on my journey I will bring you home, mother, be sure. I am not going to London, and shall not meet any thief-catchers——"

"Now, Richard, don't be laughing at me; it is too serious."

"Dearest mother, I am not laughing; and, of course, it is serious. It is time for me to put up my greatcoat and be ready to go. Kiss me now, mother; not in the hall. And, mother, you will see Helen every day?"

"I will. Good-bye, my son. I feel no more fear for you than if you were crossing the street. There is something that tells me you will return safe and sound, and successful."

But after Richard rode away, Mrs. Fenthorpe went to her room and prayed. Her faith did not melt away; faith, hard and firm and unreasonable, is not like wax. That kind of faith, too, that is intimately allied with hope, and is little else in reality than a form of hope, is closely allied with courage. Pitt had it in no common degree. At the very moment that Mrs. Fenthorpe was expressing her faith in her son's safety, and fortifying that faith with prayer, without which true faith cannot live, Mr. Pitt was saying to a timid member of the Cabinet that, if the impending battle should be lost, and ten more battles too, and London and Portsmouth taken, he would be for fighting on, "Aye, if we shall have all to take flight to Scotland."

The only thing that Dr. Fenthorpe took with him of which he did not tell his mother was a double-barrelled pistol of the best make. It was raining at five o'clock, when he and John Hunter quitted Norwich by the Wymondham road, and very few people saw them. When they reached the village it was dark. The door of Mr. Tomlinson's house was opened when Richard knocked by the master himself. For many days so many of the enemy had been quartered there and in the neighbourhood that servants were afraid to open doors.

"Dr. Fenthorpe!" said Mr. Tomlinson. "What chance, good or ill, has brought you here? Not that you are not welcome. Come in. Jock," he called out, "come here and take this gentleman's horse."

"You know," said Mr. Tomlinson, when they were seated by a fire, with candles on the table, and brandy and rum, and were waiting for hot water, "you know of the disaster we have met?"

"We know nothing," said Fenthorpe. "We have heard, for a fortnight, nothing but the most vague rumours."

"We were defeated in a great battle near Ipswich, on the fifth. After the battle, they did not go to London, as was feared, but came in the direction of Hertford and Cambridge. During all yesterday and to-day, numbers have been passing through here, coming from Yarmouth. There are none here now, which is a great relief. The last passed through about noon, or a little later."

"It must be what we heard in an indistinct kind of way," said Fenthorpe. "Do you know anything more than that there was this battle, and that we were beaten?"

"Very little more; but I am satisfied it is true. There was a man here from Thetford to-day, whom I know well, and he confirmed it. Our loss was very severe, but the army was got away—not flying, you know—in pretty good order. Now, Dr. Fenthorpe, you'll stay all night?"

"I thank you, Mr. Tomlinson; will you allow that to depend on what you recommend me to do?"

"Me recommend you! I don't understand."

Fenthorpe then told him what he had left Norwich for. "And now, where should I go? My object is not merely to get information, but to bring to Norwich, and I may say to Norfolk, instructions from Government what we are to do. Do you think things are so bad that we can actually expect no help?"

"I think, Dr. Fenthorpe, you are doing a thing that the people of Norfolk ought to be very grateful to you for. If I should give you advice, it would be to go home, straight; that is, in the morning, for, of course, you stay here to-night. But I conjecture you would not do that?"

"I should look very foolish."

"Perhaps you will look just as foolish when the French have you a prisoner."

All had not been explained, and Dr. Fenthorpe showed his friend his safe conduct. "They may recognise this or they may not," said Mr. Tomlinson. He rang the bell, and when it was answered, desired the servant to go up the village street for Mr. Partring. "He is the clergyman. I suppose you know him?"

"Not personally."

"He is a very good man to consult. After the last of them went through to-day, with ever so many pieces of artillery, we were talking about it. He thinks that their bringing up all their force from the coast—for they hold that there were very few left at Yarmouth—that that shows they are going to fight another battle soon. They have gone towards Ely and Cambridge. The Thetford man I told you of says there were never any of the enemy there, but there are some at Newmarket. If that is the case, this Norfolk army of theirs, as we may call it, must have been pushed forward to join with the main army that took Ipswich. Mr. Partring remarked that, if there was going to be a battle, there must be English to fight it on the one side as well as French on the other, and he guesses that our army is at Cambridge or in that neighbourhood."

Here the clergyman came in, and Mr. Tomlinson asked him before he had sat down, "Did not Waddy say that there never were any French at Thetford?"

"He said there are none there now; they had a few, I understood him to say, till the other day. They must have had, because they had some in every village on the border between this county and Suffolk. They have none there now. That was what he said."

M

When Mr. Partring had been put in possession of all we are
already aware of, and after he had uttered all the exclamations
of surprise becoming to the occasion, the three gentlemen
proceeded with their council of war in a regular manner.
"Dr. Fenthorpe's notion has been," said Mr. Tomlinson, "to
go almost due west from here, and get into Cambridgeshire.
His horse can swim, and he thinks of getting over the Ouse
unperceived. It would be dangerous to try a bridge. What
do you think, Mr. Partring?"

"I think it most dangerous, if not impossible. There is a
large French garrison at Wisbeach, and you may depend on
it they have patrols all the way from that to their position
near Ely. I certainly don't recommend that. Dr. Fenthorpe,
do you know the roads beyond here?"

"I know the road to Thetford."

"Do you know the roads beyond Thetford?"

"No."

"I suppose, Mr. Tomlinson, you would advise Dr. Fenthorpe to return to Norwich, only you know that he is a man
who, once having put his hand to the plough, will not look
back. I should recommend you to go to Thetford and make
inquiries there."

"Dr. Fenthorpe will be no nearer the English army at
Thetford than he is here," said Mr. Tomlinson.

"That is true. But he will be nearer London."

Richard started. He had said a few hours ago to his
mother that he was not going to London. Could he be sure?

"I am not saying this to alarm you, Dr. Fenthorpe," said
Mr. Partring. "It appears to me that, even here, you are
in reality nearer London than you are to our army at Cambridge, or wherever it may be. And there is this
consideration—I think it a very much safer undertaking to
go to London than to try to go right through the whole
French army."

"Do you believe they will not recognise my permit?"
asked Richard.

"I think your permit, when you are not using it to move
about visiting your patients, may be a danger to you."

This was a new idea to the physician, and it staggered him more than anything that he had heard said yet. He asked Mr. Partring did he think he should be in danger of being shot if taken prisoner.

"Not in the least danger; they do not do that sort of thing. Dr. Fenthorpe, have you any knowledge of the history of the French wars in Italy—Bonaparte's war there?"

"I have no minute knowledge. I know that they conquered Italy to change its Government; and I believe that the object of this invasion is to make a revolution."

"Exactly so; which they won't succeed in. But, that being their view, they will not act as some invaders do, laying the country waste with sword and fire. Indeed, they have not behaved here with harshness, except in the matter of the horses. They will try, of course, with no effect, to make friends. Mr. Waddy, that you heard us speak of, told me that one or two of the officers at Thetford had been talking to a man there that knows French about the chances of a revolution."

"You think, in fact, Mr. Partring—I must consider this in a personal light—that I am not travelling, as it were, with my life in my hand?"

"I think it very likely that you may travel through the country already occupied by the enemy, or already cut off, the part, that is, where fighting is not going on, with safety even from capture. You would be questioned; but I do not see what object they would have in taking a gentleman prisoner who was going to London on his own private affairs."

"I am not travelling on my own private affairs."

"You have no compromising letters or documents, except that permit, which I should recommend you to burn."

"I shall want it," said Richard, "when I am in Norwich again; that is, if the enemy are still there."

"If we win the next battle," said Mr. Tomlinson, "will it not deliver Norfolk?"

"It will bring the deliverance of Norfolk and of all

England within sight," said Mr. Partring. "But I was going to say to you, Dr. Fenthorpe, that the way Bonaparte has generally carried on war makes me think that most of the country behind this, between his army and the coast, is pretty clear. Bonaparte burns his boats; you know what is meant by that. When he had conquered the King of Sardinia's dominions, he quitted them at once, and did not attack the Austrians in front, but by the south side of the river Po. He, what is called, gave up his communications. I think he is doing the same here."

Mr. Partring was wrong in his interpretation of Bonaparte's strategical system, however shrewd may have been his guess that there were very few French at that moment in Suffolk and Essex. He went on, as his listeners did not reply. "If you try to get to London after you leave Thetford, through Bury, I think you have a very good chance of a successful journey."

So it was settled. Richard wrote to his mother from Mr. Tomlinson's that night of his change of plan, charging her, for obvious reasons, not to let it be known that he was going to London, or had gone in that direction, until it should be necessary, to calm the minds of the people, that they should be informed. The Mayor was to be told, and Helen; no others. Mr. Tomlinson promised to have the letter brought to Norwich at the first opportunity. He kept his word more than faithfully, for he sent a messenger on foot, when he found that no other thing would do, and Mrs. Fenthorpe received the letter on Wednesday evening, not much more than forty-eight hours after it had been written.

At six in the morning our traveller quitted Wymondham on the faithful John Hunter. Against about noon, he reached Thetford, where he stopped to bait his horse and himself, and enquired for Mr. Waddy. That respectable shopkeeper told him that he thought there were no French at Bury; he could not be sure.

Five miles from Bury he met a man coming out of a wood with a bundle of sticks. Were there any French in Bury?

There were plenty of them a week ago; he was certain sure
there were none now. He had not been in the town, but he
heard of the numbers that had passed through it, with great
cannons; and, after the soldiers had left, more cannons had
come, and passed through the town without stopping. That
was all he knew.

It seemed satisfactory, and Richard proceeded. In about
an hour Bury was in sight; and so was a French dragoon,
emerging from a lane on the right side of the road.

"Halt!"

Richard pulled up. He had his pistol in his greatcoat
pocket, strapped to his back; but had he had it in his hand,
it would have been of no use, nor would he have fired it.

"Rendez-vous; vous êtes mon prisonnier."

CHAPTER XII.

Mr. Partring, shrewd as he had been in surmising the where-abouts of the French, had forgotten one thing. Hospitals are always in the rear of a marching army.

"Quel êtes-vous? the dragoon asked his prisoner.

"Je suis un gentilhomme."

Now, a gentilhomme is not the same as what we mean by a gentleman. To put it in the form of a statement in the rule of three, a gentilhomme is to a gentleman as a gentleman is to a gent. Gentilhomme means nobleman, or of noble birth.

The dragoon looked at him, and did not disbelieve him. Indeed, Richard Fenthorpe was much more noble in appearance and manner than two or three of our acquaintances who get their livelihood on the strength of their titles. They rode together to the Court House of Bury St. Edmunds, where Richard was desired to dismount, and was brought into a room that served as a kind of guard-room. All the soldiers who were about had hurts or wounds, wraps round their legs, or their arms in slings. Inside were the severely wounded, and Richard perceived easily the nature of the establishment.

Within a few minutes he was brought into another room, where a major, as he knew by the uniform, sat at a table, his left arm in a sling. The major rose and bowed, and desired him to be seated.

"You are a gentilhomme," said the major.

"Yes, monsieur," Fenthorpe replied.

"What is your purpose in travelling?"

"I am on my way to London concerning business."

174

"It is necessary, but merely a matter of form, to search you. Have you any written papers or letters with you?"

Richard rose up, drew out his watch and his purse, and also his pocket-book. The officer handed him back his purse without taking an inventory of the contents. He even smiled and said that was not necessary. But he looked at the watch, and observed with interest that it was of great size and apparent value, and had a coat of arms engraved on the case. The same coat of arms was on one of the seals. "I have," said Richard, "some linen in my greatcoat pockets, and also a pistol."

The pistol was sent for. It was a remarkably handsome one, silver-mounted. But nothing made such an impression on the major as the Norwich Commandant's permit to have a horse. That document, which the clergyman had warned its owner not to rely on, was really not in the least compromising. He was styled in it Monsieur, not le Docteur, Fenthorpe, and was not described as a physician, or described at all; and he was licensed to "voyager librement et faire les visites."

"This must be a person of consideration," said the major to the dragoon who had made the capture, "to be allowed to retain his horse."

They were a little puzzled by the case of instruments, and agreed that the English are a strange people. It seemed that it did not occur to them that the prisoner was a surgeon.

"We must detain you, monsieur," said the officer, "till we shall have received instructions about you from headquarters. You shall be well treated, but we must confine you to this hospital and its precincts. I, and the other officers, are to have our supper at nine o'clock. I hope that we may have the honour of your company."

Richard bowed, wondering why he was treated with so much deference. The major took him to two or three small rooms, in each of which were two or three beds or shake-downs; but, not feeling satisfied, found, with a little search, a room which the prisoner could have to himself. It had a mattress on trestles, a chair, and a table. The major com-

manded a basin and jug to be brought, and the jug to be
filled with water. Then he left him with a bow, saying, "à
neuf heures."

There was no soap. The prisoner could not remember the
French for soap, and, after the supper, and when in bed,
racked his brains for it. As he awoke in the morning, it
came to him suddenly. He asked for it; and in about half
an hour, a soldier having been sent into the town, and having
inquired at a grocer's, a haberdasher's, and a stationer's, and,
at last, at the right shop, it was brought to him. This
demand for an article of luxury raised him in the estimation
of his captors, who were more and more deferential. Another
trifle had an influence of the same kind. When the soldier
brought him the article of luxury, a cube of yellow stuff three
inches every way, nearly all resin, he asked what was the
price. The man thought this the absurdest thing he had ever
heard in his life, and laughed at him. But he told the
circumstance to the rest, and all agreed that the prisoner must
be a great milord to think of paying for an article that could
be got for the taking.

After breakfast, Richard asked the major if he might be
allowed to write to his friends if opportunity of sending a
letter should occur. For the first time he was answered with
sternness of voice and manner. Certainly not. The major
even cautioned him against making the attempt, which put
him from the idea of offering one of the invalids a couple of
guineas to take a letter to Thetford. It was as well that he
did not try this, for he would have been insulted. These
soldiers, who understood neither soap nor the propriety of
paying for it, would not—no, not one of them—have done
such a thing for two guineas, nor for two hundred. They
were all Republicans, not Imperialists. A French soldier at
a later and more corrupt time would have done it for two
shillings.

It was on Tuesday evening that he was taken prisoner. On
Friday morning there arrived from the side of Newmarket
a waggon-load of wounded men, and, during the day, many

more; and by night, the Court-House was filled in its every corner, and some granaries and other buildings in the town requisitioned. Professional zeal, or natural humanity, or both, surged in Dr. Fenthorpe's eager spirit. He almost wished for a moment that he was a French surgeon. He had heard of what military hospitals are; now he saw part of it. Only the beginning, however, and not the worst; for in another week Bury St. Edmunds was a pestilential charnel-house, from which arose the smoke of the torment of six thousand dying men.

Near midnight, he was about to retire to his little chamber, when the major sent for him, and told him that he was instantly to proceed to headquarters. The major also told him that there had been a great and bloody battle, in which the French army had been completely victorious. He did not brag, and he looked on the prisoner with a kind of compassion. We believe that even the most unfeeling of men, and those most disposed to gasconade, do not talk big about their victories in hospitals.

John Hunter had been well fed and groomed while in Bury. His pistol was returned to the prisoner; the twelve charges he had for it were not. He rode off on his good old horse between a slightly wounded ensign and a dragoon to Haverhill.

CHAPTER XIII.

WHEN it was known in London, on Wednesday the sixth of March, that the English army had been defeated at Ipswich, the exodus, which had paused for a few days, was hurried on almost with panic. Everybody that could left town during that day and the rest of the week. The Houses met, as usual, at four o'clock, and adjourned for a month, to meet at Oxford. The King, determined not to leave his capital before the break-up of Parliament, departed on Thursday for Worcester.

In the House of Commons a conversation took place that gave Mr. Pitt very great pleasure. Mr. Fox rose to ask the right honourable gentleman a question, when Mr. Sheridan interrupted him to call the speaker's attention to the presence of strangers. The gallery cleared, Mr. Fox asked what was the object of the military and engineering proceedings on the Surrey side of the Thames. Mr. Pitt, perceiving that the exclusion of the reporters had been arranged by the Opposition, gave a reply rather less evasive than usual—he was a master of evasion—and complimented honourable members opposite on their care for the public interest, in securing that no information about the plans of the defence of the country should reach the enemy through the publication of the debates.

A still more provident precaution of the same kind had been taken by Mr. ——, Lord Camden's buffer, who had gone, on Monday, to the editors of the *Times*, the *Morning Chronicle*, and the *Morning Post* (we do not remember if there were any other daily papers then), and conjured them not to publish anything about the military preparations in the Borough. Accordingly, it was three weeks before Bonaparte knew anything about them.

The treasure of the Bank was removed—six millions of

gold, and more than two millions of silver. As the Londoners saw the long train of waggons that bore it depart, many of them were surprised to learn that the weight of this bullion was four hundred tons. It was stated in the newspapers that it was sent to Portsmouth; it was really sent to Dorchester. We are not without a suspicion that the thoughtful Mr. —— made a communication to the newspapers concerning its destination. We questioned that gentleman's youngest son, who was living twenty years ago, about this, but all that we could get him to say was that it was a very likely thing for his father to have done.

In the removal of the executive Government from London, no arrangements for which were even thought of till the abandonment of the Metropolis was, in a manner, compelled, there were the greatest difficulties in the very setting about the business. The Horse Guards, the War Office, the Admiralty, as well as Lord Camden's department and the Foreign Office, were transferred to the English general's headquarters, which, by the end of the week, were fixed at Royston; or, more correctly, the skeletons of those departments were transferred. Nearly all the members of the Civil Service were left behind; and most of those gentlemen, being unable to quit London, remained there, terribly against their wills, during the rest of the war, and till the departments were restored to their old habitations. A few prominent noblemen and others found it impossible to leave town owing to illness and other reasons.

The Horse Guards practically ceased to exist, except as the mere instrument of giving orders for the movements of troops to the scene of action, orders that really proceeded from Lord Camden. The Duke of York showed the highest patriotism. He was a good administrator, and a good soldier, but the worst commander in the world. He resigned himself to the inevitable, swallowed his pride and jealousy—no great dose, for he was anything but a mean man—and bargained for nothing but that he should command his own favourite regiment. In the battle that followed, he bore himself as bravely as his great grandfather had done at Oudenarde and Dettingen.

There was, in truth, among all public men, a profound and almost awful political calm, like the calm that precedes the bursting of a tornado. Old hostilities between politicians who had accused each other of bad faith and public criminality and treason, and who had menaced each other with impeachment and attainder, were dropped. Every man watched with intense anxiety while the sails of the good ship England were being furled, and her rigging made taut and her hatches closed down. For a while, the names Whig and Tory and Jacobin were unheard. If any distrusted the ability of the man at the helm, they did not distrust his good will, and they were silent about former faults and failures. All knew that a crisis was coming. Some, perhaps, feared the result; very few feared the final result. The ship might reel, but would not go on her beam ends.

Against Wednesday, the twentieth of March, the English general had under his command, disposed from near Saffron-Walden to beyond Ely, seventy thousand soldiers of our regular army, hastily drafted from all parts of England, from Wales, from Ireland, and from Scotland, and seventy thousand volunteers, of whom a large fraction were from the Metropolis. Of all these, more than twenty thousand were horse, of the regular cavalry, of yeomanry, and of volunteers. Cambridge was his centre, although headquarters were still at Royston, the inconvenience of moving the executive Government and its machinery being too great to shift headquarters so frequently as may possibly have been desirable for military convenience. The defence of the line of the river Cam had been resolved on as the most opportune measure in making a stand.

Bonaparte had his whole army right opposite, with a narrower front, extending from Haverhill to a little beyond Newmarket. The right wing of his army was the force that had come from Norfolk. He himself directed the centre, and the left wing was under Berthier. On Wednesday morning he made a general forward movement, and a little before four o'clock his centre was little more than a mile from Cambridge. Making a hasty reconnaissance, he ordered an attack on the town, hoping to take it with a rush.

There were fully twenty thousand in and close to Cambridge, and the streets and bridges were barricaded. Outside the town there were six battalions of regular infantry; the garrison proper was of regulars and volunteers mixed. Batteries of artillery were disposed so as to sweep the level ground and the roads. The volunteer corps from London, thirty in number, were all placed in the right English wing; the left contained a larger proportion of volunteers. But no distinctive portion of the English line was exclusively of either one military class or the other, except the extreme left, towards and beyond Ely.

The attack on Cambridge opened with a cannonade, which was well replied to; then infantry, and a close fight. By six o'clock, when twilight was coming on, the French were beaten back with loss, never having reached the town. The six battalions in front of it were severely handled, but quite unbroken when the action closed. It was too late for Bonaparte to do anything more that evening.

The English general was advised by many of his staff, when it was seen that the French front was comparatively narrow, to imitate them, and to concentrate both wings nearer the centre. He did so, leaving Saffron-Walden empty of troops, and making a like disposition on his left. But orders were never despatched to, or never reached, the extreme left, and a gap of five miles was left between the battalion of regular infantry furthest in that direction from Cambridge, and twenty volunteer corps, which remained behind Ely, north of the Ouse, which there makes a bend.

This omission, whether it arose by mischance or blame, was not the only fault in the drawing up of the English army. They were to defend the river Cam; in other words, to prevent the enemy from getting over it. There were four bridges between Saffron-Walden and Cambridge, and four between

Cambridge and Ely, some of these eight being of strong and heavy pontoons. Now, the way to prevent an enemy from crossing a bridge is not to let him get across it and then fight him, but to stand in front of the bridge and fight him there, keeping a reserve behind it, so as to give the enemy a hot reception in case he should, unfortunately, succeed in pushing you back. But Sir D—— put less than a quarter of his force on the east side of the river, and kept the bulk of his army, both wings, in the rear of it. He made another error, not unusual with commanders of the school of Frederick the Great and Marshal Dann, although those great generals knew how to correct it when its consequences threatened to be mischievous. The various volunteer corps were of various numerical force. Sir D—— made the front of each and all the same; so that some corps were columns six deep and others ten deep. Under a cannonade, accordingly, the more numerous a corps was, the more in proportion it suffered from the same amount of fire.

Wednesday night was fine, but at seven on Thursday a drizzling thick rain came on, which was not over till after nine. Instantly on its clearing, Bonaparte attacked as he had the evening before; but he assailed not Cambridge only, but the whole English army, with the whole of his, except that he, of course, attempted, as yet, no cavalry movement.

His left attack, that on the English right, was much more vigorous than the attack by his right wing under Davoust. From the very first, the English battalions suffered badly from the fire of the French artillery, while the enemy's infantry, not being in position, and not being advanced very early in the day, suffered far less from our guns. Every now and then there was a pause in the artillery fire; and about twelve o'clock two of the bridges, those next Cambridge to the south, were assailed. After an hour and a half of stiff fighting, the assailants were driven back.

Cambridge town, however, was the vital point of the battle. Bonaparte directed, from ten o'clock till half-past two, four separate assaults upon it. The first two were repulsed without the French getting into the town; in the third, they penetrated some way in, but were stopped by the barricades, and drew off; in the fourth, they surmounted two barricades, and came within sight of the sluggish river, to cross which was their object, but at last were driven back. Then Bonaparte wound himself up for a final attempt. He harangued his forlorn hope, and told them that the fate of two nations depended on them. And he did another thing besides.

If it did not succeed, this new idea, he would at the utmost lose two battalions of infantry and a few squadrons; if it did, and if he at the same time took Cambridge, he would gain a victory ten times as great as Marengo.

He sent orders to Berthier to cause the two battalions farthest but one on his left to defile behind that furthest one, and turn, after marching a mile south of it, sharp to their right, and suddenly rush at the bridge over the Cam, the nearest to Saffron-Walden; in the meantime, moving as many guns as he could to bear upon that bridge till the moment the rush should take place. A good force of cavalry was to follow, and to charge the extreme English right. Bonaparte would never admit that this manœuvre was a copy from Marlborough, who rolled up the French army at Ramilies in a similar way.

By this time, when half the day was over, the English behind the bridges were becoming terribly impatient with being shot at and kept standing still. Sir D——, observing that, except in Cambridge town, the battle was hitherto little more than an artillery fight, in which we were getting the worst, ordered an advance from two of the bridges, moving up infantry to reinforce it. Had he done this earlier, it would have been better. As it was, this advance had a good effect, and Berthier's line was, in the course of a short time, nearly broken. Our supports came up, suffering still under a heavy artillery fire; but the men did not mind this half so much as when they were standing still. Two French batteries were forced to limber up and retreat, in fear of capture.

This was on the English right, and a similar advance was

made on the left, with results not equal, although not very
different. The resistance of the French under Davoust was,
however, not nearly so vigorous as the resistance of the other
wing, and he withdrew some battalions that ought not to have
been retreated.

At half-past three, Bonaparte hurled forward his fifth
attack on the town. Larger columns than those employed in
any of the previous attacks were pushed forward. They
reached the barricades that had been taken, but there their
heads began to melt away, as when one tries to light a tallow
candle at a slow fire. Those behind pushed on those before
them, and at last, marching over the bodies of the dead and
dying men, the French reached the river. They had taken
that side of Cambridge by mere weight, and they took one of
the bridges by mere weight too, and that in no long time.
One of our colonels, seeing the disaster, weakened the defence
of the next bridge by half a battalion, and that bridge was
forced also. The colonel paid with his life for this almost
insane attempt to retrieve an irretrievable loss.

All that the remainder of the garrison of Cambridge could
do was to retreat, in good order if possible. With such speed
as perhaps no other army could have matched, the French
passed infantry, guns, and some cavalry through the town;
they branched to right and left, and a new battle began on
the west side of the Cam—two new battles, for the English
army was cut in two.

The English on the right side of the Cam were recalled,
and nearly all got back before the enemy had reached any
of the bridges. Our left wing made the best fight; for, just
about when Cambridge was taken, Berthier's two battalions
seized the Saffron-Walden bridge, and assailed our right
flank. The cavalry followed, and there was terrible disaster,
the result of their charge. But they made but one other
charge, for we had plenty of horse there, and many of those
six hundred French dragoons were unhorsed or killed.

But more infantry crossed the Cam, and the battle then
became hotter, though terribly losing for us. Just before

sunset, there was, as it were, a quiver through the whole of the line of the English right wing, and a general retreat, to avoid absolute rolling up and almost utter destruction, commenced. Had the French had time and light and more cavalry, the ruin would have been complete; as it was, our army was shattered, divided, flying, as the enemy called it, in three branching directions, after losing twenty-five thousand men and all the guns in Cambridge.

The sun set upon an England such as had not been for three hundred and fifty years, on that day when the Lancastrian baronry was buried in one huge grave at Towton field. But on the morning after Towton, the sun rose upon an England of a new and renovating birth. The feudal anarchy of four centuries was over, and order, and liberty, and law reform, and church reform, and progress, and expansion, were coming. Was that grand order then founded, the highest political and social civilisation that the world had yet seen, to perish in the vigour of the first years of its maturity by the hand of a foreign pirate, the destroyer of nations and their liberties? Or was England to rise, stronger for this blow, as iron grows harder between hammer and anvil, and, though with her sword arm maimed, in the fulness of time to beat down and destroy this new anarchy, ten times more devilish than the old?

Bonaparte, as was his wont, rode over the field of battle the next morning. The sight of Cambridge streets was almost too much even for him. As soon as practicable, and there was but little delay, he ordered pursuit of the enemy. It had to be excentric, and he directed three separate attacks on Huntingdon, on St. Neots, and on Bedford. For anything that he knew, the river Ouse might have been fixed on by the English for a second line of defence.

The English headquarters and executive Government were withdrawn, during Thursday night, to Bedford. If there was consternation, it did not manifest itself openly. If Bonaparte expected a flag of truce, proposing an armistice, he was disappointed. Men said, some perhaps despairingly, "let us fight on."

N

During the next day, as accounts came in of the different battles, which, put together, made the one great battle, it began to be thought at Bedford that there was something unaccountable. It was not astonishing that Cambridge should have been forced, nor that the flank movement of Berthier's division should have surprised the English right; but why were one hundred thousand men kept standing many hours for nothing but to be shot at? Why should not a hundred thousand men have been boldly launched against ninety thousand? And why, said officers who had seen some other wars, why were the bridges defended by a method unknown to the military art?

But when it came to be known that twenty thousand men had been waiting all day five miles from the northern end of the English line, not one of whom had fired a shot, and some of whom were too far off to hear the noise of the battle, there was something more than questioning. There could be no doubt how the battle had been lost.

The Cabinet, which was virtually a council of war, was summoned, and Sir D—— desired to attend it. Lord Macaulay relates that Lewis the Fourteenth's courtiers said of King James, when he took refuge in France, that no one who heard his Majesty's story from his Majesty's lips could be surprised that he had been dethroned. Lord Chelmsford is not deficient in some of those qualities that belong to a soldier; but no one who reads his despatch giving an account of Isundula can wonder at what happened there. Of such a nature was Sir D——'s explanation of the battle of Cambridge and its issue.

He was requested, in the least wounding terms that could be employed, to resign his command. General Wallerton, whom Lord Camden esteemed very highly, and whom he knew to be highly thought of by others whose opinions he valued, among the rest, Colonel Blessingburn, was made Commander-in-Chief in his place. A few days after, the King sent for Sir D——, and told him, in that hearty and gracious, if not graceful, manner which made so many love him, that his confidence in his general was undiminished, but the confidence of others was not, and it was necessary that the army should be in harmony with their commander. He proposed to make Sir D—— a peer so soon as Bonaparte should be a prisoner, or out of England; which Sir D—— wisely declined.

The council of war gave general instructions to General Wallerton not to bring on again so great and critical a battle as that just lost. To this he replied that, did he wish to do so, it would be beyond his power.

"Why?" said Pitt.

"Bonaparte is a better man of war than I am, sir, and I shall not be able, in ordinary circumstances of equality of forces, to bring on a battle unless he wishes to fight; and he will not bring on such a battle as that of yesterday a second time."

"Why again?" said Pitt.

"Because he cannot afford a second loss such as he made yesterday."

"What was the extent of his loss yesterday? What means have we of knowing?"

"It is impossible that his loss yesterday can be less than half of what ours was. I am confident that he has not with him more than seventy-five thousand men. Their loss, in Cambridge, was greater than ours. Their loss in cavalry was greater than ours. That arm of theirs is crippled."

Hope springs eternal in the human breast. Pitt and Lord Camden exchanged glances.

"And what are you going to do now, General Wallerton?"

"He is marching here, I am sure not with the whole army. I will make ready for him; he cannot be here till the afternoon of to-morrow, unless he marches all night. I will send orders to resist, to the very last, all attack along this river. I will make no attempt to keep him out of London; for I cannot keep him out of London."

"What amount of force have you here in Bedford?"

"Fully forty thousand, counting cavalry."

The council separated. It is fit that we should describe here the comparative behaviour of the regular troops and the

volunteers. In open fighting in the field they were about
equal in conduct and merit. In standing fire at
long bowls, much of which was so disastrously endured
in the early part of the battle, the volunteers were
not nearly so steady as the soldiers. It was the
general opinion that, had the fighting in Cambridge
itself been confined to the volunteers only, they would have
given way at the third, certainly at the fourth assault. They
had been severely shaken by the cavalry charge on the right
wing, more so than older troops would have been. But they
had kept together during the retreat, both in companies and
battalions, without exception, better than the regular troops
had. It must be added that there was no jealousy whatever
between the two branches of the service. The yeomanry had
done good service in covering the retreat.

When the council met on Monday, they had something to
congratulate each other about. Bonaparte had attacked Bedford in person with an insufficient force, and been repulsed;
St. Neots had been attacked with an insufficient force, which
was repulsed; and Davoust had attacked Huntingdon, and
been driven back after a murderous fight. But Bonaparte
was thought to be in full march on London, notwithstanding
which the ministers were in higher spirits than they had
been in since his landing.

Bonaparte committed, after Cambridge, the same error, or,
at least, met the same misfortune, that was repeated eight
years afterwards in Saxony. After he had overwhelmed the
allied army at Dresden, he sent out detachments in all
directions in pursuit; and he lost four battles, or his
lieutenants did, in a few days.

On his way to London he learned about Davoust's defeat
on the Ouse, and sent for that general and reprimanded him.
Davoust confided to him that the men and officers of the
Norfolk army were amazed at the bravery of the volunteers.
They had behaved at Norwich with great folly but with great
courage; and now there were countless numbers of them.
Bonaparte ordered Davoust to return to Norfolk; and on the
twenty-eighth of March the first division of the French army
entered London unopposed.

CHAPTER XIV.

GUILDHALL.

Dr. Fenthorpe arrived with his escort at headquarters duly; but Bonaparte was not there, nor were there any orders as to what was to be done with the prisoner. He was kept at Haverhill for a few days, being well treated, just the same as at Bury. The eating and drinking at the officers' mess was better.

On Tuesday, the twenty-sixth, orders came to remove head-quarters to a village, the name of which Richard did not know; but when he started on his ride, escorted as usual, he perceived that the journey was to the southward, and on asking where the army was going, was scarcely surprised to hear in reply, "to London." The men and officers were in the highest spirits. They knew that the English had been defeated in a tremendous battle, and they thought the conquest of the country was on the point of consummation. They had heard of the minor battles of Saturday and Sunday as victories of their own. They were exultant, and did not conceal it.

They arrived in London in the rear of the first division after dark on Thursday evening. Coming into town from the direction that they did, and being considerably behind the body of the army, it is not surprising that the commanding officer of the three or four companies of the very hindmost of the detachment should have lost his way. All that he knew was that he should keep well to his right; and, trying to do so, he blundered upon the Angel at Islington. There he halted, and determined to stop for the night. The guests of the inn, not very numerous, were ordered out of their rooms,

189

and the landlord commanded to find a messenger to conduct the officer and his suite into the city. Boots was summoned, and desired to guide them to the house of the Lord Mayor.

"The house of the Lord Mayor! I don't know where he lives."

Richard was standing by, and told the man that they meant the Mansion House. We believe that this man was the brother of Antony and uncle of Sam Weller; at all events, he had the sharpness and love of action, and of very decided practical jokes, of the latter, and looked as if he would like to play the French a trick. Richard remarked his face, and warned him that such a thing would certainly cost him his life. In the morning Boots thanked the gentleman for his advice, and described the rough manners of the enemy down in the city with much disgust. Thirty years after this, when Pickwick was published, Dr. Fenthorpe, then an old man, on examining the illustrations, was positive that he recognised a likeness.

He got a room in the Angel to himself, and, with some trouble, ascertained that John Hunter was housed in a neighbouring mews. When getting up in the morning, some fancy inspired him to put his pistol in his coat pocket. There had been various noises during the night, which had not kept him from sleeping, and which he did not much remark. He was surprised to learn that there had been much firing of heavy cannon, at which the French officers were as much puzzled as himself.

At about one or two o'clock he was directed to come into the city, escorted as before. On reaching the Mansion House, he dismounted, and the dragoon held his horse. Crowds of French soldiers were in the streets; there was no traffic. At first he hardly knew what part of the town he was in. It was nine years since he had been in London, walking the hospitals. He had then lodged on the Surrey side, near Guy's, and had never frequented any of the hospitals on the Middlesex side, except St. George's. He had known but few people, and the only house where he visited much was in Palace Yard, which he reached by crossing Westminster Bridge. Thus he was but little acquainted with the city, and, indeed, could not easily find his way about it.

He was brought into a room where three general officers sat at a table, with three or four secretaries or clerks. The ensign who had accompanied him from Bury, his arm still in a sling, came with him into the room. The generals rose and bowed.

For the life of him he could not understand all this. What did it mean, this respect he had been paid ever since the major at Bury hospital had made him take out his watch and pocket-book, and refusing him leave to send a letter to his friends? Was it not far more like the treatment due to a prisoner of state than to a mere prisoner of war, and a nobody? Were they under some mistake? Were they taking him for somebody else?

He was soon enlightened. "Monsieur le gentilhomme Vantorp," said one of the generals, who, by the way, was Berthier, "sa Majesté l'Empereur va publier un manifesto, addressé au peuple Britannique, et il desire qu'il soit contre-signé par autant de personnes de consideration de votre nation que soit possible. Déjà, un grand nombre des citoyens les plus considerables de Londres, et aussi de votre noblesse, viennent de signifier leur approbation. Si vous voulez nous signifier votre consentement, ou vous mettra tout de suite en liberté; au contraire, si vous refusez, vous resterez prisonnier. Voici le manifesto."

The general handed him a printed paper, at the top of which were the words "Republique Britannique." He read no further, and threw it down on the table. He was going, as any Englishman would have done, to say indignantly that he would not sign it, when he suddenly perceived the mistake that had been made about him.

"Pomiquoi," he said, "m'appelez-vous le gentilhomme Fenthorpe?"

"N'êtes vous pas gentilhomme?"

"Oui, je suis gentilhomme; mais on n'addresse ainsi les

gentilhommes Anglais; aussi je ne signerais rien; et mon nom serait tout a fait inutile à vous, je ne suis qu'un medicin obscure de la ville de Norwich."

"Un medicin! N'avez-vous pas declaré au dragon que vous êtes gentilhomme?"

"Sans doute, je suis gentilhomme."

"Bah!" exclaimed Berthier, suddenly recollecting his English, and turning to the others, "il a vent dire chentelman, ce n'est que monsieur ordinaire! Bah! Pst! Allez! Allez! Entendez-vous?"

Richard turned his back and walked out. He mounted his horse. In two or three minutes the ensign came down, but not alone; Berthier was with him. "Descendez," shouted the general.

"Descendre du cheval, voulez-vous dire?"

"Oui, descendez."

He saw, with a very keen pang, what was going to be done. Berthier, who was a good judge of a horse, walked round John Hunter, and made the dragoon show him his feet. He was no charger, but would be a good hack.

"Amenez le à l'ecurie; un des soldats vous conduira." Berthier said to the ensign.

Richard Fenthorpe had only once before, during his life, been so enraged; that was when an awkward student at Guy's had volunteered to tie up arteries, and made a mess of it, after he himself had warned him. He forgot himself a little; he caught Berthier by the arm and said, loudly, and, he thought afterwards, as he said when he told the story, menacingly, "Vous avez pris non cheval, mais moi, suis je libre?"

Berthier was as angry as he was, and replied, "Allez! Allez! Entendez-vous! Nous n'avons plus d'affaire avec vous."

So there he was, not knowing what turn to take or what to do. French soldiers filled the streets. He could not ask the way. Neither could he remain standing where he was. He thought of returning to Islington, but dismissed the idea.

There he would still be considered a prisoner; the ensign
might not return to set them right. He would lose his
instruments, and his greatcoat and shirts and razor; but all
that was nothing after losing John Hunter. He turned down
a narrow street and got as far as Cannon street. He did not
know where he was. He traversed many streets, meeting no
one. The houses were all shut up. Now and then he saw a
head thrust out of an upper window; and he had made up his
mind to call to the next person whose head he should see,
when he came to what he thought looked like an eating-house.
He knocked at the door, and a man's head appeared out of the
window of the second floor. "What do you want?"

"I am a stranger in London, and I have lost my way. I
want something to eat."

"Lord save us!" said the man. He came down, and opened
the door, which was barred. He looked up and down the
street, but saw nothing suspicious, nor anything at all. This
looked like a gentleman, and he told Richard to come in.

"Is not this a house of entertainment?"

"Yes, sir." The man did not tell the name of the tavern.
Very likely it was Joe's or Sam's. "And you're a stranger,
sir?"

"I am. I have not been in London for years. And I came
now in a curious way." He thought it judicious to give an
account of himself before he was asked to do so.

"What would you like to take, sir? There are only two of
us in the house, but there is plenty to eat and drink."

He asked for a beefsteak, which the man said would be
ready soon. This waiter, however, did not bring the dinner
when it arrived. Joe or Sam (this is not the correct name, for
it was a woman) brought it himself—we mistake, herself.
She was more curious about this strange guest than the man
had been, and was properly amazed at his story.

"Now, can you tell me how I can get out of London?" he
asked, when he had related his adventures.

"They do say, sir, that nobody will be allowed to leave
London. I don't know what you can do. Dear, dear me!"

"Madam," said Richard after a pause—the landlady had sat down, and his dinner was over—"would it be possible for you to keep me here all night? I have nowhere to go to, and don't know the way anywhere."

"Oh, sir," she answered, "we're going, me and Ben, as soon as it is dark, away from here. I couldn't bear the noise of those cannons another night; and a cannon ball might come into the house any time and kill us. We are going to Islington."

"Islington! Why, that is where I was last night, at the Angel. What part of Islington are you going to?"

"It is just close by the Angel. You might come with us, sir, and you would just be going back; that would just suit you. And we would be three in the streets, instead of two."

"I am sure, madam, I thank you very much; but, you see, if I was seen there, I might be taken again. But you are safe here, I should say, far safer than going through the streets at night. If you are really going to Islington, you ought, I think, to go now, in daylight."

"If the French saw us, they might cut our throats."

"I don't think they would; they were civil enough to me. I really don't think they would." He saw that reasoning would produce no effect on her, though persuasion and reassuring talk might. "And there will be French about after dark as well as now."

She said she would see what Ben thought. Richard rose to go. If he could not stay in this house, he had better look out for another place to lodge in during daylight. The worst of it was, every house was shut. He had had no idea that the popular consternation would be so intense.

The landlady would take no payment for the beefsteak and pint of wine; she said she had not entertained the gentleman in the way of business. He thanked her, and shook her by the hand, and asked her for some instructions how to get anywhere. She directed him how to reach Cheapside, which he knew, or thought he knew.

It was growing dusk and foggy, and he got into Cheapside,

not knowing that it was the street he wanted. The lamps here were lighted, and for the first time since he had left Islington, at noon, there were some of his countrymen moving about. Still in perplexity, he turned down a street where there were Englishmen not only moving about, but some standing together in groups. The lamps in the street gave more light, or there were more of them, than in the other street, and he walked on, looking at faces to try to find a likely-looking person to consult. We have observed that people who know London and Londoners a little are far more backward in addressing a stranger when they are in a scrape than Londoners themselves.

He soon came to the end of the street, which was a *cul de sac*. A wide door that he had never seen, and a building that he did not know, stopped him. But no! The door was open, and two French sentries guarded it; and he saw, what he had missed in the fog, that there were several soldiers more in the street. One or two Englishmen came out at the door: two went in; so he thought he might go in also. Looking at the sentries, who were unmoved and, to all seeming, unmovable, he entered.

He found himself in a large and lofty hall, empty of furniture except a table at the left end from the door, which was near one corner of this great room. Some candles were on a table, and a man in a cocked hat, like that of a French general, sat on a chair at one end of it. The floor of the room was occupied, not thronged, with English gentlemen in groups and French soldiers. Walking towards the table, Richard Fenthorpe saw beyond it two gigantic black figures, seated. He thought they looked like idols in an Indian temple. Suddenly, he remembered Gog and Magog, which he had heard of but never before seen, and he knew that he was in Guildhall.

A group of Englishmen were beyond the table; they did not seem to be conversing with each other, but waiting for something. As Richard stood, his personal difficulties forgotten for the moment, in the difficulty of understanding the scene before him, the man in the cocked hat lifted his head, and the light of the candles shone full on his face. It is not usual to call masculine features beautiful, but Richard thought that he had never seen a more beautiful countenance. It was full, without being fat; not very dark, but darker than that of most Englishmen; very close shaven, commanding in its expression, and, in the very highest degree, intellectual. He did not see the man's legs, but his figure, as he sat on the chair, gave the idea of a person of fully middle height. It was a face and a figure that could not be seen by the least observant without attention and almost fascination. But as Richard continued to look, although not a motion of the features of this remarkable face could be perceived, it appeared to him as if the face itself changed. For a moment he admired, and was entranced by its beauty, power, and intellectuality; then, while the power and the intellectuality remained, the beauty seemed to die out of the face, and be replaced, as by transformation, by something far transcending mere human ugliness, something whose origin could be ascribed to nowhere but the depths of the bottomless pit.

Some one who came in from the street, a little out of breath, and crossed the hall in his direction, whispered to Richard, " Is that he? " He turned and said, " I am just come here." The new arrival then whispered another person, and Richard heard the name Bonaparte. At the same instant the man in the cocked hat, whose identity he could not but recognise, called out, " Venez donc." The group of Englishmen standing beyond the table came to the end of it opposite Bonaparte; one of them stood in front of the rest, a small man, with rather a mean-looking countenance. The people in the hall began to press towards the table, and Richard heard one or two whisper, " The Lord Mayor." An officer took his stand at the table half-way between Bonaparte and the Lord Mayor, his back to Gog and Magog. Bonaparte addressed a few words to him in a low voice. He was the interpreter.

" His Majesty desires to know if you have considered," said the interpreter, handing a printed paper, which Richard saw to be the same as that which Berthier had shown him in the morning.

"I have," replied the Lord Mayor. His voice was firm and clear, slightly Cockney; as his features moved in the act of speaking, the effect of his countenance improved.

"And what answer do you give to his Majesty?"

"The same that I gave before. I will not."

This was repeated to Bonaparte. His dark face darkened; it did not become blacker in colour, but it darkened in expression till it was like what might belong to a being whose birthplace was farther away, if it be possible, than the regions of hell.

"Ne savez-vous pas que je puis vous faire fusillé?"

"His Majesty asks do not you know that he can make you to be shot?"

The little man drew himself up, and his face seemed to dilate as did his form, and become noble. He looked like Paul when he pleaded his cause, and the cause of the truth of God, before Festus and Agrippa; and he answered, in a voice that rang to the furthest part of the hall:

"My lord, I know that you can shoot me; but there is a thing that you cannot do—*you cannot hang me for high treason to King George.*"

Had the occasion not been too solemn and portentous, the London aldermen, merchants, and shopkeepers who heard these words would have cheered. They hummed their approval; perhaps it was more expressive than noise would have been. There was not one of them that was not proud of their fellow-citizen, and that was not proud of being an Englishman—aye, though Hannibal was within their gates.

A moment after, at a sign from some officer, the soldiers began to clear the hall. They shoved the Englishmen out of it rudely, and used the butt ends of their muskets to expedite their departure. They continued this brutality towards the retreating crowd even in King Street. Richard Fenthorpe was one of the last to get out of the hall, and at about twenty yards from the door, he was struck on the back of the head, and fell heavily, stunned.

How long he lay on the pavement he never knew. It was known afterwards, by the evidence of persons who had looked at their watches, that Guildhall was cleared by the French at half-past six, and that Bonaparte left it for his quarters immediately. The probability is that Richard remained lying on his back for nearly three hours. He remembered wakening and feeling the pistol in his pocket under him. That was safe; and it reminded him to feel for his watch and purse; they were safe, and so was his pocket-book. None of the dangerous classes were abroad in London streets that night. Satan, for a moment, had cast out Beelzebub.

Richard got on his feet, and found he could stand and even walk, though he was hurt and dazed. He walked down King Street, and away he knew not whither. He must have crossed Cheapside without turning into it, for he remembered that he did not meet any soldiers, at least to recognise them; and Cheapside was being patrolled all night. The fog was thicker than ever. He walked on and on, stupidly, and hardly able to think.

He was roused by a man coming out of what seemed a hole in a wall, who presented a bayonet at him, and said, "What word?" He stopped. Behind the man was a lantern, which gave light enough for him to see that the hole in the wall was a niche in the parapet of a bridge.

"What word?" he answered, not knowing what was meant, and hardly what he said himself.

"Are you drunk?" said the sentry.

"No; I have lost my way. Is this London Bridge?"

"How in the name of —— did you get here?"

"I don't know. The French had me prisoner, and I was hurt."

He put his hand to the back of his head.

The sentry took a good look at him, and observed that his coat and all his clothes were black. "Are you a clergyman or a gentleman?" he asked him.

"I am a gentleman. Where should I go to? I want to go to bed, if I can find one anywhere."

" You can't go back to the city, that's sartain. I'll pass you on to the next sentry."

He did so, taking him by the arm. " Brown," he said to his comrade, " here's a gentleman that has escaped out of Bonaparte's hands, and he's hurt. He ought to be sent to headquarters. Pass him on."

Private volunteer Brown passed him on to ditto Jones, Jones to Thomson, and Thomson to another, till he was fairly in the Borough. He grew in importance as he proceeded, and was at last an important prisoner who had been badly wounded and had miraculously escaped, and Bonaparte was looking for him up and down London. He must be sent to headquarters, in a coach if one could be found.

Against eleven o'clock he was in bed in a room of the Elephant and Castle, going to sleep after being bled, plastered, and all other things necessary.

CHAPTER XV.

"How is the French prisoner that came in the other night?" said Commander Groves to his orderly on the Monday morning after the Friday when Richard Fenthorpe arrived in the Borough.

"I don't know, Commander. Shall I send Dr. Tarring?"

"Yes; he is here, I suppose?"

Dr. Tarring came in, and informed the Commander that the prisoner was doing well, but was comatose.

"What is that? Stupid?"

"He is inclined to sleep, and has not opened his mouth to say a word since he came. But, Commander, he is not a Frenchman."

"What is he, then?"

"He is an English gentleman, possibly a clergyman, for he was dressed in black. It seems he said to one of the sentries on London Bridge that he had escaped from the enemy. We have not examined his clothes, and we know nothing about him."

"It is very curious. Do you think, Dr. Tarring, that it would do him any harm for me to see him—I mean, to question him? If he was in the enemy's hands, and escaped, he may be able to tell something worth our knowing."

"Commander, as his physician, I would not recommend that. But I do not know—I am not certain—that any mischief would supervene. I have just come in; I have not seen

200

him since about eight. I will go to his room and see him now, and tell you."

Dr. Tarring went to where his patient was lying in bed, neither asleep nor awake, as he had been for two days. As he opened the door, which was opposite the bed, the wounded man (wounded by bleeding in the arm as severely as he had been wounded by the French soldier's musket on the back of his head) looked at him intelligently.

"Where am I?"

"You are in the Elephant and Castle inn. Are you better?"

"Yes, thank you. Have you been attending me?"

"I have. Let me feel your pulse. Better. Is there anything you would like—tea and toast?"

"I don't know; I think so."

"I shall send you some. I shall come later in the day. By the way, the Commander wishes to see you, if you are equal to it."

"Commander! Commander of what?"

"The Commander of the Kentish volunteers. I did not tell you, till I should see how you are, that you are at headquarters."

"Headquarters of our army? Did you not say the Elephant and Castle?"

"This is the headquarters of the force that is defending the bridges. Bonaparte's army is in London. I suppose you know."

The patient smiled, or laughed. "I know that. I came with them, and they told me to go about my business when they had done with me; and I have been wondering how I got here. What day is to-day?"

"Monday, the first of April."

"I was in London on—Friday, as well as I recollect. Yes, Friday; and I remember nothing since. The first of April, doctor? You are not making a fool of me?"

"My dear sir, things are much too serious here for anything of the kind. I am delighted to find you so much better.

o

I will send you your breakfast." Dr. Tarring turned to
leave.

"I say, doctor! You've been bleeding me?"

The Doctor returned to the bed. "Yes," he said.

"What did you bleed me for? It is lowering; it is not
what I would have done."

"My dear sir, you hardly expect a physician or a surgeon
to tell his patients the reasons for treatment."

"My dear sir, I expect you to tell me, for I am a physician
myself."

Dr. Tarring thought it better to turn the conversation.
"Bless my soul, that accounts for it! They told me when you
came in that you were a clergyman, I suppose because your
clothes were black."

"I am a physician, and a surgeon too, I assure you. You
have gone, I daresay, according to rule; I do not know what
symptoms I showed. How much did you take from me?"

' Only six ounces. You were not a bad case."

"Doctor, if it had not been for those six ounces, I should
have been as much at myself thirty-six hours ago as I am
now. But we need not talk about that. I am detaining you."

Dr. Tarring sent Dr. Fenthorpe his breakfast, and Dr.
Fenthorpe ordered for himself his dinner, at three o'clock, of
two mutton chops and a pint of claret if it could be had. His
tea and toast consumed, he tried to settle himself to sleep till
dinner-time, but could not.

A knock at the door. "Come in."

A gentleman in volunteer uniform, by no means young,
pretty tall, and most winning looking, entered the room.
He bowed, and Richard sat up in his bed.

"Don't rise, sir! Don't rise, I beg! Dr. Tarring has told
me I might visit you, and don't incommode yourself. You
were wounded?"

"I was felled by the blow of a musket in the city somewhere, and can hardly tell you anything since."

"I am told you were a prisoner."

"Yes; how do they know?"

"It was the account you gave of yourself. You were challenged while crossing London Bridge on Friday night, and you said you had escaped from the enemy, and been hurt, and did not know where you where or how you got there."

"All that is true, except that I did not escape. They set me at liberty. I was more than a week with them. But, sir, allow me to ask, what is this the headquarters of?"

"This is the headquarters of the volunteer and other forces, but chiefly volunteers, engaged in the defence of the bridges. You heard nothing about this in London?"

"Nothing. I was dismissed by my captors at the Mansion House. It all comes back to me now; I have been asleep, almost comatose. I was dismissed at some time in the afternoon of Friday. I found, with some trouble, a house where I got something to eat. I wanted to stay there all night, but they could not keep me. I wandered about till dark, and got, I don't know how, into Guildhall. Sir "—here Richard sat up suddenly—"it would have done any Englishman's heart good to see the way the Lord Mayor behaved!"

The Commander smiled. "We know all about that," he said. "Yes; it was great. We know everything that goes on, on the other side, you know."

"Aye! You have communications with the other side?"

"We hold the heads of the bridges."

"And you hope to prevent the enemy from passing the river?"

"We hope it."

"That," said Richard with animation, "is the only good news I have heard since I left home. Sir, it makes me well! It will be good news to take home. Thank God! Thank God! How long am I away? Monday—this is Monday! A fortnight, and I heard nothing but about a great battle."

"Aye, sir, a great and disastrous battle, and then they came here. But that is the last of their successes. We had a great fight in the city on Saturday. They attacked the bridges three times, and we beat them off. My men tell me part of it was stiff work, and I almost wished I was a young man."

"Sir! Sir! I should call you Commander—I beg your pardon. Tell me about it."

"We hold the whole of this side. We removed all the shipping, and boats, and wherries, from the other side. You never heard of this? Where were you taken prisoner?"

"At Bury St. Edmunds, where their hospitals are."

"At Bury St. Edmunds! And when you left that, were the hospitals full?"

"They were beginning to fill. I was removed from that to Haverhill on Friday night—Friday week. Then, on Thursday night I reached London, with them, you know. But I am interrupting you."

"We hold, as I was telling you, all this side as far as Richmond, and they cannot cross for want of boats. We have batteries the whole way. The only way they can get into Surrey is by the bridges. We have all the houses three or four hundred yards beyond them, you understand, every house in Bridge Street, Blackfriars; and every house in Fish Street Hill, and the whole of Thames Street between them, both sides of it, every house full of men. They attacked both bridges on Saturday, in columns; they have nowhere to plant cannon. Well, the columns got as far as Thames Street, at both bridges, and there our men took them in flank and sent them back. That happened three times, and we gave them more than we got."

"But, sir, Westminster Bridge?"

"Yes, I was more afraid of that than of here—I mean, I was more afraid of that than the city bridges. You see, this, the Elephant and Castle, is just where the three roads meet; that is why we made it headquarters. But Colonel Blessingburn, who is in command of the artillery, has great faith in his own arm, as he calls it; and he has batteries everywhere that a battery can be erected. And when they began to come down Great George Street and the other streets, and deploy, so as to form in Palace Yard—though I don't think they tried to deploy at all—we sent such a shower of shot on them that they could not reach the bridge. He says it is the safest of the three against anything but a surprise at night; and we have such a barricade at the Surrey end, I think, as they would find insurmountable."

"It must have been your guns that we heard on Thursday night."

"It was. Bonaparte got into London on Thursday morning, and went with a troop of horse himself to the Mansion House. The army went to the parks, where they are encamped. They got in their second and third divisions on Friday. They have the Tower, and they have some of the squares occupied, and some points round the north side. About two thousand at Islington, and as many more on the Edgware road. They have pickets on all the roads out of town west from Kingsland Road, and prevent egress and ingress; but they cannot entirely prevent communication. We have a post twice a day between this and headquarters at Bedford. It goes by a circuitous route, through Kingston and by Aylesbury, for they have a strong force of cavalry at Hertford, and the direct road would not be safe. The first thing Bonaparte looked for was the river, and it is certain he never knew that it was to be defended. He rode that day down as far as Blackwall and as far as Hammersmith; and he saw batteries everywhere. He took Northumberland House for his headquarters; we knew of it before an hour was over, and that night we played on it with eighteen-pounders and made it too hot for him. His headquarters are ·now in St. James's."

"And, sir, will you tell me about where our army is now? I left home to get information, and bring instructions what we were to do."

"You left home? Where? When? I do not understand."

"Norwich. You know, perhaps, that they seized all the horses they could find in the whole of Norfolk. I had the only horse but one other in Norwich; you see, I am a physician, and I and another got permission to keep our horses. Norfolk is closed in from the rest of the world, or

was when I left it. Our volunteers were cut up and dispersed.
You heard of that?"

"I heard there was a skirmish."

"It was such a skirmish as destroyed or dispersed three
thousand volunteers, who ought to have gone to the interior.
It was the maddest thing—three or four thousand men thinking they could obstruct Davoust's whole army. I was there.
I am, or was, surgeon of the Loyal Norwich, and our corps
lost three officers killed, and I don't know how many men.
Then for a fortnight we heard nothing—nothing. The Mayor
of Norwich came to me and proposed that I should try to
reach wherever the executive Government was, and bring
intelligence and instructions, and, of course, urge that something should be done to relieve us. The people were getting
excited, and the garrison was reduced, and he feared there
would be a rising, and more slaughter. I thought about it,
and I came. I left Norwich this day fortnight, intending
to try to get into Cambridgeshire; but I was advised to try
London. And the next night, at Bury St. Edmunds, I was
taken prisoner."

"And where is your horse?"

"General Berthier stole him. I was brought before him on
Friday at the Mansion House. He showed me the proclamation about the Republic, and wanted me to sign it, amongst
others he said had done the same. Of course, this was all lies.
I said I would not, and asked them what use a country
doctor's name would be to them. Some fool—I suppose the
major at the hospital at Bury—had taken it in his head that
I am a considerable person. Well, when General Berthier
found that I am—nobody, in fact, he nearly kicked me out
of the room. But he kept my horse."

"One of the most extraordinary adventures I ever heard,"
said the Commander. "And you actually left Norwich on
this public enterprise? It is most patriotic; but, sir, you will
pardon me for saying, most quixotic. And you are a
physician?"

"Yes; M.D., of Edinburgh. Fenthorpe is my name."

"Fenthorpe! Did you say Fenthorpe?"

"Yes, Commander; Fenthorpe."

"This is most extraordinary," said the Commander, as if speaking to himself. "I know the name—Fenthorpe, of Norwich. I became acquainted with it in a curious way. May I ask, Dr. Fenthorpe, are you related to the Reverend Henry Fenthorpe?"

"He was my father. Did you know him?"

"He was your father, do you say? Is he not living?"

"My father died in the year 1794."

"I never heard of his death. I never knew him personally. I became acquainted with circumstances connected with your family in a curious way. I wrote—I suppose the letter was not received— it must have been a month ago, to the Reverend Henry Fenthorpe."

"Sir," said Richard, again sitting up, "Commander, it is ignorant of me not to know, but is it possible that you are Mr. Groves?"

"That is my name. I see, you have heard nothing the last week or two, or you would have heard."

"This is amazing! How excited my mother will be when she hears this. Mr. Groves—I beg your pardon, Commander —that letter was received. It was delivered to my mother's house in Norwich—I live with her—and she opened it. She was my father's executrix. It brought the whole thing up again. You read the document, I presume?"

"I did, and it interested me very much. I am, perhaps you know, a lawyer——"

"I know," said Richard."

"It interested me as a lawyer. The loss of a will that is known to have existed at one time——"

"Pardon me, sir, you remember, if you have the contents of old Mr. Armitage's memorandum in your mind, he doubted if there ever was a will."

"I am not of that belief. I am of opinion that there was a will. What has become of it is another thing."

"When I come, if I ever come," said Richard, "to tell my

mother of this, my meeting with you, it will confirm all her impressions. I need not, however, speak of that. You see, when this began, I was an infant, and never heard of it till the time of my father's death. But my mother has had it always in her memory. She has never flinched in the belief that there was a will, and I think she believes that it will turn up yet. I do not, but I do not say so to her."

"It is very interesting," said Mr. Groves after a pause. "There are one or two points that the memorandum does not make clear. What was the relationship between the testator and your father?"

"They were distant cousins. They were brought up together, living in the same house, Fenthorpe Hall, till my father went to Cambridge. Then there was another relationship, for my grandfather, my father's father, married the widow of Mr. Fenthorpe, the lawyer, the father of the testator Charles. People often spoke of him and my father as half-brothers, so I have understood; but they were not, for Mrs. Fenthorpe, the lawyer's widow, was not Charles Fenthorpe's mother, but his stepmother."

"I see. Now, what relation was Mr. Mortland to Charles Fenthorpe?"

"His sister's son. He is Scotch."

"I am aware of that. His public character is not what one likes, though that has nothing to do with this. I asked you about this relationship, Dr. Fenthorpe, so as to judge, so far as relationship may have had influence, is it intrinsically likely that Mr. Fenthorpe would have bequeathed his property to one rather than to the other. There are sometimes, also, family quarrels, and things that have influence on people in making their wills. It is plain to me that he volunteered his information to your father, and that must outweigh any consideration based on probabilities only; at the same time, one is not to neglect probabilities. What was Mrs. Fenthorpe—your mother's—maiden name?"

"Grayswell."

"I do not know it. I should tell you, I found——"

"Sir," interrupted Richard, "will you pardon me?" He proceeded to detail Mrs. Fenthorpe's investigations, her interviews with Allonby, and her meeting with Robert Mortland. He told Mr. Groves, also, that Mr. Mortland had systematically treated his mother with avoidance—not overt hostility, but avoidance, and a species of hauteur. The rest of the Mortland family did not imitate this, but there was, naturally, no great intimacy.

"Were I to regard this merely as a lawyer," said Mr. Groves, when Richard's narrative was concluded, "without its being brought before me as it has been, it would be interesting. As it is, it is profoundly interesting, the more so because every particular that you have told me is confirmatory of my belief in the existence of a will. At the same time—you will repeat all this conversation of ours to Mrs. Fenthorpe, whom, I doubt not, you will see soon; you must return home so soon as ever you are able to move—all this brings you no nearer to the will. It may be impossible to convince a lady of that; but we lawyers are logical. I do not think I ever heard of a will being lost for thirty years and then found. I have known deeds to be lost for nearly as long, and, after it was thought they were destroyed, to reappear. A will is different."

"Will you tell me where lies' the difference?" asked Richard.

"A will is always searched for at the time that there are the fewest probabilities against its being found. The loss of a will that is known to have existed is the very rarest thing. The mislaying of a deed is not a very unusual thing. I must not forget to tell you I found another memorandum in old Mr. Armitage's writing, relating to Mr. Mortland having removed his business. Mr. Armitage evidently thought that an excuse was made."

"And that the design was to get rid of him?"

"He believed so, I think. It is not very material. From what you tell me, it is to be expected that Mrs. Fenthorpe will think that it points in the same direction as all the rest; as it does."

"My mother will say so, I daresay. You have not that memorandum in your possession?"

"It is in Armitage's old house in Bloomsbury; at present, inaccessible. You are much better, Dr. Fenthorpe, than I had expected to find you from Dr. Tarring's report. I hope you may be able to travel shortly."

"I thank you, Commander; I hope the same. Now, will you tell me what is being done to recover London and defeat Bonaparte? Was the battle that I heard of so disastrous that we can do nothing?"

"It was a terrible defeat; but it divided our army, and did not by any means destroy it. They took Cambridge, and have fortified it since, so that it is thought it could not be taken except by a regular siege, which would require fifty thousand men, and guns in proportion. We find the greatest difficulty in knowing the exact force of the enemy in various places. If they have sixty thousand in London, it is the very utmost, in my opinion, and in General Langton's also."

"Who is General Langton?"

"He commands this defence; I am under him, and so is Colonel Blessingburn. Most of the organisation of the defence on this side has been left to me; the regular troops, nearly ten thousand, are directly under General Langton's command. Well, the great battle was on Thursday week; on Saturday and Sunday, there were three minor battles, in all which we were successful, and punished Bonaparte. You see, his want of cavalry is against him, though he has no end of guns. The determination of our Government is to leave nothing to chance, and to gather the remaining strength of the kingdom into one mass, and then pour it on London. General Waller-ton, the new Commander-in-Chief——"

"What! Is Sir D—— no longer Commander-in-Chief?"

"No; the storm raised against him was too great. I do not know the merits, but more confidence is felt in General Wallerton than ever there was in Sir D——. There have been hardly any of the volunteers of the western counties employed yet. They are now being assembled at Reading and the neighbourhood, and the project is to add to them all of the regular army possible, and then move on London by both sides of the Thames. If we had fifteen thousand more than we have here now in Surrey, General Langton would attack the enemy across Westminster Bridge. We are getting materials together for a pontoon bridge at Chelsea, and we believe that a joint attack across the river and from Hounslow side must be invincible."

"You are sanguine, Commander."

"We are all sanguine. But we are going to be cautious. You see, there are so many volunteers, more liable to fluctuation of spirits than old troops; and another heavy defeat would discourage them awfully, and must not be risked. Every day we are improving, and Bonaparte is making no way, at the very best for him."

"Another thing. Why is Yarmouth not attacked by sea?"

"Yarmouth has been evacuated. It is supposed that the neighbourhood is infested with them; but the King's ships need not be sent to batter down one of our own ports that there is no enemy in."

"I see; and is anything really known of the condition of Norfolk?"

"I cannot tell you what is known at headquarters. Unless there were something considerable, it would scarcely be communicated to us here. I almost think that some trading from the Thames to Yarmouth has recommenced. If so, will you try to return home that way?"

"By sea?"

"It would be your speediest way, if you could get some vessel sailing from Gravesend. I will have inquiries made if you like. After the way you have acted, Dr. Fenthorpe, you are entitled to all, and more than all, that can be done for you."

"But I should not be fulfilling my commission. It is nothing that it is self-imposed. I regard it as my business, my duty, to bring word to Norfolk what is being done for the county, and to bring such instructions as I can get for the people, what they are to do. Now, Commander, you have no instructions that you can give me, have you?"

"I have not, indeed, nor authority to give any; nor could General Langton give any. I see how it is; you must travel by Bedford. I will give you a letter to Lord Camden, who will attend to you; and I will give you also a letter to an artillery officer there, who will explain to you the military position, which none of us more than half understand. Now, Dr. Fenthorpe, I must take leave of you for to-day; I have to go to the other side. And get well as fast as you can."

"You have to go to the other side! Can you cross safely?"

"Perfectly, except for a chance shot, a very chance shot. They cannot get a gun to bear on us. On Saturday night they erected a battery on the terrace of Somerset House; and in the morning, with our eighteens and thirty-twos, we dismounted every gun in three-quarters of an hour."

"Now, good day."

CHAPTER XVI.

THE OTHER WITNESS.

DR. TARRING, on visiting his patient in the evening, found him restless, and his pulse much higher. Fearing feverish symptoms, he gave him a strong sedative, which produced a good night's sleep, the first which Richard had had for many nights. In the morning, Dr. Tarring pronounced him convalescent, but another day of rest was necessary before it would be prudent for him to move.

On Thursday morning, being provided with a good horse vice the lamented John Hunter, Dr. Fenthorpe quitted the Elephant and Castle on his journey to Bedford. He took with him the Commander's letter to the Secretary of State and also that to Major Tomlinson of the artillery. "That is a Norfolk name," he remarked when he received the letter.

"I do not know if he be of Norfolk or not," replied Mr. Groves. "I have asked Colonel Blessingburn about the means of trying to clear that part of the country of the enemy. He says that Bonaparte is making a military error in continuing to occupy it, and that it is one that he has made before, to keep a grasp on everything he once seizes, whether its continued possession be important or not. Colonel Blessingburn says also that, for an English force to penetrate into that country, while they hold the almost impregnable position of Wisbeach, is very difficult at present. The only way is by Ely, and the rivers are very high."

"If that be so," said Richard, "I may have to get into Norfolk from one of the small ports in Lincolnshire."

"They can tell you more at headquarters than we can. I will write to you, Dr. Fenthorpe, under cover to Major Tomlinson at Bedford. You shall wish to know what is going on here. Now, good-bye, and may we meet again at a more propitious time."

The traveller reached Bedford the following night. Several times on the road he met the mounted post of four dragoons galloping past him and galloping by him. There was no other sign of the country being engaged in a war for its existence.

He sought Major Tomlinson on Saturday morning before presenting his letter to Lord Camden. That officer was a Norfolk man, as he had supposed, a relative of Mr. Tomlinson of Wymondham. He knew Dr. Fenthorpe by report, although he was ignorant of the remarkable expedition on which he had left home. All this was to tell before they began to discuss military matters.

"There is a letter for you, Dr. Fenthorpe," said the major. "I forgot it till this moment."

It was from Commander Groves, and was very short. "To-day, after you left, there was a general attack on all the bridges, and they have made a lodgment in Thames Street. We hope to expel them to-morrow."

"You have not heard of this?" Richard asked, as he handed the letter to the officer.

"No; it is not good news. No doubt they have it at head-quarters. Do you understand the plans of defence?"

"Only generally, and I know nothing about military affairs but what I have heard. I know that Commander Groves regards Thames Street as a very important part of the system."

"It will be right," said the major, "not to speak of this, either of us, unless we hear it spoken of. Now, about the relief of Norfolk, about which, as a Norfolk man, I am more interested, perhaps, than most. We have force enough of volunteers to attempt it by a double operation, which I will explain to you. But it is a principle to mix the regular troops and volunteers in every undertaking. I heard yesterday that two battalions on the way from Scotland are to be diverted from the great rendezvous on the Upper Thames to help an attack on Wisbeach; but it is not authentic. My plan would be—the plan is, you understand, to make a simultaneous attack from Ely—my plan would be to cross the Nene in boats below Wisbeach, when it would become untenable without our having to fire a shot. If the Ely force, at the same time, could avoid entangling itself in the fens and rivers, and could reach the solid country, we could make all their forces in Norfolk and Suffolk surrender."

"Well," said Richard, his face brightening, "you know about this better than I, but I am delighted to hear what you say. I am much impressed, Major Tomlinson, by the confident tone with which both Commander Groves and yourself speak; cautious, at the same time."

"The firm determination at headquarters is to do nothing rash. A rash act, if successful, might gain a day, but, if unsuccessful, might lose a week. Are you going to my Lord Camden's?"

"I must deliver my letter and crave an interview. I suppose it is very unlikely that his lordship can see me at once."

Major Tomlinson walked with Dr. Fenthorpe to Lord Camden's residence, and on the way told him that there was an utter uncertainty as to the number and localities of the enemy's forces in the whole country east of Cambridge. It was believed that there were fifteen thousand French in that town, with a great force of artillery. The whole west side of it was a row of batteries. They had three or four thousand horse between Cambridge, Hertford, and London, which made incursions ten and fifteen miles round. On the line from Wisbeach to London, in fact, the enemy were ubiquitous. They had never been nearer Ely than on the day of the great battle, but their position in front of the Isle of Ely was covered by the nature of the ground. "That whole country," said Major Tomlinson, "is just like Holland and Flanders, and, even without artificial defences, is extremely strong."

Lord Camden could not be seen on that day. During the afternoon a rumour spread that a messenger had arrived from London with proposals from Bonaparte. Richard heard it, and hastened to Major Tomlinson's quarters to learn if the rumour were true.

All that was certain was that a carriage and four, with a coat of arms painted out, had arrived in Bedford at about six o'clock, and had driven to Mr. Pitt's residence. The occupant of the carriage had not been recognised. He had returned to his carriage after a short interview with Mr. Pitt, and had then driven out of the town, not in the direction of London. Mr. Pitt had visited Lord Harrowby and the Duke of Rutland.

Nothing more could be learned. Richard could only hope that he should be able to see Lord Camden on the next day, Sunday, and then depart for home; by what route had yet to be determined.

It was five o'clock on Sunday before he saw Lord Camden. The Secretary could tell him not very much more than he had already heard, but he confirmed most of it. An attack on the enemy east of the Fen country was being organised, and the precise day that it would be commenced depended on the arrival at Peterborough of two battalions from Scotland. It would be made with such a force that success would be placed beyond reasonable doubt. Some information oozed out now and then from Norfolk and Suffolk. There was no force of the enemy whatever in the latter county, excepting such as was required to guard the great hospital at Bury. About Norfolk less was known. The force of the enemy there, altogether, was estimated at from eight to sixteen thousand. Lord Camden thought it could not be so much as the larger figure. Many disorders had taken place in Norfolk, particulars unknown, and all plan of conciliating the inhabitants had been utterly relinquished by the enemy.

" Can your lordship inform me if the enemy occupy King's Lynn ? "

" Our information is that it was never occupied by them, and it probably is not now, for it is their obvious policy to concentrate at Wisbeach. They know of our projected advance in that direction. Are you thinking, Dr. Fenthorpe, of your best route for reaching Norwich ? "

" I am, my lord."

"Then I think you should get into Lincolnshire, and cross to Lynn over that arm of the sea. But I speak in much ignorance, for all information from that distance is a day late. I will give you a circular-letter to all general and other officers to assist you, actively and by advice, in every way. The services that you meant to do your country, Dr. Fenthorpe, and your fellow-citizens, although their issue has been unfortunate to yourself, are such as your country ought to be grateful for. Dr. Fenthorpe, they place you, if I may so say, on a pinnacle."

"My lord, you flatter me, and I hope——"

"I do not mean to flatter you, sir. Your behaviour, when it comes to be known, has been so uncommon, so—— I assure you, sir, the mere contemplation delights me. Not a word, pray. Is there anything now that you desire to suggest?"

"I think it would be desirable that your lordship should, by a letter to the Mayor of Norwich, signify that his Majesty's Government have been solicitous for the deliverance of his subjects of that county; and that you should counsel them to rely on the relief that will shortly be sent, and not on doubtful and irregular efforts."

"It shall be done, Dr. Fenthorpe. You intend to depart to-morrow?"

"To-morrow early, my lord."

"I shall have such a despatch ready, and also the letter for yourself, at nine this evening, when perhaps you will come. Now, sir, God speed you on your journey."

Nothing more could be learned about the negotiation, if there had been any, with Bonaparte. Many officers whom Richard met thought it must be a mistake. But late on Sunday afternoon he had a letter from Mr. Groves, saying that the communication between the bridges was restored. When he told Major Tomlinson of this, the major, who was overjoyed, said that perhaps there was some connection between the two circumstances, a remark that Richard was unable to understand.

On Monday he started early, intending to reach Peter-

P

borough that night. But eight miles short of that city, his horse went lame. For four miles he struggled on, till he came to a house that had the look of an inn, although there was no sign. It was close by the roadside, large, with large windows, and a large yard, with stables, at one side. The door was shut. Richard knocked.

A most respectable looking man, of perhaps fifty years of age, and with the look of one exposed to weather, as farmers are, opened the door. "Perhaps I make a mistake," said Richard, "I took this for an inn."

"It was, at one time," said the tenant of the house. "It is not now. Your horse gone lame, sir? You must be travelling about some business in earnest to be travelling now. Come in, sir, and I'll see what can be done."

"Thank you," said Richard, and dismounted. He had replenished his wardrobe in the Borough, and had on his greatcoat, with a shirt or two in the pockets.

The farmer led the horse to the yard. "Jack," he cried, "where's Bill?"

"Here, master," said two voices.

"Come and see what's the matter with this horse."

Bill lifted his feet one by one and pronounced the near fore foot to have been hurt by something, and went for a smith, two hundred yards off, to remove the shoe. The shoe off, the smith and Bill agreed that the horse ought not to travel that evening, nor the next day either. The farmer went to tell the traveller the extent of his misfortune. While doing so, which he did less concisely than we narrate it, he opened a cupboard, and produced strong waters of various nationalities.

"This is troublesome, I fear, to both of us," said Richard. "I must go on immediately to Peterborough. How far is it?"

"Take something first," said his host. They sat down. A woman, tall and handsome, though not young, well, and some would say expensively, dressed for a farmer's wife, came into the room. She had on her bonnet and shawl. Richard stood up, and bowed.

"There is no meeting to-night, William," she said. "Sir," to Richard, "I hear that your horse is lamed. This is a dispensation; but if you are on the Lord's work, it will be found a blessing and not a misfortune."

"It is a misfortune at this moment," answered Richard. "I am on a journey that I must accomplish with the least delay, and I must go to Peterborough and buy another horse, and leave this horse with some one that will take care of him."

"Is your journey so important as that, sir?" said the lady. "Though I should not ask, for no one would travel for nothing at these times. May I make so free, sir, as to ask where you are journeying to?"

"I am on my way to Norwich."

"To Norwich!" exclaimed the man. "And how can you get to Norwich?"

"I shall ask my way at Peterborough. I suppose that I shall have to get into Lincolnshire, and cross the water to King's Lynn. I was so advised at Bedford."

"At Bedford! Where the army is?"

"Yes; I came from Bedford to-day."

"But you're not an officer?"

"No; I am not. You, sir and madam, have received me very kindly and hospitably, a stranger, and I should tell you that, though I am not an officer, I am travelling to Norwich with a despatch from the army. That is the reason I must not delay."

"Then you are upon the King's business?"

"I am a private person. This opportunity offered for the despatch being sent. I live in Norwich, you see."

"And, sir—I am inquisitive—may I make so free as to ask what brought you to the army at Bedford?"

Richard smiled. He had no secrets to keep. "I came to Bedford from London."

Both the man and his wife stood up. "From London! Where Bonaparte is! And how did you escape out of his hands? The Lord," said the lady, "surely hath you in his keeping."

"I believe that He has," said Richard. "He has us all in His keeping. He has England in His keeping, though this evil has fallen upon us."

"Bonaparte is the Man of Sin," said the lady. "He is the Beast of the Revelations. His number is six hundred three score and six. It cannot be the Lord's purpose that England should be delivered into his power. And how, sir, is the war prospering?"

"Those persons," answered Richard, "who know the most, and can judge the best, are now very hopeful. Yesterday evening, I heard from good authority of a defeat that Bonaparte received the day before in London."

"In London! Is there fighting in London streets?"

"There has been very hard fighting. London, you know, is on the river Thames, and Bonaparte's army has only the north side of the river. The bridges are armed to keep him out of the south side; and that is where the fighting is."

"On the very bridges of London?"

"In the streets on the north side of them. Our army and volunteers have both ends of the bridges, with cannon, and they are confident that they can keep the French from passing."

He told them all his adventures. The farmer's wife was more impressed with the manner in which General Berthier had dismissed him than with any other incident. She called it being delivered out of the mouth of the lion. The farmer was more struck with the manner in which Berthier stole the horse. At that period, horse-stealing was the climax of wickedness in the judgment of the agricultural mind.

"And you live in Norwich?" said the host, after the history was told. "I lived near Norwich once, when I was a young man. Four miles out of Norwich it was, at a place called Fenthorpe. I suppose you know it, sir?"

"I do," said Richard, rather surprised.

"I suppose Mr. Fenthorpe, the clergyman, lives there now —that is, if he is alive?"

"Mr. Fenthorpe, the clergyman—my father! Did not I

tell you my name is Fenthorpe? No, he is not living there. He never lived at Fenthorpe Hall, except when he was a boy."

"Your name is Fenthorpe, sir!" The farmer took a good look at him. "This is past the common. I remember well of your father, seeing him in Norwich city, and two or three times, or may be oftener, out at the Hall. I thought Mr. Charles would have left him the estate. And who is living there, sir?"

"Mr. Mortland."

"Is that Mr. Charles's sister's son?"

"Yes."

"And Mr. Charles Fenthorpe left Fenthorpe Hall to him?"

"He did."

"I never would have thought that. I certainly never would have thought that."

"Why," said Richard, curiously interested, "did you think Mr. Fenthorpe had left my father the estate?"

"I did think it. He made a will, you know."

"He made a will, leaving it to his nephew. "

"He made a will, just a short time before he was drowned; and most surely I did think he left his estate to Mr. Fenthorpe, the clergyman—the same name, and everything."

We can hardly tell whether Richard was more amazed or puzzled at this. "He made a will," he repeated the words, "just a short time before he was drowned?"

"He did, sir; surely you must know that?"

"How do you know that he did?"

"How do I know? I signed it for him."

Richard Fenthorpe's amazement at this was greater than his puzzlement. He stared at the man, and then at his wife, and then at the man again, till his blue eyes were nearly black. "You signed Charles Fenthorpe's will as a witness."

"Yes, a witness—that's what he called it."

"And what—you have not told me your name."

"My name is William Bannox. My father was bailiff on Fenthorpe estate. You can't have known him, sir?"

"No; I remember hearing his name. Mr. Bannox, you

were not at Fenthorpe Hall at the time that Charles Fenthorpe lost his life by drowning?"

"I was not, sir; or would you rather for me to call you doctor?"

"Thank you, Mr. Bannox; most of my friends call me doctor."

"Well, doctor, I had a good education; and at that time Norfolk farming was thought the best, far over everything, in England. I heard of a place as bailiff in Lincolnshire, a long way beyond Lincoln, and Mr. Fenthorpe, he recommended me for it; and I was engaged, and I went away to Lincolnshire, it may be a month, more or less, before Mr. Fenthorpe was drowned, on his journey. I heard a great many months after about his being drowned; and from that day to this—and it is nigh thirty years ago—I never heard the name of Fenthorpe, or of Fenthorpe Hall, spoken. And I did think that Mr. Charles—he was always called that—left the clergyman, that is, your father, the estate."

"And tell me, Mr. Bannox, how long before you left that for Lincolnshire was it that this will was executed?"

"Executed?"

"You witnessed Mr. Fenthorpe's signature; he signed it in your presence?"

"He did; leastways, he did it this way. He sent for me, and brought me into the large room in the Hall; and there was a man of the name of Toby Allonby, that was—what surprises you, sir?"

"Toby Allonby; that is what surprises me. I will tell you presently."

"Allonby was sexton of Brandwood Church; that is the name of the parish, and there is nothing in it but Fenthorpe Hall and Squire Tronford's estates, but there is no house on it. He—that is, Allonby—had the name of doing some things that he ought not; no matter about that. Well, Mr. Fenthorpe took a sheet of paper—it was thin paper—out of a desk, with writing upon it, and showed me his own name written at the bottom of it, and Allonby's name written below it—not straight below it, but crooked below it. Then he took a pen without ink in it, and passed the pen over his name, like as if he was writing his name, and he desired me and Allonby to witness that he had signed it. After that he took wax—there was a candle on the table—and made a seal and pressed it; and then gave the pen to Allonby and told him to pass it over his name in like way as he had done; and last of all, he dipped the pen in ink and made me write my name."

Richard Fenthorpe had never heard of such an execution of a will before, and wondered if it were according to law; but the chief interest to him of this account was the light that it threw on Allonby's varying statements. That clever prevaricator, when asked about his signature, had answered one set of questions as if they were about his signing when the pen had ink in it, and had answered another set of questions as if they were about the final signature in the dining-room of Fenthorpe Hall. What was the man's object in these lies was a question still impossible to answer.

"How long," the doctor asked, "before you left Fenthorpe was this?"

"I left Fenthorpe two days after that. Mr. Charles sent Allonby out of the room, and he made me a present of three guineas, and he told me he hoped I would do Norfolk credit where I was going. And I think I did, for there I found her"—here Mr. Bannox regarded his wife steadfastly—"which she is as good a wife as ever a man had, and a trifle of money besides; except only that she holds by the Methodists, and I hold by the Church. For all that, she comes to Church on Christmas Day and Easter Sunday, always, and I go to the Meeting when they have a greater man than the common. But for all that she is real good."

Mrs. Bannox looked at her husband somewhat sternly when he began his eulogium, but her countenance rather changed to softness as he concluded; and Richard felt disposed to believe that the eulogium was both deserved and sincere.

"Mr. Bannox," he asked next, "you know, perhaps, that your father did not remain long after Mr. Mortland came?"

" He can't have stayed very long, for when I had been two years in Lincolnshire I had a letter from my sister to say they had gone to Marlborough, in Wiltshire—it had that post-mark. And ten years after, I had a letter from her to say he was dead. And about three, or it may be four, years ago, I got a newspaper by the post office, that was printed in Bristol. Who sent it I don't know. I gave it to her to read, and she found of my sister's death in it, Sarah Bannox."

" You remember the year, the year you witnessed the will, and when you left Norfolk? "

" Certain; the year of our Lord one thousand seven hundred and seventy-five—thirty years ago come this summer."

" Mr. Bannox," said Richard, after a pause, " I have now to tell you what you, as a witness of that will, are entitled to know. Charles Fenthorpe visited my father a day or two before he left home on that journey in which he met his death. He told him he had made a will bequeathing him his estate, and that the will was in his attorney's hands. When the body was recovered, it was brought home for burial, and the attorney, Mr. Armitage by name, came from London for the funeral. He had not the will; he had another will, made several years before, leaving the estate to Mr. Mortland. The will that you witnessed was searched for, but was not found, nor has it been found from that day to this."

While he was speaking, the mouths of Mr. and Mrs. Bannox opened, and continued to expand till his statement was con-cluded. Then Mr. Bannox shut his mouth, and opened it again instantly for the reception of some brandy and water. Mrs. Bannox, when she had collected her faculties, which were, however, never very far off, uttered this very unlawyer-like opinion:

" But it can't have signified, when your father knew what it was."

" Oh, no ! " Richard corrected her; " it made all the difference."

" Do you mean, doctor," said Mr. Bannox, " that your father did not get the estate? "

"Certainly not, because Charles Fenthorpe's last will did not leave it to him. We know now that there was, at one time, a later will than that last will; but it has not been found, and has no existence—none in law, even though we knew its contents by a person who has actually seen and even witnessed it."

"But that is not justice."

"It never appeared to me," said Richard, "that it is not just. The law has provided wise safeguards about the making and proving of people's wills. If a misfortune has happened to my father and to me by the loss of a document, it is not a wrong because it is a misfortune. If the law permitted laxity in the matter of wills, many injustices, greater than any that we suffer, would almost certainly be done."

"Sir," said Mrs. Bannox, "you seem to take this in a Christian spirit, without murmuring. May I ask you, sir, have you never murmured?"

"I do not think I have. I met no disappointment. I was more than twenty years old when I first heard of this, at the time of my father's death. It was not to me that Charles Fenthorpe promised the estate. My father suffered from the disappointment, as I suppose any one would; and he suffered, too, so my mother has told me, from a doubt whether his cousin had not been deceiving him. Mr. Bannox, what kind of a man was Mr. Fenthorpe?"

"He had the name of being slippery and secret, but those that served him liked him. If he saw a man doing anything wrong—shirking, or the like of that—he would watch the man and come down upon him in the way of serving him a trick; and he would laugh at the man, and make people laugh at him, till the man would go away with a flea in his ear. Pray, sir, what did Allonby say about this? Is Toby Allonby living?"

"He is living. I saw him about a month ago, professionally, as his physician. Allonby was asked was there a will, for Mr. Fenthorpe had been observed with him three or four times just before he left home on that journey. He gave very crooked answers, and told more than one story. Nothing could be made out of him, and he was not believed."

"Just the kind of man he was; he was a regular bad case. And he's living yet? Well, well!"

"Dr. Fenthorpe," said Mrs. Bannox, "have you any hope or expectation of finding that will?"

"None; I have no ground for any such thing. It is not till now, this very hour, that I know certainly that there was this will at all at any time. Mr. Armitage, the attorney, believed that my father had made a mistake, and that Mr. Fenthorpe only told him he would leave him the estate, not that he had done so. A lawyer, a very eminent lawyer, has told me that to find a will, lost so long as this has been, is a thing that never happened, or never happened that he heard of."

"If the attorney was not an honest man?" said Mrs. Bannox. "My father had a dispute with a neighbour about his cattle trespassing, and he went to an attorney; but he could get no justice, and the attorney made him pay eight pounds. I don't believe attorneys are honest."

"Mrs. Bannox, if you were sick and ill, and you sent for me and I did not cure you, but nevertheless made you pay me a fee, would you say I was not honest? Mr. Armitage was a man known and trusted by every one that knew him. And if he was not, he is dead this many a year. And there is an end of the whole matter."

"I shall not be surprised if you do find it some time," said Mrs. Bannox. "It is a remarkable dispensation. If it be the Lord's will that you should come into your lawful estate, you will come into it; and if it be not His will, you will not."

With this absolutely safe prophecy, the discussion ended. If Mrs. Bannox had been told that it was as much a dispensation that Mr. Mortland had received the property as it was that Mr. Fenthorpe had not, she would have been puzzled. People find it hard to believe that the sun rises on both bad and good, and that rain falls on both righteous and unrighteous. Large words, like dispensation and Mesopotamia, often pervert people's ideas of Scripture truth. The same influence is occasionally exercised with effect, in a similar way, when an expert witness gives evidence before a stupid judge and an ignorant jury.

Richard rose to go. "What do you recommend me to do, Mr. Bannox," he said, "about my horse? Shall I take him round and leave him with the smith till I can send for him?"

"Doctor," replied Bannox, "leave your horse to me. Must you go at once to Peterborough?"

"I must not delay. You see, I am not on my own business."

"No, doctor; you are on the King's business. Look here! I will lend you a horse—least ways, that is, a mare—and you will return her when you can. I am proud, doctor, for to do so much."

"Mr. Bannox, be sure I thank you; and I will not say nay. You may be long till you get your mare back. But I am unknown to you, and you are behaving to me as if I was known to you. I will buy your mare. What do you put on her? I can go as far as thirty guineas." He took out his purse.

"Doctor, did you ever hear that it takes two for to make a bargain? Well, I won't sell my mare."

Richard laughed. "When the French general took my horse, the bargain was made without two to it."

"Well, doctor, if so be if you are going to steal my mare, then it would be a case similar. Come out and see her. She'll carry you well. We are nigh Peterborough here; four miles and a half, it may be. You are not hurried."

He lodged in Peterborough that night, and learned that preparations for the attack on Wisbeach and deliverance of Norfolk were in a forward state. He crossed the river Nene by the ferry where Charles Fenthorpe was drowned thirty years before, by night, and arrived in Norwich, without having seen a French soldier since he had been in London, on the evening of Thursday, the eleventh of April.

CHAPTER XVII.

THE TIDE TURNS.

THE hour at which Mrs. Fenthorpe received her son's letter from Wymondham on the evening of the Wednesday after the Monday when he had started on his journey, was too late for her to communicate its contents to Helen that evening. Early the next day she found an opportunity of telling the Mayor of Norwich of Richard's change of plan. Household engagements prevented her from going to Mrs. Cardwain's till that time of the day when the ladies were in the habit of receiving visitors.

Robert Mortland was in Mrs. Cardwain's drawing-room when she entered it. She sat down, after greeting her sister and the rest of the occupants of the room. Mr. Mortland poured out small talk in a large voice to Fanny Tronford; but Helen was absent. In about ten minutes, after casting sundry glances at the door, he took his leave.

At the very instant that the butler closed the hall door on Mr. Mortland's back, Helen came into the drawing-room. " My dearest Helen," said Mrs. Fenthorpe.

They kissed each other. It may not be known to the present generation, but so it was, that for a young woman and for an older middle-aged one to kiss each other meant more at that time than it does now. " Helen," said Mrs. Fenthorpe, " come here." They withdrew into a recess or back room.

" Helen," whispered the elder lady, " Richard is gone to London."

" To London ! " exclaimed Helen in a subdued voice, yet agitated.

" He thought it safer. You are not alarmed, love ? "

228

"No; he knows best. Oh, Mrs. Fenthorpe!"

"Helen, love, command yourself. You, only, are to know this. You, and the Mayor, you know, who knows about it. Not your aunt, nor Fanny."

"Mrs. Fenthorpe, is that all?"

"That is all. He was advised that it is impossible for him to travel to the west, and this side is clear of the enemy. Love, as you say, he knows best. I have no doubt we shall hear soon again. Now we will go and talk to them. But oh, Helen! I remarked you did not come into the room till this minute."

Helen Tronford glanced round. "Mrs. Fenthorpe," she said, still whispering, "Mr. Mortland has been going on, I can hardly describe it to you; and, Richard being away, I thought it best—you understand."

"My dearest, I do, thoroughly. You are quite right. But, Helen, don't be too distant."

"I cannot be rude to him, because he was so useful, you know, Mrs. Fenthorpe, about that time they wanted to remove us; and he behaved so well, and has behaved so well. But you know one can't—you know, there are lengths—you know——"

"I know perfectly, Helen. Now, let us speak to your aunt —my sister, I mean."

Helen smiled. Mrs. Cardwain was not her aunt, but Mrs. Fenthorpe habitually forgot that. "Isabella," said the latter, "I have been remonstrating with Helen about the encouragement——"

"Encouragement!" exclaimed Miss Dorkington, who had seen it all, "encouragement!"

"Well, Miss Dorkington, perhaps not that. You know I am not a person——"

"You are a person!" exclaimed Helen. "You are the dearest person in the world!" She rushed up to her and embraced her, and fled from the room.

"I don't think you can have scolded her very severely, Elizabeth," said Mrs. Cardwain. "I was quite pleased at her not coming down. He comes here every day, the idle fellow; she said last night she would only see him every other time, so she began to-day."

"Mrs. Fenthorpe," said Miss Dorkington, after they had done with this subject, which took a longer time to discuss than any result from the discussion justified, "do you know that the French garrison was changed this morning?"

"No. Changed?"

"The four hundred soldiers that have been here since the rest went, last Saturday or Sunday, left this morning, at or before daylight, and are replaced by a larger number, that are supposed to have come from Yarmouth. It is the butcher that told us."

"Yes," said Mrs. Cardwain; "I wonder if he knows."

"I will go and find out from the Mayor," said Mrs. Fenthorpe, rising. "Don't you see how important it may be to Richard when he comes back? If they all are new soldiers and officers, his absence will never be perceived. Don't you see, Isabella?"

"I hope," said Mrs. Cardwain when her sister had left the room, "I hope he may ever come back. Jonathan thinks he must be mad."

"Mrs. Cardwain," said Miss Dorkington, "Richard Fenthorpe knows what he is about."

"I hope so," said Mrs. Cardwain, sighing helplessly. It is no wonder that people sighed helplessly in those times. Let us not despise her, nor even her husband.

The butcher's intelligence was correct, excepting that the relief garrison had come from Lowestoft, not from Yarmouth. At the same time, the garrison of the latter port was advanced three miles inland. Two or three craft, which the French thought suspicious, had appeared on the coast, and they thought it judicious not to give our sailors and marines an opportunity of showing what they were made of. It was of even more importance to Richard's personal safety than his mother supposed, that his absence should be unremarked by the enemy. There were no spies among the English, as the

Mayor of Norwich had feared. But, even without them, any-thing at all that would not bear explanation according to his lawless code would have been no protection to an Englishman from such a ruffian as Davoust.

Robert Mortland did not leave off visiting at Mrs. Card-wain's although he did not see Helen every time that he came. When he did see her, he rather dropped his impetuosity. Then, after a few days, he began again. By that time, Helen was becoming anxious, for the week that Richard had allowed for his absence was considerably over-passed. She feared to betray herself, for their secret was still religiously kept; and for mere weariness, she allowed Mr. Mortland to become more pressing, not that he ever allowed his suit to develop itself into words.

Still no news, except that every one knew now. about the battle of Ipswich. But on Saturday evening there was a grand salvo of artillery fired at the Castle, and it came to be surmised, and then known, that the enemy had gained a great victory. Then it came to be known that the last battle had been fought at Cambridge.

Mrs. Fenthorpe saw here the hand of a protecting provi-dence over her son, who had been diverted from his journey to that country, and had gone to London. But Monday came, and he had been away for a fortnight, and did not return; and Tuesday and Wednesday—no news.

Yes, some news. General Davoust had come back to his old quarters at Fenthorpe Hall, to Mr. Mortland's great dis-quietude. He came in as he had gone out, without a word of greeting or politeness. He could not have behaved with less ceremony at an inn. He brought back Captain Balutin with him, and that officer rode into Norwich almost every day, Robert being in his company.

Mrs. Fenthorpe was walking one day with her brother-in-law, when they encountered the Mayor. They stopped and spoke of Richard. "When I see you, Mrs. Fenthorpe," said the Mayor, "I am filled with remorse that I helped to send your son on that errand."

"It is for the best," she said. "I have no fears. He will return safe and sound. He has escaped one danger; he will escape them all." She looked as she believed what she said; and she did believe it, though the tension was growing extreme.

"More knowledge is trickling in," said the Mayor, "of what is going on in England." People had come to that by this time that they spoke of England as the Scotch islanders habitually do of the mainland. "We think it is nearly certain that their victory at Cambridge was not followed up. Bonaparte has gone to London, and one report is that it is because he had nowhere else to go to."

"I am told," said Mr. Cardwain, "that there are far more horses to be seen in some parts of the country."

"A great many must have been secreted—I don't know how—and escaped capture. I heard that this general Davoust was sent here because he is the best man Bonaparte has for ransacking a country. He is a brute. Speaking of horses, Mrs. Fenthorpe, there is a dealer at Ely, who brought twenty horses from that, since the battle, right through the French, into Suffolk, and he sold them, sound and unsound, for a hundred guineas each."

"I hope Richard will bring back his," said Mrs. Fenthorpe. She said it only in order to say something. She was under a terrible strain. Her faith did not waver, but she did not know what might happen before her son would return. Her impressions did not guide her beyond the bare fact—fact it was to her, though it was no fact at all—that he would return. Those persons who believe in impressions, omens, and coincidences are not shaken or staggered when they come to a fault, as geologists say; but their nerves are tried. They nourish their faith, too, with prayer, mixing up true spiritual prayer with that which is more of the earth—earthy. People who do not pray cannot understand this; if you are certain of a thing, they say, why do you pray for it? They do not understand it, because prayer is the offspring of faith, not of doubt.

"Have you heard," said Mr. Cardwain to the Mayor, as Mrs. Fenthorpe went on towards her house, "that there have been disturbances in the neighbourhood of Yarmouth?"

"No particulars; have you heard any particulars?"

"Nothing beyond the mere report; perhaps it is not true."

"I do hope so sincerely, Mr. Cardwain. How wonderfully she bears up!"

"Wonderfully. Mrs. Cardwain and I are amazed at it. We are very anxious too. She is truly a Roman matron."

This innocent, yet slightly pompous remark of Mr. Cardwain saved the Mayor and Mrs. Fenthorpe from an annoyance and mortification. The Mayor was a widower of forty or thereabouts, without incumbrance. Mrs. Fenthorpe had five hundred a year. It would raise him socially, and he admired her excessively. But, as he walked home to dinner, the Roman matron stuck in his throat. It was an English wife he wanted; a Roman matron, he feared, would not exactly do. So, after dinner, and against he had finished his wine, he resolved, with the kind of sigh that men utter when they are not entirely dissatisfied, he resolved to give it up. These things go on amid wars and rumours of wars. In Noah's time they ate and drank, married and gave in marriage, flirted and jilted one another—though the Bible says nothing about that —to the very last. And so it will be till the end of the world.

It was true that there had been disturbances near Yarmouth. When Davoust came back to Norfolk, the system of conciliation, such as it was, when people's horses were stolen right and left, and when they were not allowed to walk along the roads freely, was discontinued, having been found to bear no fruit. Another system, more congenial to the general in command, was adopted. At first, when necessaries had been taken for the use of the French army, acknowledgments were given, so that the persons supplying the food and other things should have claims on the British Treasury. This was stopped, and goods were taken from stores and shops, and cattle from farms for slaughtering, without system, and at hazard, as momentary convenience or caprice might dictate.

Q

At the same time, discipline was a good deal relaxed. The soldiers of the enemy had been kept as much as possible from mixing, hostilely or otherwise, with the peasantry; and the same course was pursued in Norwich and the occupied towns. Now the rein was thrown loose on their necks, and some horrible consequences followed.

Outrages against women, of such a nature that it is a sin to forgive them, became, if not common, occasional. Of course, there was no redress. One particular instance, about four or five miles from Yarmouth, created fierce popular wrath over the extent of country where it was known. Two or three days after the outrage had been committed, four private soldiers came into the hamlet which had been its scene and commanded a certain fat ox to be slaughtered. A few of the inhabitants gathered round, and the animal was led out of the stall. The butcher came with his axe; but he felled, not the ox, but a Frenchman. It could not be told if this were the result of design, or a sudden insurrection. There was a fight, and the three remaining soldiers were killed. One story, adopted by the French, was that after this their bodies were taken and hanged on the branches of a tree. Whether this be so or not, when the thing was known at headquarters, Davoust ordered the burning of the hamlet and the slaughter of its population. Somehow, they got warning, and fled. Their houses, and what was in them, were destroyed, but no lives were, or could be, taken.

Then Davoust, in rage, committed a crime contrary to the laws of war as carried on even among barbarians. The seventeen young peasants, survivors of the eighteen who had foolishly plunged into the battle outside Norwich, were his prisoners. He brought two battalions into Yarmouth, escorting these seventeen youths, bound with ropes, and shot them in the market-place. He watched the execution from the inn window. Then he marched the battalions back to camp, leaving the corpses of the murdered prisoners lying where they had fallen. The people of Yarmouth buried them, devoting their murderers to the infernal gods. The father of one of the young men was that day in Yarmouth, and witnessed the execution. He went straight to a magistrate, and swore informations against the officer that had given the word to fire. He did not know his name, but said that he could identify him amongst ten thousand.

Such was Norfolk. Turn we to London. We know already, from Commander Groves's letter to Dr. Fenthorpe, that on Thursday, the fourth of April, the bridges were attacked a second time. Bonaparte, before this attack, reconnoitred the English position, and detected a flaw at a point that Mr. Groves thought had been made secure. The Commander had put up a barricade near the end of Queen Street, where, at that time, it met Thames Street, so making Thames Street one continuous close line from London Bridge to Blackfriars. None of the narrow streets opening on the north side of that line furnished a proper avenue for attack. At the time when his attack on the two bridge-heads was fully developed, and the houses of Thames Street were thinned of defenders in order to take those attacks in flank, Bonaparte suddenly ran forward into Queen Street as many of his heaviest guns as the street would hold, and battered at the barricade. It was not levelled, though the guns were loaded to their mouths; but a rush of infantry followed the firing, coming down from Cheapside, where there was a reserve held, practically unlimited in number. They climbed over the barricade, and cut Thames Street in two. Before the arrival of relief from Blackfriars, which is the nearest of the two bridges, and from whence relief could be badly enough spared, the French turned our men out of eight houses, four on each side of the street, and occupied them securely, actually cramming them with soldiers.

Although the attacks on the bridges were beaten back, as before, this was a very serious inconvenience, not to say source of danger, to the English. Desperate hand-to-hand fighting went on round and under those eight houses till night. Very few eminent commanders have favoured night fighting, but on Friday morning the battle was resumed, and continued, with great loss of life on both sides, during the day. At one moment the French reached nearly half-way to Blackfriars, but the fire from the windows drove them back. By evening, the English had retaken one house, which was equivalent to making no progress. It was observed that, when it grew dark and the fighting slackened, the French left but a small number of men to guard Queen Street, between the battery and the barricade.

At about half-past eight that evening, Commander Groves was standing near the door of the Elephant and Castle, waiting for a report, when Captain Gulder, of Folkestone, came in for a drink. The smugglers had done nothing that day, having been in the thick of the fight at Blackfriars on Thursday, and part of the Commander's system was frequent reliefs, as no men can fight day after day continuously from sunrise to sunset. The sight of that captain inspired Mr. Groves with an idea. "Where," he asked him, "is Captain Blugg?"

"Hard by, Commander."

"Fetch him."

On Blugg coming out of the inn bar, Mr. Groves consulted both these brave men about his plan, which, they said, was prime.

"Then, at half-past four."

"With sarvice to you, Commander, I would say four."

"Very good; four o'clock be it. And, if too dark, we can easily wait."

Not many minutes after four the next morning, twelve or fifteen boats, with as many of the two hundred men of Dover, Deal, and Folkestone as were still to the good, perhaps one hundred and eighty, left the Surrey side and were rowed across to Queen Street stairs. The Commander was with them, the last to embark. As the men saw him coming aboard, they were raising a cheer, and had uttered the hip! hip! that precedes the hurray! when he lifted his hand. "Let us not give them a chance," he said. "They may hear you." Then, in silence, the oars were dipped in the river.

Arriving at the Middlesex side, they swarmed up the stairs as no landsmen could have done, and rushed up into Queen Street without forming. In like style they mounted and descended the barricade; then, flying past the French, not very numerous in Queen Street, they reached the guns, cut down the gunners and the rest of those holding the battery, and spiked the guns. They were followed by a great sally from Thames Street, and the barricade was wrested from the enemy. It was some time before the French in Cheapside could get down to the scene of action. The seven houses were cut off. Two of them, first assailed by men laid off for the attack armed with crowbars, were soon taken, when the other five surrendered.

This all happened in grey morning light. By seven o'clock, Bonaparte, at St. James's, learned it. He instantly sent for General Berthier; but what orders he gave him can only be surmised from the conversation that Berthier lost no time in holding with another person.

We have related how that, when a general flight took place of all persons that could leave London, a few still remained, some of them people of consideration. One of these was Lord Naresbrook. There were some other peers who remained besides him, but he was the most important political personage who did so. Nearly all the gentlemen of the Civil Service were also in town, most of them from necessity and not choice, and among these many were a kind of followers or partisans of Lord Naresbrook. A nobleman who has never held Cabinet office, but who has held at various times three or four subordinate situations, and who has presided at Commissions, has usually an extensive following in the Civil Service. Such a nobleman is the sort of man who is, at the present time, likely to be chosen as the head of a Commission of Inquiry into the public services and their efficiency. When this occurs, and a mass of evidence is brought forward which shows that Mr. A. has twelve hundred a year for doing nothing, and Mr. B. a thousand a year for assisting him, a report is generally appended to the evidence, recommending that a third shall be appointed at fifteen hundred a year to increase the efficiency of the department. The public read the report and neglect the evidence. It is a system that produces a warm attachment between commissioners and civil servants. Much of this kind of proceeding, exactly, did not go forward ninety years ago. But the salaried official gentlemen were a good deal more of party politicians than they are now, when, indeed, we do not tolerate that species of partisanship. They were nearly all Addingtonians; and Lord Naresbrook was a leader of the Addington party in the House of Lords.

At the beginning of this century, the Civil Service was in as bad a condition in all respects as it is at the present time. The most corrupt department was the Admiralty. Mr. Pitt and Lord Spencer, during the time of Pitt's first ministry, had effected a considerable reformation, which, however, was little more than superficial. Under Mr. Addington, things speedily sank back into the old ruts. The worst case of malversation was an enormous sale of naval stores, effected under pretence of economy, when the Peace of Amiens was concluded. Those stores, great part of which was never even removed from the dockyards, were bought back when war broke out again for six times the sum at which they had been sold. There was an outcry when some of this inquiry came to be known, and it was one of the causes of the fall of the Addington Ministry. But the real malefactors were never punished, or made to disgorge.

The Treasury, the War Department, and the Ordnance were not so bad, but were bad enough. There is, at the present time, a very general belief that our Civil Service has been greatly improved of late years. This is a delusion. The system of auctions of condemned stores still continues. Ships are still sent to sea that are known to be unseaworthy, as they were in the time of Rodney, and longer ago no doubt. Now and then a ship is built that cannot safely cross the Bay of Biscay in rough weather. The ablest officers are systematically kept out of favour, and thwarted, as were Rodney, Nelson, and Cochrane. The Ordnance still serves out swords that will not cut, and that are, with reason, suspected of being made of zinc, or of anything but steel. It serves out heavy guns that burst at the first discharge; other things in proportion. The Treasury still makes contracts for commissariat stores that will feed neither man nor beast, and for medicines that have been denounced by those who have to administer them as fitter to poison than to cure. As guardian of public economy, it rejoices in all that false and ruinous economy which is the worst form of extravagance. The Board of Trade makes rules of the road at sea that cause treble the number of collisions that there used to be. They refuse to allow lighthouses to be illuminated with gas, known to be the best illuminant, because some of them have shares in a patent for a new oil lamp. Under the Merchant Shipping Act, when a sailor dies at sea, his wages due must be paid to his relations through the Board of Trade. Fraudulent deductions are systematically made from these moneys. The Inland Revenue people take up three months in examining a claim for excess taxes of such a nature as any bank would settle in half an hour. They strain their lawful powers, and insist upon methods which they know that they have no legal right to employ; and oppress, when they can, every one with whom they have to deal, treating the inferior persons in their own employment, who are not properly of the Civil Service, with peculiar malignancy. The Irish Department is very bad. Dublin Castle, in not long past political times, was filled with persons who contributed articles to the rebel press, and betrayed police secrets to the moonlighters. As for the War Office, its iniquities are so notorious as to require no specification. The Post Office is, as all know, an almost perfect establishment. But it is perfect, or admirable, not owing to the administration by the civil servants who constitute the "department," but in spite of them. Those persons oppose, and have always opposed, every improvement in carrying on the public business, and occasionally practise the meanest and most dishonest tricks to defeat the purposes of improved methods forced on them. There is a standing conspiracy

among all the service to keep their doings in the dark; and
when information has to be given in reply to questions asked
in Parliament, it scarcely ever occurs that a perfectly true
answer is given, while it often happens that an absolutely
false answer is given. Of nine questions about naval affairs
asked in a recent session by one member of the House of
Commons, the replies to eight were direct falsehoods. Of
course, the Minister who gave them did not know this; the
deception was practised on him as well as on the public.
When, in the conduct or misconduct of business, anything
more outrageous than usual takes place, and comes to be
generally known, it is usual to have what is called a depart-
mental investigation. But this is never a judicial inquiry in
any case. Notwithstanding the jealousies which exist
between the sundry departments in their conspiracy against
the public, their members always stand together; and the
proceeding that we speak of is like trying a burglar by a
jury chosen from the swell mob. Any one who should believe
that the Civil Service is not corrupt is very credulous. There
are more ways of administering bribes than with bank-notes.
If England shall ever come to be ruined, that ruin will be the
work of the Civil Service; and they will manage to make a
profit out of the transaction.

In the crisis of the invasion of 1805, however, the Civil
Service could do little or no mischief. When Colonel Blessingburn went to Woolwich with Lord Camden's written
authority to get whatever he should ask for, there was no
passing on his requisitions from Mr. A. to Mr. B., nor was
there any reference from Mr. B. to Mr. C. in London, with
directions to do nothing without consulting Mr. D. For all
practical purposes, the Civil Service ceased, during several
weeks, to exist. Its candle was blown out none too soon, and
stopped sputtering when Parliament adjourned. For about
two months the army was its own war office, its own ordnance
department, and its own treasury; and the army did its work
so well that one wonders how it occurred to so very few
persons, of the thinking as well as unthinking intelligences,

that, if the army could be its own civil service to the public advantage during war, it would not be otherwise in times of peace. It is worth remarking that a similar neglect of what is obvious was repeated in our own times, not long ago, when the south of Egypt was conquered; on which occasion the army did everything except supply itself with boots, the War Office taking to itself that branch of supply, furnishing boots about as fit for the feet of men as walnuts are for the feet of cats. Thus, while our ancestors learned nothing from the lesson of 1805, we, their great-grandsons, are little, if at all, wiser.

Lord Naresbrook, being prevented from leaving town by circumstances over which he had no control, the details of which he never disclosed, considered that it was his duty to wait upon the conqueror when the French army took London. He might have an opportunity, under an over-ruling providence, of doing a service to his country, either, who knows, by mitigating the wrath and vengeance of the conqueror, or else, and more likely, by acting as a mediator or instrument in bringing about a lasting and honourable peace between two great powers. There were two noblemen who had remained in London, men of about the same intellectual and moral calibre, as, for instance, the late Earl Granville, who followed Lord Naresbrook's example in leaving their cards on Bonaparte. Their example was followed by many of the large and small fry of the public offices. Bonaparte received these people politely, but, of course, had no political conversation with any. He left that to Berthier. These visits did not commence till after it had proved evident that the Britannic Republic would not go down with the British public.

Lord Naresbrook had more than one conversation with Berthier, the substance of which, on the latter's part, was that the Emperor was most desirous of making peace between the two powers on terms honourable to both. When asked to be more definite, he became rather less so, if that were possible, and spoke of the commanding position that the Emperor occupied, and the power he had of inflicting severe wounds on England. He wished Lord Naresbrook to converse with a person much in the Emperor's confidence, who would wait on his lordship. This person talked bigger and more menacingly than General Berthier. He asked if the domestic enemies of England had not, more than a century previous, set London on fire, and remarked that it was a greater city now, and would make a greater conflagration. Lord Naresbrook had dignity enough to reply that that kind of talk would not do. But the threat stuck in his mind, and he did not hold his own with General Berthier on the next occasion that they met. The general pressed him to lay his views before the English Ministers; but Lord Naresbrook represented that it was impossible to expect any reply to a proposal before there was a proposal to reply to.

On Saturday morning, at an early hour, Berthier visited Lord Naresbrook at his house, and told that nobleman that he thought he was in a position to lay something before him which would make it his absolute duty to communicate with the English headquarters. He could take it on himself to say that the Emperor was prepared to make peace with England on the terms of a restitution by the latter power of all conquests made from France and her allies since 1792, and the retention by France of all hers. On these terms, he (Berthier) was certain that his Imperial Majesty would be prepared to evacuate England. Questions, of course, might arise about guarantees and other minor matters. In case, however, that the war was to proceed, the Emperor was physically unable to divest himself of the powers and rights of a conqueror, and the destruction that might fall on England and her capital might be such as the English people and Government should have to deplore.

Lord Naresbrook pressed Berthier to put down in writing what he proposed. Berthier had nothing, he said, to propose; he threw out these suggestions in the interests of peace and humanity, and on his conscience and honour he did believe, and was as sure as he was of his own existence, that he was speaking his imperial master's mind. He urged Lord

Naresbrook to lose not an hour in seeking an interview with the English Ministers.

On this lame errand this lame political duck was fool enough to start. He arrived at Bedford the same evening, and drove to Mr. Pitt's residence. Mr. Pitt received him with some hauteur. On hearing what Lord Naresbrook had to say, he remarked:

"I understand, then, that your lordship does not come with a proposal from Bonaparte?"

".I have had communication only with General Berthier and another, an inferior officer. General Berthier is certain that such a basis as he speaks of affords a certainty almost absolute of peace. It appears to me that, as Englishmen, we ought to make sacrifices for peace, and to avert the dangers of a terrible calamity falling on London, which, remember, is in the enemy's power."

"Have any threats been held out to your lordship that the enemy will work destructive mischief upon London?"

"Not threats, but——"

"I understand, my lord. It is from no intention to behave discourteously that I have to desire that your lordship will not see any other of his Majesty's Ministers now at headquarters, nor even remain in Bedford. It is desirable that your lordship should proceed to some place, immediately, not less than five miles from here."

"I will stay at ——," naming a village in the country, not far from Bedford.

"Very well, my lord. I wish your lordship a good evening."

"And when, sir, may I hope to be favoured with the views of his Majesty's Ministers?"

"It appears to me, my lord, that, there being no proposal, there is nothing to reply to. It is late now. In case that any communication with your lordship is resolved on, it shall be made to-morrow."

Lord Naresbrook left Mr. Pitt feeling small. He was to feel smaller before twenty-four hours were over.

Mr. Pitt was not a man given to laughter, but he watched the envoy's carriage as it drove away with a very grim smile. Then he went to Lord Harrowby's, and, not finding him, to the Duke of Portland's. Lord Harrowby was there, and Mr. Pitt had to tell his story only once.

"Let your Grace and your lordship and myself," he said, when all the points had been gone over, "resolve to keep this disgraceful business to ourselves. I am disposed to let Lord Naresbrook know, the first thing in the morning, that we have nothing to say to him. What says your Grace? Shall we write him to that effect, or shall one of us wait on him? If the communication is to be personal, it will be a great relief to me if I can be saved the burden of it."

The Duke smiled. He had not the least objection to give Lord Naresbrook a snub, and was quite competent to do it. But Lord Harrowby shrewdly observed:

"Perhaps, before we communicate, it may be well to wait a few hours, and then we may know what disaster Bonaparte has met, that has prompted this advance. General Berthier visited Lord Naresbrook early this morning; is it not so, Mr. Pitt?"

"That is what he told me," replied Pitt.

"Then something, I do believe, has happened," said Lord Harrowby. "As for keeping this to ourselves, I entirely agree with you. It is quite needless to have a Cabinet meeting. Besides, I should be sorry to expose Lord Naresbrook."

The Duke and Mr. Pitt would not have been in the least sorry, but they did not say so. The triumvirate separated, to meet again the next day when the despatches from South London should arrive. They were late, many hours later than they ought to have been, for Bonaparte had sent a strong troop of cavalry as far as the road between Aylesbury and Bedford to intercept the mounted post. Thus one post was lost, and also the time that the next was delayed by keeping still farther west, and more out of the way, than by Aylesbury.

At last it came in. In possession of the welcome fact that

the defence of the bridges was again secured, and, they were persuaded, permanently secured, the Duke of Portland and Lord Harrowby proceeded to Lord Naresbrook's quarters. The Duke was the orator.

"We are now," he said, "aware why this precise moment was chosen for despatching your lordship on what can hardly be termed a mission. Your lordship has brought no proposal, and no reply is called for. But although there has been no proposition, there has been a kind of intimation that it is in the power of the enemy to work much mischief in London. London is an open town, and the laws of war do not allow of the sacking or burning of an open town. We send no message; we do not request your lordship to communicate anything to the enemy or to any of his officers. But if Bonaparte should violate the laws of war in the way that has been insinuated, as it is evident to us that it has been, to your lordship, or in any other way; and if Bonaparte should come, as he very likely may, personally into our power, it will become the duty of his Majesty's Ministers to determine in such event what course to take with him. My lord, my Lord Harrowby and I have but to say, in addition, that it is with regret that we witness a peer of the realm, and a Privy Councillor, the bearer of such messages, if they be messages, as your lordship has burthened yourself with."

The mediator between nations who left London on Saturday left Bedfordshire on Monday in very bad spirits.

CHAPTER XVIII.

"Richard!"

"Mother!"

"At last."

"At last."

An embrace, and no more words for two or three minutes.

"I knew you would come, Richard. My faith has never wavered. Every day I said to Helen, it is but a day nearer."

"Mother, I wish I could have such faith. But I have never been in real danger. And you have kept her spirits up?"

"As well as I could. And now, tell me about yourself."

"I wish, mother, you would go and tell her. I will follow you immediately. It would be a shock if she did not hear first."

"I will go. But, Richard, were you taken prisoner?"

"Yes; and dismissed."

"Dismissed! Then you did not escape?"

"I was dismissed, and afterwards I escaped. I will tell you when I am there. Dearest mother, go now."

He was right in sending Mrs. Fenthorpe to announce him. If two lovers, separated as Richard had been parted from Helen Tronford, should meet now unexpectedly after their separation, they would fly into each other's arms. Such a proceeding would have been impossible ninety years ago. The proprieties were too strong. Lovers now, of the middle, and even of the higher classes, keep company. In the beginning of this century, that practice was confined to the common people. We are at fault, when we are called on for a judgment, which system is the best. When we were a young gentleman—we shall not be expected to say in what decade—the usages of the lower classes in these premises were beginning to prevail amongst those above them. We adopted them in the case of the lady who became, and still is, our wife. We took walks with her, sat in rooms with her, etc., even travelled in railway trains with her. We are free to admit that we enjoyed it much. We even pitied the benighted grandfathers and grandmothers who had never had such enjoyments. However, we don't know. People were as happy under ancient forms of living, perhaps, as they are now. When our own experience was proceeding, there was still a soupçon of impropriety about company keeping that gave it a great zest. We repeat, we don't know. Be all this as it may, considerations of the kind never entered into the heads of Richard Fenthorpe and Helen Tronford. They met, in Mr. Cardwain's drawing-room, in the presence of that lady, Fanny, Mrs. Fenthorpe, and Miss Dorkington. They shook hands together, that was all—squeezed them, no doubt, but that is not in the record, although theoretically admissible under the now obsolete code.

Richard, of course, had all the talk to himself, for, since he had quitted Norwich more than three weeks before, nothing had been heard of him. There was not much to tell him. He heard more of public current events from the Mayor, whom he had to see and to whom he had to deliver Lord Camden's letter, before any long number of hours should elapse. The first thing to be decided at their interview was how much should be told. There might be an imprudence in letting the French know that an attempt was going to be made to deliver the eastern counties. Lord Camden's letter, of course, must be made public.

The Mayor sent for a number of the principal inhabitants to meet him and the corporation. Dr. Fenthorpe was present, and thought it judicious to say that, while he was unable to tell in what state of progress the preparations were, no long time would be allowed to pass before something would be undertaken. He had seen several military men in the confidence of the Commander-in-Chief and the Government, and, seeing that what was at stake was not the deliverance of Norfolk only, but of all England, operations had to be made to fit into each other; and the disorganisation of the army since the battle of Cambridge had all to be put to rights before anything certain to be successful could be attempted. Dr. Fenthorpe was careful to speak in a tone such as could not but be reassuring, although particulars must be vague.

We are not going to repeat all the handsome and grateful things that were said to him. We follow him home, to the home that, once or twice in his journey, he feared he would never see.

"Now, mother, I have to tell you about what I could not at my aunt's. I have obtained certain proof that the late Charles Fenthorpe made a will about the same time that you supposed."

"From Mr. Groves?" Mrs. Fenthorpe, of course, was excited.

"No; otherwise." Then he told her of his meeting with Bannox.

"It is a most remarkable thing. You remember, Richard, I told you I knew your journey would be in some way connected with this." When people's presentiments are fulfilled, as they sometimes are, what they had formerly expected or hoped for then becomes actual foreknowledge. When they are not fulfilled, as generally happens, they are silent. But it gives them far more gratification to be right than annoyance to be wrong. "To think that, after all these years, we should at last be assured of the truth. I see it coming, Richard. The clouds are gathering, blacker and blacker, and it will be very strange if they do not break."

"But, mother, this brings us no nearer to anything. This does not find the missing will."

"Where is it? Where is it? This does bring us nearer, now that we know it and can prove it. But I have been patient a long time, and I can wait a little longer. I do not know how it will come, but come it will."

How can one argue with a person with impressions? One cannot argue; one can only soothe, and sometimes not even that.

"It will only make us unhappy and restless to be thinking of what may happen," said Richard slowly.

"One cannot help thinking of it. One must think of it."

"We have, just now, enough to think of without this. Till the enemy are driven out of Norfolk, everything else is trivial. Mother, have I not told you that there is an attempt to be made soon?"

"Yes; from Ely and Wisbeach. But you do not know when. We must possess our souls in patience. I suppose it is now nearly over. We have suffered less from this calamity than one might have feared when first it came upon us. I feared—I did not know what. I feared about you. There was that terrible battle, when so many were slain. I feared terribly for you that day. But I have never feared since, never all this time you have been away. I don't know why. There has been something sustaining me."

"And will sustain you still, mother, no doubt. I have no fears now, either, for the ultimate result. There is a spirit of hopefulness and confidence among all I met—Mr. Groves, Lord Camden, everybody at Bedford—that infects one. Even that Mrs. Bannox, though she had never seen any of the war —it has been so far from that side—the confidence that she spoke with was infectious, about how the uncircumcised and the unclean should not conquer England."

"Oh, Richard, about Mr. Groves! Did you ask him has he the sheet of paper on which Allonby was made to write his name that day, you remember?"

"He has; I asked him. His papers are not in his possession now; he has them in a house in Bloomsbury. It is curious, too, the interest he took in this affair."

His mother's last remark showed how the mystery of the will was the main thing that filled her imagination. Richard did not wish for more conversation about that subject, and they bade each other good night.

R

What a hero and lion Dr. Fenthorpe was the next day we need not enlarge on, nor what congratulations he had from friends and mere acquaintances. Saturday was the same, and on Sunday the Dean preached on him.

On Monday morning, Mrs. Fenthorpe went out about ten o'clock to market. Her marketing took up, as marketing generally does, a good deal of time, and, looking at her watch, she perceived that she would not be home till near noon, when Richard would certainly have gone out. She suddenly met, in the principal street of Norwich, a gentleman who did not often come into the city so early, or indeed often at all.

" Mr. Mortland," she said, " it is a considerable time since I have seen you."

" It is indeed, Mrs. Fenthorpe, with all these troubles."

" Do you remember," she asked him, " a person that was, at one time, at Fenthorpe Hall, called Bannox? "

" Bannox? Bannox, did you say? "

" A farm servant, or bailiff, at the time when you came there? "

" I—I think I do remember his name."

" Do you remember his son? "

Mr. Mortland gave a little gasp. " He had no son that I remember, Mrs. Fenthorpe."

" He had a son whom, I dare say, you never saw. Will you be so good as to tell Mr. Robert Mortland, when next he visits Allonby, to inform him that I know where William Bannox is to be found."

He gave another gasp, and turned pale, yellow, or green, or the colour that some people turn when they are alarmed. Mrs. Fenthorpe looked at him for a quarter of a minute, bowed, and said good day, and walked home, eminently satisfied with herself. Less and less, however, as she neared her house. Would Richard not disapprove of this attack? She should tell him of it at once, of course.

The butler opened the door before she had done knocking. " Ma'am," he said hurriedly, " the doctor is gone away with Miss Dorkington, on the new mare."

"Gone away with Miss Dorkington!"

"Gone away, with her riding behind him. Ma'am, I am afraid there is something wrong at Mrs. Cardwain's. Thomas came here in a terrible state, not long after you went out, ma'am, and ran into the doctor's room; and the doctor, he shouted for Sam to bring the mare round, and he sent Thomas away; and, just at the minute master was mounting of the mare, Miss Dorkington came up, and she said she would go with him; and he sent Sam for a pad there is in the harness-room, and they fastened it on; and master put on a belt, and she got up behind master, and they rode off."

"Where? Where did they go to?"

"I don't know, ma'am; that way it was." The butler pointed to the left; this street led towards Mr. Cardwain's, towards the Cathedral, towards Ipswich, towards Yarmouth, towards anywhere.

Mrs. Fenthorpe ran—rushed—to her sister's. Mrs. Cardwain was in a fright, in tears, almost in hysterics. Miss Dorkington was not there, nor the girls.

"Isabella, what is it?"

"Oh, Elizabeth, what are we to do? What are we to do?"

"What is it, Isabella? What is it? Where are Richard and Anne Dorkington gone to? What is it?"

"Richard and Anne Dorkington!"

"They are gone away, on Richard's mare. Where, where have they gone to?"

Mrs. Cardwain, having heard something that surprised her, pulled herself together. "They must have gone after them," she cried.

"Gone after whom? Isabella, will you be coherent? What has happened?"

Mrs. Cardwain again burst into loud sobbing. "Helen and Fanny—they are carried off."

"Helen and Fanny carried off! Isabella, tell me at once what it is. Who has carried them off? Is it the French?"

"I was not up," said, or panted, Mrs. Cardwain, a little more collected. "I was not very well, and I asked Anne to to go out to market. And Jonathan was out, gone away to Burnham. And there was suddenly such a noise and Fanny screaming; and she rushed into my room and told me—I wonder I understood her—that soldiers had come for them, with drawn swords——"

"Come for her and Helen?"

"Oh, is it not dreadful! And they took them away in a carriage. They said something about Yarmouth. What are we to do? Jonathan went at nine o'clock to Burnham, and I don't know when he will be back. What are we to do?"

"Did you see the soldiers, Isabella?"

"No; I was just out of bed, going to dress myself, and Helen came into the room, and kissed me, and they were gone in five minutes. Oh, is it not dreadful!"

"I can't understand it at all," said Mrs. Fenthorpe. "Did nobody see the soldiers, or see them go?"

"Thomas saw them, and he says the officer said something to Helen in French, and his sword was drawn, and he heard him say Yarmouth; and I thought Anne would be in, and—what did you say about her and Richard?"

"William told me—I did not go into the house—that he and Miss Dorkington had gone away on the mare, both of them. How did Richard hear about it?"

"I don't know. They would not pass that way going to Yarmouth."

Mrs. Fenthorpe rang the bell. "Thomas," she said to the butler, who answered without delay, "you saw these soldiers?"

"It was just a quarter past ten, ma'am," said Thomas, "and an officer and four dragoons came here, and they had a carriage with them, a close carriage, ma'am; and he asked for Miss Tronford, and came into the house, and shoved me to one side, and he spoke quite arbitrary; and the Miss Tronfords were both in the library, and he went in to them, and he took off his hat—leastways, his helmet—and spoke to them in French; and Miss Fanny began to cry, but Miss Helen spoke to him calm, and she turned to me and told me they were going to take them to Yarmouth; and I went to the hall door, and the dragoons had their swords drawn, and they came downstairs and got into the carriage and drove away. And I couldn't think what to do, and I went straight and told Dr. Fenthorpe. And I am so taken, ma'am, I don't know what to think about such a terrible thing."

"And did you see Miss Dorkington?"

"No, ma'am; Miss Dorkington was out. When I told Dr. Fenthorpe, he just called out loud to Sam, the groom, for to saddle the mare; and he told me for to say nothing, and he desired me to go back here."

"She went with him, you see," said Mrs. Fenthorpe to her sister. "They have followed them. What kind of a carriage was it?" she asked Thomas.

"A close carriage, ma'am, with two horses; common hacks they were."

"Did the officer speak rudely?"

"Well, ma'am, I couldn't tell; they don't speak like Christians."

"What did he look like? Did he look like a gentleman?"

"Lord bless us, ma'am, what gentleman would come and take away two young ladies with soldiers, and them their swords drawn? He just looked like one of them; a pack of scoundrels they are. But I would know that gentleman again, I would."

"How long do you think Dr. Fenthorpe would be before he could overtake them? You told him you heard the man say it was to Yarmouth?"

"Yes, ma'am, I told him. Well, you see, ma'am, he might pick them up in half an hour; but he has a new horse—leastways, a mare—and I don't know that mare. But I think she might pick them up, if so be as he doesn't miss them, in half an hour or a little more, pretty tidy."

"He would be longer, with Miss Dorkington on the mare behind him," said Mrs. Fenthorpe to her sister. "And then they would go with them to Yarmouth. It is terrible. Is it possible to get any one that has a horse to send to try and know something?"

"There's not a horse you could get in all Norwich, but just by luck, ma'am," said Thomas.

What could they do? There is no situation so fearfully depressing as helplessness. But if they were helpless, what were not Helen and Fanny. The more they thought of it, the worse they thought of it. Then they remembered that Richard and Miss Dorkington must by this time have overtaken them.

For a long time Mrs. Cardwain and her sister remained together, the former frequently weeping. "Isabella, was Helen as terrified as Fanny?" Mrs. Fenthorpe asked.

"No; she has wonderful self-command."

"She has. It will be of service to her in this. I hope she may have been able to calm Fanny."

Let us follow those two outraged girls. The carriage was a close one. The officer had been more rude than Thomas had described. When they were quite out of the city, Helen had put down one of the carriage windows, when he stopped the cavalcade and required it to be closed. Then Helen sat back on her seat, while her sister, no longer crying or hysterical, but trembling, leaned forward and looked out of the window. They said nothing to each other. The coachman drove his horses at a quick pace, nine miles an hour at least. The officer twice commanded him, so well as the imprisoned sisters could make out, to increase his speed.

Four miles from Norwich, just across the bridge where the battle had been fought, Fanny, knowing the locality, was looking at the scene of it up and down the road as well as she could. Suddenly she called out, "Oh, Helen, there is Mr. Mortland," and pulled down the window.

"Don't," said Helen; "what can he do for us?" But Fanny had put her head and shoulders out of the window and called to him loudly. He was riding, at a walking pace, towards Norwich. He pulled up. "Miss Tronford!" he exclaimed. "Hold! Hola! Arrêtez-vous, monsieur, s'il vous plait!"

The officer—Fanny said this—turned to him at once.

"Why do you want us to stop?" he asked in French.

"Where are these ladies being taken? I pray you, monsieur, stop! I am acquainted with them. I pray you to be allowed to speak with them."

"I am taking them to Yarmouth, where they are domiciled. I have orders to do so. Do you wish to question them, monsieur? They will confirm what I say." He called, "Halt!"

Robert Mortland came to the side of the carriage. "Miss Tronford, what is this outrage?"

"What you see, Mr. Mortland," answered Helen. She pressed her sister's hand, and desired her, with a look, to leave her to conduct the conversation. "An hour ago we were ordered to get into this carriage to go to Yarmouth; we could not resist."

"This is an outrage, after Dr. Fenthorpe and I had pledged ourselves for you. Oh, Helen!—she started as he addressed her as he never had before—"would that I had the right to protect you! You know, you must have seen, my devotion! At a moment like this, I cannot but speak. Is there no way to save you—to save you both? Let me speak to this man."

The officer and the dragoons were twenty yards or more in front of the carriage. Mortland rode up to them before Helen could speak, and conversed with the officer for two or three minutes. The sisters, now one and now the other, looking out of the window, could hear nothing, but saw the eager gestures of Mortland and the officer's shrugs.

Mortland at last shook his head at something said by the other, and rode back slowly to the carriage. "There is," he said, "a way for you to avoid this terrible thing—how terrible I tremble to think of! Helen, you know my devotion, and I have presumed to hope——"

"Mr. Mortland," she said, "I cannot listen to this."

"I have presumed to hope—you must needs hear me, at this moment I cannot be silent; you are in danger, and it cuts me to the heart. I told this man—I fervently hope you will—but you must—forgive me—I told him, to soften him, that you are my betrothed. Listen, let me finish "—he raised his voice to overpower hers and Fanny's exclamation—" and he answered—he answered, I say, that were you my wife it would be different, for then you would be of Norwich, and not of Yarmouth. Marry me now, Helen, here at Brandwood Church, and you will save yourself and Fanny from an awful danger, and make me, and, I think—I hope—I pray—yourself happy."

Astonishment, and the nearest approach to rage that ever rose within Helen Tronford's bosom, prevented her from interrupting Robert Mortland with anything but exclamations. His speech done, he was out of breath with excitement, and she was able to say, "It is impossible."

"Not impossible, dearest Helen—may I call you so?"

"You have no right to call us by our names," exclaimed Fanny. "Helen, don't do any such thing. Mr. Mortland, if I was she, I wouldn't for——"

"You must pardon my precipitancy," he went on, as though taking no denial. "It is not, you will allow me to say, impossible, and it is the only way out of this danger. The road lies through the camp, and you don't know what it is. For your own sake, for your sweet sister's sake, Helen——"

"Eh bien," interrupted the officer, riding up, and making a grimace, "quel chemin? Ah, je vois bien. Fermez cette porte, cocher. En route. A droite au petit chemin le plus proche."

Neither of the girls caught this. The carriage moved on, Robert Mortland riding beside it, saying more to the same purpose, incoherently enough. Helen put up the window; but when the carriage turned up the road leading to Brandwood, she screamed and pulled it down. "Mr. Mortland," she called out, "are you trying to force me?" Fanny put her head out of the other window, and called for help which did not come.

Mortland had ridden on, beyond the dragoons and their officer, and either did not hear or did not choose to hear.

"Fanny," said Helen, "all we can do is to be quiet and do nothing. Better go to Yarmouth ten times than this. It is atrocious, Fanny. Do be as quiet as you can, love. Let us not get out of the carriage."

It was less than half a mile, and the rapid motion of the carriage, with its rattling windows—inn chaises, like London cabs, always rattle—impeded even such conversation as theirs. At the church door, where they stopped, Mortland came to hand them out. Helen said quietly that they would remain in the carriage.

"But do you not see," he urged, "do you not see the necessity—it is no less than necessity. What are you to do, exposed as you will be? And, Helen, I know you don't hate me. Think of everything—of your sister, the——"

"Mr. Mortland, cease." She could not raise the window, for the door was open. "We will not get out. We will go to Yarmouth. Send the officer——"

"My dearest Helen"—she looked indignation, but he went on—"this is perfect madness. I will!" He was now on foot, and he started away suddenly. He exchanged a few words with the officer, and went towards the back of the church, where the rectory was, about a hundred yards off. They watched, and, in a few minutes, Mortland and the rector appeared. The latter went into the vestry, as they guessed, and Mortland returned to them.

"It is an absolute necessity to you," he said, again addressing Helen. "But you cannot be married without witnesses; and I am going for my mother."

"It is useless," said Helen, commanding herself, though more terrified than ever. "Set me free; we will not stay here. Why did you say that to that man? You know it is not true. Why do you put a force on us? Why——"

"It would have been true had I had courage," he said. "I refrained then, but I cannot refrain now. For your sake, do you not see it, not my own——"

"I will not," said Helen. "You shall not," echoed, or screamed, her sister.

"I am going now for my mother. I shall be back in a few minutes." He was off before they could reply with more than powerless exclamations.

The moment that he was out of sight, the officer came forward, and, bowing, desired them to descend from the carriage.

"We prefer to remain here, monsieur," said Helen. "We are to proceed with you to Yarmouth."

"Ah! peut-être," he answered. "Descendez, mesdemoiselles, descendez."

"Non, nous resterons."

"Il faut que vous descendez," he said peremptorily. "Descendez! Descendez!" He compelled them, with tone and gesture, to comply, and to enter the church.

"Oh, Fanny," said Helen, "what does it all mean? Is this a planned thing?"

"I don't know," answered Fanny, sobbing. "That insolent man! But I would go to Yarmouth ten times, twenty times, sooner. Oh, Helen, let us go to Yarmouth."

"Fanny," she whispered, "this is a sacred place; let us be silent, and pray."

They waited for they knew not what. Helen feared that the rector would come into the chancel; then, as she thought again, she was going with her sister, without telling her why, into the vestry, to claim his aid, when Mrs. Mortland and her son appeared.

"Oh, Miss Tronford," said Mrs. Mortland, "what a situation for you. But Robert is right, and there is nothing else."

"Are you, Mrs. Mortland, against me?" said Helen. "I tell you, I will not. To put force on me! I will not."

Mrs. Mortland whispered to her, and Helen, as her sister thought, who did not catch the words, seemed stunned. But she drew herself up in a moment, and said:

"Your son has told that man that I am his betrothed. It is false! Richard Fenthorpe is my betrothed. And you say this to me!"

"Richard Fenthorpe!" exclaimed Mrs. Mortland. "Richard Fenthorpe will be in no haste to fulfill his betrothment with a lady that has allowed herself to be carried away by a French officer. Save yourself, Miss Tronford, while you can."

Helen turned on her not a look of anger, but of reproach, that one woman should so speak to another under a most dire affliction.

"You speak so of Richard Fenthorpe!" she cried. "You do not know him! I know him, and I know your son—now. Richard! Oh, that you were here! You would save me! Hark! What is that? I hear the sound of horses' hoofs. Yes, Richard Fenthorpe has come to save me!"

She rushed out of the door of the church, still left open. Fanny followed her. The officer did not oppose them. He was looking at something else. He had never seen a man riding a horse with a woman behind him. And, as the riders drew near, he recognised one of them.

"Oh, Nunnie, Nunnie, dearest Nunnie!" the two sisters cried, as Miss Dorkington slid with the activity of a circus rider from the mare's back. "You are come to save us! Nunnie, Nunnie! Take us from this dreadful place."

"Monsieur le Captaine Balutin," said Richard, dismounting, "que veut dire toute cette chose?" Then, seeing Mortland and his mother within the church door, the truth burst upon him. "This is a plot," he said to Mortland, raising his whip. "If this rascal has an order to remove ladies of Yarmouth from Norwich, why did he not take Miss Dorkington?"

"I know nothing about his orders," said Mortland.

"You know nothing about them, because he has no orders to remove ladies that have General Davoust's protection. This is a plot got up between you and him, and I will denounce it. I will go straight to General Davoust and tell him. The French army has got more serious business in England than to help to carry away ladies against their will and marry them." Then he turned to Balutin, who looked rather scared, and threatened him. "You have been bribed by Mr. Mortland to do this. You have no orders to arrest these ladies; if you have, come with me and exhibit them to General Davoust."

Balutin remembered that this was the gentleman who had obtained the order from Davoust for the protection of ladies domiciled in Yarmouth. Robert Mortland had given him no instructions how to act in the circumstances that had arisen. To accuse a French officer, or any Frenchman, in the times of the Republic and the Empire, of taking a bribe, was not an unpardonable offence, nor indeed is it at this time, unless you can prove it, and it gets into the newspapers. "Monsieur Mortland," he called out.

Robert went to him, and they whispered together. Fenthorpe strode up to them and said, "It is too late for you to plot any more now. Let these ladies return home, and on their account, not on yours, we shall say nothing about this infamous business. Make up your minds at once, or I go to General Davoust."

No person could have looked more shocked than Mrs. Mortland did. Fanny whispered to Miss Dorkington how she had threatened Helen. Miss Dorkington was slow in taking up a thing, but, when once alight, she burned steadily and was hard to put out. Just as she was going to speak to Mrs. Mortland, the rector walked down the aisle of the church from the vestry and joined the group.

"Dr. Fenthorpe," he said, "I should address myself to these ladies were I acquainted with them, while I believe that the Misses Tronford are, in a manner, my parishioners, but I wish to say that I have had no hand in this affair."

"Have you not?" said Robert, with a sneer. "Why did you call the banns, then?"

They all stared at this. The plot was deeper than they had thought, apparently.

"Why did I call banns on the instructions of a gentleman, the son of my principal parishioner, whom I could not suspect of something very like an abduction? To be sure I did, and

will do the same again, on any honest man's instructions.
But, Dr. Fenthorpe, it is perfectly evident that you are right.
On account of these ladies, whom every one who has heard of
them honours, let there be a perfect silence about this affair.
Mr. Mortland, for his own sake, will say nothing. Mrs.
Mortland, we must all regret that you have been misled."

"No person," said Miss Dorkington, "was ever so much
misled as to justify the language Mrs. Mortland used towards
a young woman in the most dreadful position that ever a
woman was. Mrs. Mortland, this is the last time that I will
ever speak to you, and any friends that I have I will warn
against you if there should be need. Ah!" she went on, in
a triumphant tone, for the first time in her life speaking with
studied scorn, "the Fenthorpe Hall and Brandwood estates
are not going to be united in this way, you'll find, in whatever other way they may be. Take my warning, Mrs.
Mortland. Now come, Helen and Fanny, my lambs, my
doves, saved from the claws of the lion and the fangs of the
vulture (she was getting mixed), come home with your
Nunnie." She broke down, and cried loudly enough to be
heard across two fields, now that she saw the danger was over.

Mrs. Mortland turned homewards. Balutin said nothing;
he had nothing to say except to Mortland, and what he had
was best said without witnesses. Richard handed Miss
Dorkington and the sisters into the carriage, when he recognised the coachman, who was from a second-rate livery stable.
"Hold your tongue about this," he said, "and I will make it
worth your while." He saw that the man had been pressed.
Robert Mortland walked after his mother as the carriage drove
away to Norwich.

"Mortland! Wait!" called Richard, when it was out of
hearing. He turned. "You are too vile for me to wet my
hands in your blood. But I have an account to settle with
this fellow. Vous entendrez de moi," he said to Balutin, in
his awkward but comprehensible French. Then he mounted
Bannox's mare and rode home.

CHAPTER XIX.

"ISABELLA," said Mrs. Fenthorpe to her sister in the afternoon of that memorable day, "this makes it necessary that there shall be no longer any secret about the marriage."

"I suppose so," replied Mrs. Cardwain.

"Will you tell Mr. Cardwain when he returns this evening—of course, after you have told him about the way they were carried off? Or will you wait and let Richard state his own case?"

"I hardly know how I could tell Jonathan about the terrible affair of to-day, and the way Richard rescued them, without telling him all. You see, Helen avowed it to that woman. But, Elizabeth, I had not time to hear all about it from Anne; she is with them upstairs, poor children. How was it that they did not ride past the turn to Brandwood?"

"They asked every one they met about a carriage with French soldiers escorting it, three or four; and there was a man working close to the turn who guided them. It was providential. I wonder was Mrs. Mortland in the plot? I cannot think it possible. What do you think?"

"I hope not," said Mrs. Cardwain, with a sigh. "I think it hardly possible. Yet I don't know what else could have made her say that abominable thing to Helen."

"I think that almost shows that Robert rushed up to her with some story. If she knew that it was a planned abduction—what a horrid thing to say—that could hardly have come into her head. But she will get plenty of blame for it when it all comes to be known."

"Comes to be known! How is it to come to be known?"

"Nonsense, Isabella. How is it to be kept to ourselves? We are going to tell nothing ourselves, nor you; but how many people saw Anne Dorkington on Richard's mare? And the man that drove the carriage, and the people on the road? It will be all known, depend upon it."

"Oh, dreadful!" said Mrs. Cardwain. "I never thought of that. Elizabeth, can nothing be done?"

"Why, what could be done? It is only half so dreadful as it might have been; as it was, nearly, at one moment. If they had missed that turn in the road, the poor girls might have been at Yarmouth this moment, or—what do we know? It is providential. It will pull down those Mortlands' pride," added Mrs. Fenthorpe, who was commonly free from vindictiveness. But who could be altogether so in such a case?

"And what do you think of Mr. Sayers. Jonathan has a very bad opinion of him; and he knows."

"I certainly do not understand about his calling the banns. Nobody that I know of goes to that church. Mrs. Mortland goes to the other church, and neither Mr. Mortland nor Robert ever goes anywhere. Mr. Sayers hardly ever leaves his house. A most deeply laid plot it was. And think, if Richard had not come, what might have happened."

We pause to say that we do not believe that Mrs. Mortland was in the plot. She called at Mrs. Cardwain's two days after, when Mrs. Cardwain desired Thomas to say that his mistress was at home, but did not wish to receive Mrs. Mortland. Would she have had the audacity to do this had she been guilty? She must have wished to clear herself. But we believe that the clergyman was in it, though he kept himself safe—safe every way. About a month after, he paid some money that he owed, which his creditor was about to take proceedings for; and people said there was no other way to account for it; and that he was very knowing to get paid by Robert Mortland beforehand.

Richard Fenthorpe left the door of Brandwood Church with the fullest intention of killing Captain Balutin the next day. We are not defenders of the practice of duelling. But in the

year 1805 it would scarcely have entered a man's head not
to seek such satisfaction as a duel was held to give, under the
provocation of his intended bride carried off by force and
fraud, and even treated needlessly with rudeness. He went,
on his return to Norwich, to Lieutenant Fordman of the
Loyal Norwich, who knew a little French, and who could be
trusted. The instructions were, swords if it could be so
arranged, and no apology to be accepted.

At eight o'clock that evening, Richard received word that
the parties were to meet at eleven the next day in a secluded
field, surrounded by trees, a mile or more from Fenthorpe
Hall. Mr. Fordman had tried hard for an earlier hour, but
could not manage it.

Dr. Fenthorpe was not sorry that so late an hour had been
fixed on, for it enabled him to conceal his intention from his
mother. If he had gone out earlier than usual the next
morning she would have remarked it, and might have suspected. But this concealment made him unwilling to be with
her: and though no fear for himself, for he trusted his
swordsmanship—a by no means rare accomplishment at that
time—and no fear of doing a wrong action, troubled him, the
first concealment that he had from his mother since he was a
boy weighed sorely upon his mind. He recommended her to
go to bed early, after all the excitement of the day, and
lighted a candle and went upstairs himself.

He laid the candle on a table, without observing that it
was very low in the socket. He went to the right-hand
window of his room, and looked out on where the four streets
meet. That street, straight, or nearly so, before him, was in
moonlight shadow; the crossing of the two streets was as plain
as day, or almost so. He stood a long time at the window,
and fell into a reverie—not a dream, for he heard and saw
perfectly, while what he heard and saw did not occupy his
thoughts. They were with the past and with the future. His
candle burned itself out, and he did not observe it. He heard
the trampling of horses' feet on the pavement of a distant
street, in the direction in which he was looking, yet this

unwonted sound did not rouse him. The sound grew louder, and he remained unconscious or unstruck by it. The horses and their riders, French cavalry, came into sight; they came towards the house at a walk, and he remained without moving or thinking of them. As they came to where the streets cross, just under his window, they turned to their left, and he looked down on them, bright with their arms and helmets in the moonlight. Still he did not move; but he began counting them, not knowing or hardly knowing that he did so. Four abreast, fifty times four—that makes two hundred.

But as the last four turned into the street under the window, a halt was called. Then Richard Fenthorpe saw three officers, who had not turned to the left but remained in the street straight before him, not much more than visible in the shade. He thought two of them were general officers; he scarcely knew why. The halt was followed by what seemed something like confusion, for a right-about-face was made, and it was apparent that the troop had been directed along that street in error. While the horses were being turned, the three officers came out of the street into the full moonlight for about half a minute; one of them looked up at the moon, and his features were plainly descernible. By this time Richard was a little more awake, if that should be called awake that is not the opposite of sleep, but he was still unobservant, and images seen with his eyes passed from his mind.

The officers turned back into the darkened street, while the troop turned again to their left, thus going on straight from the street that they had approached by. All went on then right, it would appear, with the loss only of some minutes. The sound of the march of the cavalry grew familiar, and died away. As it died away, Richard woke up completely.

He had a sensation of puzzlement, he did not know about what. He noticed his burnt-out candle. It was not that. It was something that recalled something which yet he could not recollect. At last he discovered what it was. It was the

S

face of the officer who had looked at the moon. He had seen
that face before. Where?

It must have been lately, for it was not an Englishman.
He began to think of the various French officers whose
countenances he remembered. No help. Then he began to
think of them in order of time, on his journey from Bury St.
Edmunds to London, till he arrived, in his mental journey, at
Guildhall.

Guildhall! That was it. He had seen that face in Guildhall; no other face was like it in the world. It was
Bonaparte.

He ran downstairs and knocked at his mother's door.

"Mother, did you hear cavalry going past?"

"I did indeed; they woke me."

"Mother, Bonaparte is with them!"

"Bonaparte! Richard, wait till I get up."

"I am going to saddle the mare; I will follow them. I
will come in and speak to you before I go."

He was not long in the stable; and Mrs. Fenthorpe met
him when he came in at the foot of the stairs.

"Richard, is it safe? And what good will you do by
following them?"

"It is safer than my last journey. What good? Don't you
see, mother, of what importance it is that Bonaparte's where-
abouts should be known. Mother, you speak of providential
things; what could be more providential than for me, the
only man in Norwich, I suppose, that ever saw him before, to
see him to-night?"

"Go, then, my son. You think he is going to escape?"

"I don't know what to think. How long is it since the
troop went past?"

Mrs. Fenthorpe consulted her watch, and thought less than
half an hour. "Yarmouth is the most likely, I suppose," said
Richard. "Now, good night; you will not expect me home
at any particular time."

He did not remember, in his excitement, till he was just
mounting, his appointment with Balutin. He returned, and

wrote a message to Lieutenant Fordman, not to wait in the city for him, but to meet him at the appointed place. He woke William, the butler, and gave him this note for delivery. Then he put on his sword and belt, and rode off.

He galloped as far as the bridge beyond which the two roads branch. Crossing it, he rode more slowly, keeping on the shady side of the road. Very soon he came in sight of the troop, which had halted. What did this mean?

It could mean nothing but that Bonaparte had gone up to Fenthorpe Hall to see Davoust. Richard Fenthorpe knew that this general was one of his most trusted lieutenants. There was a path by which he could reach the house. He tied the mare to a tree, and went there, across fields, and through a wood, as fast as he could walk, or run. The wood—it is cut down now—ended about fifty yards from the corner of the house. At nearly the last tree, hiding behind it, he saw a man, watching. The stranger heard him, and turned and faced him, grasping a stout stick.

"Hush!" said Richard, standing still. "What are you doing here?" he asked in a whisper.

The man came closer to him, but not aggressively, and looked at his face. "You be Dr. Fenthorpe?"

"Yes. What are you doing? What is going on?"

"Sir, you are a friend. I heard the French horse going through our village, and I came to see what they are after. Yonder—you can see from here—is one that came with them, talking to the French general."

Richard strained his eyes to look, and there was Bonaparte on horseback, talking to an officer whose back was towards them. Taking a wider view, he saw several French dragoons, who seemed to be waiting. The colloquy between Bonaparte and Davoust lasted for some time; it appeared as if it would never be over.

"What did you come for?" he again asked the stranger. "You seem to know me?"

"Sir, my son was murdered in Yarmouth by that bloody general. I am going to have a life for a life. I have watched him, and him that gave the word to fire, every day since. I think they are going to leave this, and I will follow them. They don't know what's before them when I am behind them."

"You are not going to attack armed men with a stick?"

"No; I am going to take a sure way. They don't know."

Richard wondered if the man had become a maniac with grief and rage for his son. He asked him his name.

"Joshua Bates; and my son was young Joshua."

"I will tell you now," Richard said, after a pause, "why I am here. That man on horseback, talking to the general, is Bonaparte." Bates uttered an exclamation. "I think he is going to fly this country, and I am going to follow him. My mare is below on the road, tied. If that is what he is going to do, he will send this general, Davoust, to take command of his army."

"The army in London?"

"Yes; the French army is in London. I think, if you wait long enough, that you will see the general and all his officers leaving this."

"I will wait, and then I will follow them to London. I have a good horse. Dr. Fenthorpe, you should have your mare up here with you."

"I thought they would see me crossing the fields."

"Where are they?"

Richard described.

"If you are right, sir, and they are to take this general with them to London, they will see your mare where she is tied. It is safer for you to bring her here and have her safe in this wood, and then you can follow Bonaparte at once. There is no mistake that's him?"

"No mistake; I saw him before, and do not forget him. I think I will take your advice. You stay here, do you not?"

"Till I see where they go."

As Richard walked back through the wood, he thought that Joshua Bates was as sane a man as he had ever met, and that he gave him very shrewd advice. He found the mare

where he had left her, and walked beside her across the fields.
So far as he thought, he was not within view of the French
troopers. When he reached Bates, Bonaparte was gone, and
there was a sound in the house and at the stables as if preparation for departure.

"What way," he asked Bates, "has Bonaparte gone?"

"The left-hand road, sir; wait a few minutes, and I think
they will be all gone."

He waited, impatient though he was to follow the fugitive,
as he now judged Bonaparte to be. He asked Bates about his
projected journey, and advised him to find by what route
General Davoust should have travelled if he did travel, and to
avoid it, as there might be a good many of the enemy about.

"When will you start on your journey?" he asked him.

"In early morning, if so be those murderers are on their
road."

"Will you leave word at your house—you live in the
village, do you not?—by what road they have gone? I think
they must go through Norwich."

"I will leave every word. You are the gentleman that
went to London?"

"I am; that is where I saw Bonaparte. Hush!"

Several saddled horses came from the stables to the hall
door of the house, led by dragoons. The moon shone full and
bright. General Davoust and several officers came out and
mounted them.

"That is him," said Bates, with a curse.

"Which?" said Richard.

The man could not describe. But among them was Balutin.
"Am I not going to meet that man after all?" thought the
challenger. They rode down to the Norwich road. The
listeners waited till they heard a movement in the troop, and
decided that they were leaving Norfolk for good. Then they
separated, Bates returning home by the path, and Richard
proceeding in pursuit of the fugitive by the northern road
to Yarmouth.

He rode as fast as the mare could canter—she declined any

more galloping—till he saw a party before him. He kept well
in rear. At a turn to the left they seemed to be at fault; but
they took the turn. Then he guessed that their destination
was Cromer. He had travelled that road, but did not
remember it. For hours he followed, and was glad that they
did not ride fast, or he should not have been able to keep
up with them. He knew that Bonaparte was a furious rider;
probably some of the horses were spent. As well as he could
judge, there were about fifteen in the party.

The moon began to pale, and dawn to show itself in the
east. Midlanders, and west country people, and Londoners
have no idea how early the spring and summer dawn appear
on the shores of the German Ocean. At last, signs of
nearing the sea were visible; those must be sand-hills, but
this was not Cromer. The pursuer judged that it must be
somewhere between Cromer and Eccles. At last, suddenly, he
saw the sea through a gap in the sand-hills. He kept himself
a good quarter of a mile from the French; and when they
were nearing the beach, still farther. He turned to his right,
the ground being now sandy and open, like a common, and
reached the sand-hills and dismounted. There was light
enough to see almost anything.

The group of Frenchmen were at the beach before him, a
good way off. They sent up a rocket—two rockets. He
looked out to the east for a vessel, but could not see one; but
two puffs of smoke on the horizon showed that the signal had
been observed.

Excited beyond measure, he determined to see the business
out, although it was five o'clock. It was half an hour longer
before a boat became visible. In ten minutes more four of
the fugitives were on board of her. Our witness could swear
to a cocked hat; and one of the others, he thought—he could
not be sure—was Berthier.

And now, was it safer for Richard Fenthorpe to wait till
the escort should leave the shore on their return, or to antici-
pate them? He thought the latter, because their horses were
tired, and, if he followed, he must accommodate his speed to

theirs. Besides, they might come along the beach towards him. Therefore, having seen, as he was certain, Bonaparte out of England, he left the Norfolk strand at sunrise exactly.

Bannox's mare began to exhibit signs of distress at the end of half-a-dozen miles. Richard did not know the roads, and he began to wonder should he be in time to fulfil his engagement with Captain Balutin. Then he doubted if that captain was going to fulfil his engagement. At length he met a peasant, who directed him to an inn, or public-house, where the mare could be refreshed and fed. When on the beach, he had not ventured to let her put her feet in the water, lest he should be seen. The publican gave him his breakfast while the mare was resting, and told him the distances. There was ample time.

Precisely at ten o'clock, he passed through the village where Bates lived. To his surprise, Bates was standing at his door. But he was booted for the road.

"Dr. Fenthorpe, you have had a long ride, sir."

"I would have ridden farther to see him out of England. He is gone; I saw his boat row away."

Bates lifted his hat, and uttered a speech that was praise, prayer, and cursing, all in one. It is better for men, no matter what they may think, not to talk so. All have some vindictiveness and righteous wrath when they witness or hear of cruelty and wrong. But let us beware, as those who have received the light of the Christian religion, of confounding our desire for righteous and lawful vengeance with any desire for mere personal vengeance. Richard did not answer this speech, but asked the speaker why he had delayed.

"The bloody general and his officers went down to the large troop of horse, and they rode off at a trot to Norwich. I was down here before them; I came through the fields. I saw the man that gave the word, in Yarmouth street, to fire. They are all gone, every man Jack of them. At six o'clock this morning I was leaving this, and was mounted; but there came a man out of Norwich that I know, and he told me they were leaving the Castle. So I could not go till I should know what road they were taking; and I sent one of my men to find out, and it is but just now I know. Sir, they are gone, clean out of Norwich Castle, on the road to Ipswich. And now I am going to London, after those bloody villains; and God do so to me, and more also, if I do not have a life for a life; and I have here "—he slapped his pocket—" what will give some of them their gruel."

Richard did not know what he meant, and was going to ask him when a horseman, coming from the direction of Yarmouth, rode past. They stopped him and asked what news.

"I am sent," he said, "with a letter from the Mayor of Yarmouth to the Mayor of Norwich, to say that the camp is broken up, and they are gone to Lowestoft, or farther."

"Thank God for all His mercies," said Richard. "Men," for several had come up, "hats off. God save the King! And tell—you may tell it from me—to all King George's subjects, that Bonaparte has left England, and I saw him go."

Half the village heard him, and a roar of joy rose from a hundred throats. The messenger rode on. Richard looked at his watch, and saw that it was time to keep his appointment with Balutin. He asked leave of Mr. Bates to stable his mare with him for an hour, and walked by himself to the wood-surrounded field. Lieutenant Fordman and a surgeon were there. For form's sake, they waited till half-past eleven.

"Now, gentlemen," said Dr. Fenthorpe as they departed, "I have to thank you for this great service; and I have to ask you to allow me to put myself under a still greater obligation to you by your observing perfect silence about this business to all persons, without exception."

They promised; and, taking the way to Norwich by the village for Richard to get his mare, all rode home together. The first thing they heard when in the city was that Wisbeach had surrendered the day before, and Norfolk was delivered from the enemy.

Much money was spent that night in Norwich in illuminations, chiefly the burning of effigies of Bonaparte and General Davoust. Several barrels of pitch were also lighted, producing that mixture of flame and smoke that so delights the vulgar and sometimes even the cultured. One of these pitch barrels was burned opposite the house of Dr. Fenthorpe, the principal hero of recent events. Another was burnt close to Mr. Cardwain's; for the populace had heard that a lady living there had ridden by herself on a bare-backed horse without either saddle or bridle, to Fenthorpe Hall to tell the bloody French general a piece of her mind. Some one in the crowd called for three cheers for Miss Dorkington, who appeared, in response, at an open window, in a most remarkable bonnet and shawl, and gracefully bowed her acknowledgments. Had she been a strong-minded lady of the present time, she would have improved the occasion by a speech; but, perhaps, a strong-minded lady of the present time would never have ridden on a pillion without a habit—think of that!—to rescue her lambs from the mouth of the lion.

CHAPTER XX.

LORD NARESBROOK, on his return from Bedford to town, was in no haste to impart to General Berthier the result, or non-result, of his mission. When, at length, the peacemakers met, all that he who ambitioned to represent England could impart was that the English Government would not treat. A day or two after, Bonaparte despatched Berthier on a similar errand. He was stopped at five miles' distance from Bedford, and, on his announcing that he was a bearer of a message from the French Emperor, word of his arrival was brought to headquarters, in the first place to Lord Harrowby. Lord Harrowby immediately communicated with the Prime Minister.

"What do you think we should do?" he said to Pitt.

"Tell him to go back to whence he came."

"I am not quite sure that that is the best course. Some time or other we shall be treating with Bonaparte; it may be next year, or the year after. It is an opportunity of judging, if not of what his views are, then of the way he will put forward his claims. I think that we had better not throw away a lesson in diplomacy."

"Whom, then, does your lordship think of sending?"

"I think of going myself."

"You! The Foreign Secretary!"

"I shall not go as Foreign Secretary; I shall go as Mr. Ryder, of the Foreign Office."

Pitt did not like this, but he found it difficult to place a negative on it. Lord Harrowby met General Berthier. We do not know the specific terms of peace that the latter

274

proposed; we only know the conclusion of the conversation, which did not occupy a very long time.

"I understand from what you said that a part of the plan of pacification proposed is that General Bonaparte's army shall evacuate England?"

"That is one of the sacrifices that my imperial master is prepared to make, in the cause of peace and humanity."

"How does General Bonaparte propose to carry out the evacuation of England?" next said Mr. Ryder.

"You ask how the evacuation is to be carried out? I do not understand," replied Berthier.

"How is the evacuation to be carried out? Where are your transports for the removal of your troops? And how do you propose that your transports shall obtain access to our harbours?"

This was a poser. Mr. Ryder went on: "His Majesty's Government will not treat at present. Your army at present occupies London, or a part of it. London is an open town. The laws of war do not permit of any violence or wanton destruction being done to unfortified towns. It will be well for General Bonaparte to bear that in mind. The Government has no further communication to make."

On Berthier's return, Bonaparte saw that the game was up. He knew that an army, greater than that defeated, but not totally defeated by any means, at Cambridge, was gathering at Reading. He knew that greater forces than his own were fronting the screen which he had interposed between the eastern counties and the rest of England. All that he could do was to get out of his scrape in the best military fashion possible, as he could not get out of it diplomatically. He had deserted an army before, and had managed to gain, rather than lose, credit, by what he would have called infamous in any other. What man has done, man may do; therefore, certainly, the same man might repeat the same thing.

He managed his flight so secretly that it was not known by the army in London in general before Davoust's arrival to take the command, on Wednesday, the twentieth of April.

Davoust had orders, which he faithfully carried out; it was not alone at the midnight interview at Fenthorpe Hall between those two soldiers that the next movement was planned.

At the moment when Davoust took the command-in-chief of all the French forces in England, their military position was this—About fifty thousand effective men, of all arms, were in London, all but five thousand in camp in the parks and squares, the rest in the Tower, and at some points held for strategic objects. Twelve thousand were in and close to Cambridge, about half that number between London and Cambridge.

The garrison of the various towns of Norfolk, Suffolk, and Essex, now collecting together to approach London, were five or six thousand more. If Davoust should cause Cambridge to be evacuated, and its garrison to be brought to London, a larger English force, probably three times larger, would be liberated for operations against London. Cambridge must therefore hold out, and make the best terms it could, after or without a siege. The Norfolk army should be in London in less than a week.

On the other side, all the available strength of England was gathering, and was now nearly gathered, at Reading, under General Wallerton. It was certain to march on London as soon as the movement should be perfectly secure. Twenty thousand foot, and nearly ten thousand horse, had invaded the eastern counties from Ely on the same day that Wisbeach had surrendered. If they should be moved fast enough in the proper direction, they would take the whole Norfolk army prisoners, and take the hospitals at Bury; and they could attack London after that, in concert with the Reading army.

Davoust resolved to wait till Monday, the twenty-second, so as to allow the reinforcement from Wisbeach to come up, before attempting anything. It arrived on that day. The army from Ely pursued it, or tried to intercept it, much in the fashion of the groom in the centre of a circular field trying to catch the horse galloping round the circumference.

When the horse is fast and the groom slow, the latter is generally much bothered. Thus the English, marching first on Ipswich, then before getting there, on Chelmsford, and before getting there, lastly, on London itself, arrived near Highgate on Tuesday. They were confronted by a small force of not more than three thousand, who, to their infinite surprise, sent a white flag with offers to treat for the surrender of London.

A day was passed in negotiations, the French having to communicate with headquarters more than once as to terms, which were finally arranged on Wednesday. The French occupying London surrendered themselves prisoners of war, the officers to be allowed to retain their side-arms, and to be free to move within twenty miles of London on their parole; the troops to pile arms after a march past, on ground laid out; and a number of guns, not exceeding fifty, to be restored to the French at the end of the war; the evacuation to be completed against six o'clock on Thursday evening, before which time the conquerors were not to enter London.

Six o'clock on Thursday evening arrived, and all the French that had surrendered were the three thousand who had met the English advancing from the north, and about eight hundred more, who, it turned out, had been guarding the northern outlets from the Metropolis. The English commander demanded explanations, to which the reply was that those who had surrendered constituted the whole garrison, and, if the English were not satisfied, they might go into London and look. They did so, and it was quite true. At first they felt ashamed of themselves for being sold, as it would be said should such a thing happen now, in having granted such terms to one-eighth of their number. But their reception by the Londoners soon put this out of their minds; they were regarded as deliverers, and treated accordingly. Very few of this army of twenty-four thousand men had ever been in town before, and for the next fortnight they had such times of it as never happened to them in later life.

Davoust, to return to him, had observed that the upper part

of the Thames, above Lambeth, was not guarded so securely
as had been reported to him. He knew of the assemblage of
a great army about thirty or forty miles from London; and
he conjectured, rightly, that it would, when ready, operate by
both sides of the river, principally by the northern. It was
out of his power to make a direct attack on that English army
by both sides of the river, as he was, and impossible to make
an attack by the northern side only, without exposing his
rear. He resolved, therefore, on an ingenious and almost
desperate movement, combining it at the same time with the
movement which his final instructions from Bonaparte had
dictated.

On Monday, at sunset, he pushed forward, on the road
towards Reading, a body of about ten thousand of all arms,
properly proportioned, and at the same time he began the
removal of his whole remaining force, including nearly all
the guns, by the road close to the Thames. The van of this
army reached Richmond and Kingston before daybreak.
They took both bridges at the first rush. Davoust caused the
bulk of the army to pass into Surrey, diverting to the right
about six thousand infantry, to join the force that had taken
the northern road, at Windsor. He timed his marches with
wonderful precision. His augmented northern or right wing
had orders to proceed at once along the Thames, and to direct
their whole efforts to the seizure of Maidenhead Bridge. When
taken, it would give them communication with the main
army in Surrey, which was advancing parallel to them, and it
would enable them to fight either an aggressive or defensive
battle. He calculated that the English right wing, south of
the Thames, would be much weaker than the left, north of it,
and was not without hopes of giving that right wing a severe
check.

Luck attended him, up to a certain point. The bridge at
Maidenhead was not occupied by the English. That being so,
Davoust halted his right wing, giving orders to its commander to keep his front as narrow as possible consistent with
having a tolerable point of natural support to his extreme

right. Owing to the shape of the ground and the curve of the river there, this was not difficult. He made the front of his left, even in marching, by using all the roads in that part of Berkshire, as wide as possible, so as, however, to keep up safe communications; and, on Wednesday, he began an attack on General Wallerton's right.

That general was perplexed, not knowing what Davoust's object was, except that it was plain that he was not avoiding battle. He did not reinforce his right, which consisted of more than thirty thousand, at first; and Wednesday's battle, on that side of the river, was indecisive of anything. But on the north side he made a direct attack on the enemy in front, and moved his extreme left so as to outflank them the next day. On that day, Thursday, there was heavy fighting on both sides of the river. The efforts of the English were directed towards dispossessing the enemy of the bridge, and towards evening they succeeded, cutting off the whole northern division, except that fraction that had previously got across. Nothing but surrender was left to the five or six thousand that remained.

But the issue of the battle in Berkshire was dissimilar. The English right wing was worse provided with artillery than their left, or main army, and the French had altogether a disproportionate number of guns. Without being defeated, for they were well supported from across the river by the bridges at Reading and Henley, as the battle proceeded, the English were very severely handled. On word reaching Davoust, some time before sunset, of the loss of Maidenhead Bridge, which it is possible he did not expect, he sounded a general recall, and the fight ceased, with no result but a great loss on both sides.

Davoust himself, for the whole time after the passage of the Thames, was on the south side, leaving the conduct of his right wing to a general who was killed. On Friday morning early, word was brought to General Wallerton that the whole of the French army, excepting a few corps of artillery, had decamped in the night. Sending out cavalry scouts, he soon

divined that the enemy's object was Portsmouth. He
instantly gave orders to move the whole army in pursuit. He
sent word to London to move whatever infantry and cavalry
were available to Chichester; and he sent orders to Salisbury,
where fifteen thousand volunteers of Somerset, Devon, and
Cornwall were collected, for them to march to Southampton.
He would thus have, in four days, one hundred and fifty
thousand men surrounding forty thousand, with no means of
escape, as he hoped. The forty thousand had a day's start,
and the best legs.

Bonaparte had planned this movement, on the chance of
Portsmouth and its forts, which were open towards the land,
being surprised at a moment when none of our Channel Fleet
should be at Spithead. His army might then be able to seize
enough of shipping to bring a portion of them at least across
the Channel. At the very worst, they could effect a great
destruction of naval stores before being compelled to surrender. Davoust added to this plan the attack on the English
right wing, in order to cripple the pursuit, and the necessary
false attack from Maidenhead Bridge.

General Wallerton kept in the front during the march, and
was overjoyed to observe that the French had not occupied
Portsdown hill. He was equally delighted to see three men-
of-war lying at Spithead. With all the speed possible, battery
after battery was brought up and placed in position, and soon
after daybreak on Tuesday, the thirtieth, more than three
hundred guns were firing on the town. No reply, or very
little, was possible. There were several fires, and it was
evident that the enemy were doing all the mischief they
could. At noon, an officer came to the outposts with a white
flag to propose a cessation of firing with a view to a capitulation. The reply was—"I have three times your force
surrounding you; to-morrow, by this hour, I shall have four
times your force. You are burning his Majesty's stores and
buildings. I will continue firing till you extinguish the fires.
It is contrary to the laws of war to destroy property wantonly.
If the fires are not extinguished in three hours, I will

decimate your army. You have plenty of fire-engines. When the fires are out, if you propose to treat, I shall be ready to tell you my terms."

The fires were soon put out, and the officer returned. General Wallerton instantly gave orders to cease firing. The officer was about to propose terms of capitulation, when General Wallerton interrupted him, and said that he would receive no proposal, but insisted on a surrender at discretion, or unconditional. If there was not an acceptance of this in an hour and a half, he would reopen fire.

In less than an hour, the officer came on his third journey. "General Davoust accepts the terms, with this modification, that arms shall be piled after a march past, and the officers shall be allowed to retain their side-arms."

"You shall march out of Portsmouth, leaving your arms behind you, officers included. Any man carrying arms shall be cut down, and any one with concealed arms shall be shot."

"General Davoust shall deliver up his sword to yourself, general."

"No; he shall come out of the town unarmed, like the rest. He has wantonly caused the shedding of much blood, and has strained, if he has not violated, the laws of war by destroying property after he knew that he cannot escape. He shall have no terms whatever."

So was England delivered. Nothing remained of the enemy but the garrison of Cambridge. They were offered studiedly honourable terms, to make a difference between them and the piratical army of Davoust; which terms they accepted.

We do not attempt to describe the acclaims of exultation and joy that rose from Britain, as the tidings of victory spread. There was no drawback; there was no discount to deduct. But there was a thing that happened which, according to the light in which it is looked at, either defiled the purity of the national triumph or shed lustre upon the national character.

A handbill was printed, without a printer's name to it, and many thousand copies distributed, chiefly

T

in London, breathing the direst and most detestable
sentiments of enmity against the French, and proposing that the soldiers that had surrendered, without
terms, at Portsmouth, should be all put to death, or at least
decimated. The authorship of this handbill was never known.
William Cobbett was not at that time so eminent a personage
as he became later in English politics; but those who knew
him and his accustomed sentiments very generally attributed
the handbill to him. Nearly all persons were horrified. On the
day after its appearance, the three morning papers denounced
it. The *Morning Post* regretted that zeal had prompted a
proposal that no civilised nation could entertain; and the
Morning Chronicle and the *Times*, in the fiercest and most
condemnatory terms which our language provides, called on
Englishmen to banish from among them, if he could be discovered, the man, if he were a man and not a devil, who could
imagine such an atrocity. On the next Sunday, voices from
ten thousand pulpits were lifted, in the name of Christianity,
and in the name of mere natural religion, against the per-
petration of a national crime, worse and more stupendous
than any that had brought infamy on the name of France
during the reign of the Convention. We repeat, it is hard to
judge whether the mere mooting of such a proposal was the
more disgraceful to the British nation, or whether, on the
other hand, its reception was the more creditable.

But one piece of vengeance there was. Joshua Bates had
travelled from Norfolk with a warrant for the arrest of the
murderer of his son in his pocket, as far as Portsmouth. He
got the warrant endorsed by two magistrates of Hampshire,
and attended the peace officers despatched to execute it, to
identify the criminal. General Davoust and his staff were
lodged in the same house, somewhere near Netley; and before
Davoust's eyes, his aide-de-camp Frederic Balutin was
arrested on the charge of wilfully murdering Joshua Bates
the younger and sixteen others. .

Balutin was tried at the next Norfolk assizes. His counsel
urged that he was not amenable to English law; that his

case was a case for adjudication according to the Law of
Nations; and that he was acting, in directing the slaughter
of the prisoners, under orders from a superior. The judge
who tried him laid down that every man in England is
subject to the law of England; that the court knew no law
but the common law; and that if the prisoner had acted under
any person's instigation, that person was guilty, like him.
The jury, composed of six yeomen of Norfolk, a Dutchman, a
Swede, and four French refugees, found Balutin guilty, and
he was sentenced to death.

Before his execution, Davoust was despatched to Bonaparte
by our Government with a proposal concerning the exchange
of prisoners. Perhaps he was a curious envoy to select. No
intimation was made in respect of the proceedings against
Balutin; but it was understood that if an exchange should be
arranged, the criminal's life would be spared. No reply came
from Bonaparte, and Balutin was hanged, a fortnight after
his conviction, in front of Norwich Castle.

CHAPTER XXI.

DISCOVERY.

THE rapidity with which England recovered from the effects of the invasion astonished numbers of persons. We have seen, in our own time, an invaded country recover with equal rapidity, and we need not be astonished at it. All that an enemy can destroy, in the course of a few months, in an old and rich country, is but a small fraction of its whole wealth. A little economy and an increased activity of production soon pull up lost way. Within a week of the surrender at Portsmouth, England had very nearly resumed its normal appearance. The houses knocked down in London and Cambridge were rebuilding, the broken windows were mended, and mail coaches ran as before all over the country.

The war had one curious effect, which attracted more attention after the defeat of the enemy than during the progress of hostilities. During the months of March and April, there were in England and Wales, with the exception of Anglesea, no marriages. The public excitement produced a social pause. Accordingly, in May, thousands of marriages having been postponed, there were more than had ever before been celebrated in any one month. It was at this time that the well-known case occurred at the Old Church of Manchester, when, in performing the marriage of more than one hundred couples with one reading of the service, two of those couples, in the confusion, changed partners, and had some difficulty in getting the mistake rectified.

We have to do with only one of the marriages celebrated in that memorable month of May. There was no reason against, and there was every reason for, the union of Richard Fenthorpe and Helen Tronford in holy matrimony. The preparations for a marriage were far less onerous to its aiders and abettors ninety years ago than they are now. Far fewer presents were made; less elaborate garments sufficed. Two bridesmaids, instead of six, accompanied the virgin or widow to church. The parson of the parish was unassisted by a colonial bishop. The guests were less numerous; the world and his wife were not bidden to an evening reception. There was altogether less fuss. But perhaps there was more of love, and faith, and hope. Generation of the present, you think your grandfathers and grandmothers were a set of old-fashioned guys, and you think you know everything. Do you ever remember that you are descended from those grandfathers and grandmothers? and that such a superior article as you are, superfine silk, cannot have been spun out of jute; while there is nothing that does not leave some offal to make shoddy with? Your ancestors, let us assure you, knew a thing or two as well as you, and tried to teach it to those that came after them, though some of you may have forgotten what they taught.

Thursday, the twenty-ninth of May, was to be the day of the celebration of this marriage. We do not enumerate the guests; indeed, we do not know all their names. Nor do we enumerate the baked, roasted, etc., meats that Miss Dorkington provided, in the commodious kitchen of Clay House, Yarmouth, for their entertainment. Nor do we look in the clergy list of the year 1805 for the name of the rector of the parish.

We limit ourselves to more personal affairs. It has been said that there never was a marriage without a quarrel connected with it. There was none connected with this, but there was very near being one.

To Helen and Fanny's consternation, Miss Dorkington insisted on being one of the bridesmaids. The moral objection to this was, of course, overwhelming, but the claimant's remarkable and almost morbid obtuseness in matters of taste was such as made her incapable of appreciating it; and the legal objection, as it may be termed, that the claimant was not herself an absolutely unmistakable candidate for matrimony, was one that Helen and her sister could not bring forward. They consulted Richard, and were still more perplexed and brought to a standstill when he laughed at the idea for a quarter of an hour, and declared that he could not object to Miss Dorkington after having run away with her himself. All at once, however, Fanny saw a way out of the difficulty.

"I have it!" she exclaimed. "We will insist, if she does, that she must be dressed exactly like me. Both of them clapped their hands, and ran to make their treaty with their Nunnie. As Miss Dorkington had already purchased twelve yards of silk, of the stiffness of sheet-iron, for a gown, the proposed compromise turned her flank; and, with a sigh, she consented to allow Miss Wyniard to be second bridesmaid, and kissed her lambs and doves.

We have said that we should not enumerate the guests, but there was an unexpected one of whom we must tell. The day but one before the twenty-ninth, a passenger arrived in Norwich by the London mail coach. After halting at the inn and shaking off his dust, he inquired the way to the post office, being an entire stranger to the city. It was not far. On arriving, conducted by Boots, he asked for the postmaster.

"At your service," said Mr. Thomson.

"I received," said the stranger, "on Saturday, forwarded to me from London, this registered letter with your post mark. I have reasons for inquiring into any particulars about it that you can give me."

Mr. Thomson looked at the address and date, and referred to a book. "Yes; I registered this letter myself. There were four of them."

"Four letters with that address?" asked the stranger, surprised.

"No, sir. Four letters that I registered, for reasons. This is one of them. The way of it is this. You know the French were here?"

"Every one knows that, I suppose."

"They took these seven houses on the day they came, and kept them till the day they went away. I found the office very dirty, and I had a complete cleaning out. The letter-box had got loose, and I had to get a carpenter to put it in its place and mend it. He took it right out from the wall, and we found—if you come this way you will see, sir—we found, between the wall and the wainscot, four letters. They were covered with dust, as you may suppose. They must have slipped through some crevice in the woodwork. I cleaned them as well as I could. Yours was one of the easiest to clean so as to be able to read the address, for its back was sloped down; so I took a memorandum of their addresses, and registered them. That's how it is, sir."

"Have you had any inquiries respecting either of the other three?" the stranger asked.

"No, sir; this is the only inquiry I have had."

"Have you any idea of the length of time that these letters have been lying there hidden?"

"I have not, and it is impossible now to reach any idea; for, you see, the French knocked the whole place to pieces almost. If I had had the least notion that there was ever, at any time, any crevice that a letter could slip through, I would have had it put to rights at once. I have taken care now that such a thing shall be impossible."

"Well, Mr. Thomson, I thank you for the information. It is possible that I may have to trouble you about this letter again."

"No trouble at all, sir."

The stranger rejoined Boots in the street, and desired to be conducted to the house of Dr. Fenthorpe. He knocked at the door, and dismissed his guide. Dr. Fenthorpe was not at home. Mrs. Fenthorpe was at home. "Announce Mr. Groves."

Mrs. Fenthorpe rose from her chair and bowed to her visitor.

"I have the honour to be acquainted with Dr. Fenthorpe,

madam," he said, "whom I presume to be your son. It is an
honour to every one to know him. You must be aware of the
circumstances under which we became acquainted."

"If you, sir, are Commander Groves, as I conjecture, I am
aware of them. It is he that is honoured by your acquaintance, and now myself. Be seated."

"I have learned from Dr. Fenthorpe," Mr. Groves said,
"that he returned home safely after his arduous journey. I
was exceedingly gratified to hear of the manner in which
Lord Camden received him at Bedford. Our troubles are now
fortunately over. My purpose in visiting him now is——"

A knock was heard at the hall door. "That is my son,"
said Mrs. Fenthorpe. "Will you pardon me for a minute?"

In two or three minutes she returned with Richard. His
surprise and pleasure at seeing the Commander made him
forget any curiosity he may have felt at the visit. After
some conversation about recent events, Mr. Groves proceeded
to inform his friends of his object.

"I received this letter," holding in his hand that which he
had exhibited to Mr. Thomson at the post office, "on Saturday. It is a registered letter, with the post mark of Norwich,
and date of the fourth of this month—the day, Mr. Thomson
tells me, that communication by the mails was regularly
resumed. It was delivered at Armitage's old chambers, and
the present tenant, not knowing my address when it was
received, did not send it on to me at Folkestone for some
time. Hence the delay. It was directed, you observe, to Mr.
Edward Armitage, attorney, Lincoln's Inn. As his executor,
I opened it. I now read it to you:

> "Fenthorpe Hall,
> "19th August, 1775.

"Mr. Edward Armitage,

" Dear Sir,—

"I have recently made a new will, which you will find
herein. I am about to travel to Scotland, and do not wish

to leave it in any less secure place than in your keeping. I hope to be in town about the end of the year, when I will tell you its contents.

" Your sincere friend,

"CHARLES FENTHORPE."

"This letter," Mr. Groves continued, "was found by Mr. Thomson, when he repaired the post office after the occupation, between the letter-box and the wall, with three other letters. This is the enclosure, endorsed, you perceive, 'Last will of Charles Fenthorpe, 3rd August, 1775,' in the same hand as the letter. I now give it to you, Dr. Fenthorpe."

He handed Richard a folded-up sheet of paper, not sealed, but gummed at the edges. This sheet of paper, and the letter containing it, were of a kind not, as we believe, manufactured now, made from linen and silken rags without adulteration of any other material, all seams first carefully cut out. It is of amazing strength, and has the highest time and weather resisting property of all paper; even the thinnest, as this was. It is nearly equal to parchment. We lately met a book by Horace Walpole composed of this paper, the material being quite as valuable as the printed matter; but it is now very scarce. These two sheets of paper, folded up in one letter for conveyance by post, were so thin that it had escaped the postmaster's observation that the letter was double.

Richard took the enclosure, and looked at his mother. She sat perfectly motionless, and unchanged in countenance, except that it looked as if all expression had suddenly left it. We do not know what sensations pass through a person's mind who suddenly finds a thing, not sought for, but expected to come, during thirty years. Most, we suppose, would break out into exclamation; some would become hysterical. Mrs. Fenthorpe did neither. She waited for the conclusion.

"Before I open this will," said Richard, "let me tell the names of the witnesses of it, if it be such as we suppose. They are Tobias Allonby and William Bannox. I shall write them down."

He wrote them down. He went for hot water, and dissolved the gum. In a few minutes, the document was opened, without damage to the paper. At the foot of the second page were written the names of Charles Fenthorpe and the two witnesses. Richard glanced over the contents of the will, and said, "Yes, mother." He handed it to Mr. Groves, who read it through.

"Let me now tell you," he proceeded, "the circumstances of the execution of this will." He detailed to Mr. Groves what Bannox had related to him of the re-writing of the names with a dry pen.

"Perfectly regular," said Mr. Groves. "It is as good a will as ever there was, drafting, and execution, and witnessing, and everything."

Mrs. Fenthorpe stood up, and threw her arms round her son's neck; and then that strong woman, for the first time since her husband died, eleven years before, wept. She wept silently; first, with excitement, and then at the thought of nineteen years of her husband's life spoiled and embittered. She composed herself suddenly, and said, "So the war did it all!" Then she left the room, saying, "Do not follow me now, Richard."

"And so," said Richard, after the pause into which all persons naturally subside after hearing astonishing intelligence, "this will has been lying in the post office of Norwich for thirty years."

"It is," replied Mr. Groves, "the first instance that has come under my notice, or that I have heard of, of a will being recovered after such a lapse of time. Deeds are often lost, and afterwards frequently found; wills are always found at once, or never. Mr. Mortland is at present in possession of this estate; is it not so?"

"He is. Does it belong to me, or to my mother?"

"If your father made no bequest of real property, to you as his heir-at-law. It is probable that he made none, I presume."

"He made none; I know the substance of his will. We

must lose no time in giving notice of this to the present owner."

"Tenant," corrected Mr. Groves.

"Tenant. In arranging terms of surrender with him, we need have no delicacy, owing to something that occurred lately. There was——"

Mrs. Fenthorpe entered the room, herself and her equanimity the same as usual. "Mr. Groves," she said, "you will stay all night; you will stay, I hope, many days. Has my son told you anything about himself?"

"Indeed, madam——"

"Has he told you that he is to be married the day after to-morrow?" .

"No, indeed. Dr. Fenthorpe, I congratulate you with all my heart. But you have been very reticent. Why did you not tell me before, and I should have gone away and not interfered with your preparations?"

"But, Mr. Groves," said Mrs. Fenthorpe, "you must not go away. You must stay with us and come to the wedding. It is to be at Yarmouth the day after to-morrow."

"Mrs. Fenthorpe, you honour me exceedingly; but I was never——"

"You were never at a wedding, you were going to say! Mr. Groves, do you know the answer I once heard when a gentleman made that objection? He was reminded that he had never been at his own funeral, but that that would not be a valid objection when the time should come. Do not, sir, I entreat, refuse us. Richard, speak."

"Madam," replied Mr. Groves, in terror, "it is impossible. I travel with a scanty wardrobe, and I have no blue coat."

"That," said Richard, laughing, "is nothing. There is in Norwich a tailor who can make a suit of clothes in twenty-four hours. Come, my dear sir, you have placed us under such obligations as embolden us to crave for more. At no cost or trouble to yourself, you will enable me to boast for the remainder of my life that you witnessed my marriage. But, mother"—turning to her—"we are not addressing our honoured friend properly.   Should we not call you Commander?"

"I believe," replied the gentleman so addressed, "that I am entitled to be so called.   No matter.   But do you really advise me to go to your wedding, Dr. Fenthorpe?   I have given much advice during my life, as I dare say you have; and now I will take it, if you say so."

They smiled, and arranged it so.   Our ancestors loved these ponderous jokes.   The tailor proved equal to the occasion; blue coat with gilt buttons, white waistcoat, kerseymere small-clothes, and top-boots, the handsomest—we had nearly said the most sublime—costume that a man can wear.   And this tailor, being a patriot and a man of substance, when he knew for whom he made the suit, insisted on paying Commander Groves the compliment that the landlord of the inn at Bristol paid to Lord Rodney, when he sent him his bill receipted, and requested the Commander to give the amount to the poor persons, sufferers by the war in Norfolk, for whose relief money was being collected.

For Mr. Groves was really entitled to be styled Commander. The King had proposed to make him a baronet, which honour he was unwilling, for various reasons, to accept.   General Wallerton heard of this, and remarked that the greatest, because the most marked, distinction that could be conferred on the Commander of the Kentish volunteers would be a military title peculiar to himself.   This was repeated to his Majesty, who had been greatly tickled with the story of the corps of smugglers; and he said, laughing, "Let him be called Commander, be called Commander."   So a warrant was made out, and gazetted, and announced in the *Court Journal*, that Augustus Groves, Esquire, Colonel of the East Kent corps of volunteers, should be, in future, styled Mr. Commander Groves; and by that title he was presented to his Majesty at the next levee.

"Where is that fellow now?" asked the Commander of Richard the next day, as they were travelling to Yarmouth in a chaise.

"In London. He is a Treasury clerk; his father got it for him during the time of the Addington Ministry."

"Aye! Well, to have been concerned in an affair like that will not injure his reputation much. Such are morals in the Metropolis. That is, if nothing is told of his employment of the Frenchman."

It was a successful wedding. The Commander in his new suit, and Miss Dorkington in a blue silk gown, yellow shawl, and pink bonnet with purple strings, were the chief ornaments, and extremely admired by the populace who attended at the church door. Dr. and Mrs. Fenthorpe departed for Cromer. Commander Groves, who loved the seaside, which reminded him of Folkestone, remained several days after the wedding at the inn in Yarmouth. He visited Clay House every day, and on Sunday accompanied Miss Dorkington and Fanny, now Miss Tronford, to church; paying always very marked attention to the elder lady, whose character, if not person, he was never weary of praising to his new Norfolk acquaintances.

Her friend, Mrs. Lyniard, was on such terms with her that she thought she might make one or two half-serious, whole-quizzing, remarks on the Commander's evident devotion. But Miss Dorkington put a stop to that by declaring that, if he should ask her, she would certainly marry him; and she hoped there was not a woman in England that would dare to think so much of herself as to refuse such a man. Two or three days after, she visited Mrs. Lyniard, and amazed that lady by her triumphant manner and mode of speech.

"Mrs. Lyniard," she said, "you remember what you said the other day about the Commander? You took him for a marrying man, did you not?"

"Oh, Miss Dorkington! And I was right! I congratulate you. Oh, how delightful! Oh, let me kiss you! I am delighted, to be sure!"

"Only," said Miss Dorkington, "it is not me. It is Fanny."

"Fanny!" Mrs. Lyniard screamed. "Why, he is three times her age."

"I said to Fanny, when she told me, that I had never boxed her ears when she was a child, but I would box them now if she would not marry him. She ought to be the proudest woman in England. But she did not require it. I have brought them both up better than that, I hope."

Such were Annie Dorkington's ideas about marriage. Like King Harry the Eighth, she admired a man. And who had a better right, for who, than she, was ever a braver woman? We need not inform the readers of this book that it turned out happily; and the Commander lived to see his grandchildren.

Cromer is a slow place now, or was when we were there not long ago; and ninety years ago it was so much more so, that its motion was unobservable. At the end of a few days, Dr. and Mrs. Fenthorpe left it for a short tour. They visited Lincoln, Ely, and Peterborough, and studied the glorious architecture of their Cathedrals; and at Peterborough returned his mare to Mr. Bannox, and told him and Mrs. Bannox the marvellous story of the recovery of Richard's estate. Mr. Mortland was not difficult to settle with. He gave up possession of Fenthorpe Hall and everything there in time for its owner and his bride to take up their residence in it on their return from their travels. On the other part, Richard released him from all liability for such profits of the estate as the statute of limitations had not already discharged him from. Mrs. Mortland and Alexander were not sorry to leave Norfolk, even with the loss of fortune. As for Robert Mortland, no matter about him, nor about his father.

What had Allonby told Mr. Mortland, or made him believe, on the morning that those two crooked individuals first met each other? Dr. Fenthorpe and the Commander sometimes discussed this together. Our conjecture is that the dishonest witness represented to Mortland—we do not say actually told him—that he and young Bannox had witnessed a will, and that he knew where it was to be found. Whatever he told him, he acquired a sinister influence, and acquired also some money, as we believe, paid quarterly.

Dr. Fenthorpe never relinquished his profession. After he and his wife took up their residence at Fenthorpe Hall, he gave up practice; but he continued on the staff of more than one hospital, and gave far more attention to such work than he was able to do when he had private patients. He always opposed indiscriminate bleeding; and sometimes said, in arguing the subject, that he was consistent, for, if the Loyal Norwich Volunteers had taken his advice in the year 1805, it would have been better for them. The professional gentlemen who listened to this scoffed, and said it was a very bad joke; but it had a most convincing effect on the laity who understood the allusion.

One Sunday, about the time that Queen Victoria was a happy young wife, and almost bride, we were at service in Norwich Cathedral, in custody, being a small boy, of our aunt. As we came out, she whispered to us, "Observe that gentleman." We looked, and saw a tall, commanding-looking, and most benevolent-looking, man of about seventy, with grey, nearly white, hair. Beside him there walked the most beautiful old lady that we ever saw; two little girls, their grandchildren, followed them. "Who are they?" we whispered.

"Sir Richard and Lady Fenthorpe. The old King, of whom you have heard, King George, knighted him on account of great public services." We went home with our aunt, and she told us the story of his journey to London and his journey back; and how he had seen Bonaparte twice; and how he recovered his father's estate, and married that beautiful lady; and it has never left our memory.

THE END.